Tales Of A Hollywood Casting Director

A show business memoir

By
MIKE HANKS

TALES OF A HOLLYWOOD CASTING DIRECTOR

A show business memoir

Contents

Tales Of A Hollywood Casting Director

Dedication

Fred Allen, the great funnyman and evolved philosopher of his era (1894–1956) said "You can take all the sincerity in Hollywood and place it in the navel of a firefly and still have room left over for three caraway seeds and a producer's heart."

This writing is dedicated to the memory of my parents, Raye and Vernon Hanks, who expounded the philosophy that a point of view is just that; another person's view, another person's interpretation, and another person's reality. Mr. Allen's observation is funny, glib, and highly intelligent, but it is just that; another person's point of view, and not necessarily applicable unless one chooses to personally buy into it and accept his opinion as truth. My parents always directed me and my brothers to examine truths for ourselves and to always question another's point of view. Mr. Allen's words were his reality, and reality truly exists in the conversation—in this case, his conversation. I suspect Mr. Allen's observation was perhaps a response to a day of not hearing from his agent, or of being truly disappointed by someone not keeping his or her word, as his remark still echoes at the farthest end of the "how to break into show business" spectrum. It's a very harsh and pessimistic observation of show business to consider. It is my opinion that insincerity exists everywhere at times, but it is not to be found in the following pages.

This writing is also dedicated to the part of the human spirit that causes us to dream, and especially to those who pursue their dreams in the face of all the adversity, negativity, and rejection that abound. It is also dedicated to those I loved and respected within this very creative artistic community. Some took my direction and went on to bigger things, and some just went on to bigger things. Most were my mentors, as I have learned and gained from the experience I had with each and every artist I spent time with, no matter how slight. I thank the many actors I read scenes with and inter-acted with all those years; the many interpretations I viewed made me a better actor, a better artist.

This work is dedicated with much love and respect to the following, with a special thank-you to those that read on: my brothers Doyle and Irv Hanks; my sons Christo-pher, Doyle, and Jonathan Hanks, daughter-in-law Syl-vie Hanks and beautiful Katerina, my most recent life inspiration; Mindy Mobley, Tim Carey, Bobbi Parsons, Jimmy and Gloria Douthitt, Bill Papahristos, Carl Joy, Chuck and Holly Essegian, Chuck Eskridge, Dorothy and Manny Oliveira, Nell Ramsey, Bob Planck, Robert Latham, Kathleen L. Smith, Wayne Scott, A. E. Marquet, Del Goodyear, Pete Loomer, John Arndt, Lou Del Pozzo, Kimberly Beck, Robert Wise, Lil Cumber, Ron Meyer, Lynley Lawrence, Doc Merman, Julie Cobb, Robert Fryer, Susan Macintosh, Nick Janos, Doug Cramer, Joe Scully, Joe D'Agosta, Jack Baur, Ann Jarboe, Sandy Thayer, Mary Prange, Garry Marshall, Tom Signorelli, Wendy Charles, Sherwood Schwartz, Liv Von Lindenland, Carl and Margie Joy, Tom Miller, Mary Ann Beck, Don Ross, Robyn Hilton, Jim Kosta, Ed Griffith, Maggie Malooly, Arthur Space, Carol Worthington, Gary Cashdollar, Her-sha Parady, Joe Mell, Jeff Cooper, Ann B. Davis, Warren

Berlinger, John McLiam, Agneta Eckemyr, Tony Giger, Patricia Morrow, Ted Wilson, Barbara Parkins, Deforest Covan, Flora Plumb, Eddie Foy III, Lynn Moody, Jack Perkins, Eve Plumb, Hal Smith, Patrick Hawley, Alice Ghostley, Lara Lindsay, James Craig, Maureen McCormack, Steven Oliver, Dorothy Day Otis, Bobby Baum, Elizabeth Baur, Larry Gelman, Patricia Parker, Ryan McDonald, Al Molinaro, Beverly Hecht, Dawson Palmer, George Furth, Gary Walberg, Barbara Baldavin, Alan Kent, Ta-Tanisha, John Qualen, Ken Sansom, Susan Oliver, Artie Lewis, Vicki Lawrence, Norm Grabowski, Vic Tayback, Jack Collins, Mary Betten, Dick Van Patten, Joanne Worley, Arch Johnson, Iris Adrian, Richard Collier, Florence Henderson, Dick Stahl, Peggy Doyle, Gene Dynarski, Jeanee Linero, Bruce Glover, Vern Rowe, Kedric Wolfe, Judy Pace, Bill Quinn, Larry Beyer, Marcia Wallace, George O'Hanlon, Christopher Knight, Marie Diane, Bobby Ross, Tracy Savage, Brad Savage, Judy Savage, Henry Jones, Bella Bruck, Tom Hanks, Dave Ketchum, John Aprea, Eve McVaugh, Johnny Silver, John Howard, Fred Amsel, Victor Killian, Joy Harmon, Steve Dunne, Jackie Coogan, Jackie Cooper, Jim York Goyette, Max Baer, Sally Powers, Billy Sands, Mike Lookinland, Ray Kark, Carmen Argenziano, Dwayne Hickman, Tom Hatton, Joe Perry, Freda Granite, Lloyd Schwartz, Howard Leeds, Annik Borel, Jimmy "I know everybody" Murphy, Woody Wilson Tolkien, Martha Tolkien, Barry and Trudi Tunick, Rand Brooks, Jodie Foster, Hoke Howell, Theresa Hunt, Harvey Ellington, Rosanne Katon, Alan Melvin, Rachele Farberman, Robin Clark, Bob Steele, Lois Laurel, Douglas Fowley, Janet Bedin,

Fred Westheimer, Caroline Ross, Gene Dynarski, Joyce Dewitt, Al Onorato, Katherine Baumann, William Benedict, Jerry Franks, Barbara Miller, Hal Baylor, David Graham, Ivan Green, Jeannie Bell, Richard Roat, Dale Garrick, Sonja Brandon, Cliff Osmond, Parley Baer, Chill Wills, Jill Wills, Alfred Dennis, Joe Plosky, Randy Rubenstein, Michael Corrigan, Sterling Holloway, Norah Sanders, Gary Marsh, Sam Laws, Arlene Banas, Hal Gefsky, Snag Werris, Sheldon Pearson, Ruta Lee, Larry Storch, Dennis Cole, Lonnie Stevens, Dee Carroll, Gary Law, Jerry Belson, Penny Gillette, Tony Randall, Mille Gusse, Davy Jones, Fran Ryan, Diane Frazen, Max Showalter, Suzanne Gordon, Ushi Digard, Dennis Murphy, Henry Beckman, Ann Bellamy, Art Metrano, Inger Stevens, Andrew Stevens, Aldo Ray, Marion Ross, Skip Young, George Leslie, Cindy Spano, Ross Borden, Ella Mae Brown, Pamela Bowman, Tom Tully, Helena Kallianiotes, Dick Whittinghill, Tracy Reed, James Jeter, Nita Talbot, Byron Folger, Gerry Lock, Iler Rasmussen, Elaine Devry, Leigh Dorgan, George Stanford Brown, Joanie Gerber, Steve Eastin, Jim Denyer, Gwynn Van Dam, Larry Stewart, Richard Hedges, Helen Baron, Joe Mell, Janice Carroll, Michael McLean, Dorothy Konrad, Irving Kumin, Ross Brown, Rosemary DeCamp, Bruce Maidy, Marlene Ross, Frank Loverde, Paul Rodriquez, Barbara Morrison, William Long Jr., Jack Coppack, Jack Frey, Fuddle Bagley, Irene Bunde, Stack Pierce, Maurine Oliver, Gary Zinn, Jimmy McHugh, Anna Upstrom, Mike Karg, Christina Cummings, Tim Karg, Shelly Novak, Renee Valente, Burr Smidt, Patty Duke, Bill Kenney, Ellen Geer, Elisha Cook, Jamie Reidy, Sharon Thomas, Peter Looney, Kathy Cannon, Oscar Rudolph, Alan Rudolph, Ester McCarroll, Chris Cain, Stephanie Faulkner, Ross Durfee, Deborah Pratt, Bong Soo Han, Don DeFore, Denise DuBarry, Loutz Gage, John Wheeler, Dean Cain, Marianne Marks, Julian Olenick, Patricia Wenig, Kaz Garas, Charlie Martin Smith, Joe Bonny, David Hasselhoff, Gene LaBell, Kitty Ruth, William Kerwin, Ed Scott, K.C. Winkler, Joe Conley, Ron Masak, Johnny Haymer, Pam Norman, Lee Corrigan, Barry Williams, John Conboy, Jez Davidson, Bert Convy, Arika Wells, David Winters, Fred Pinkard, Cy Chermak, Kandi Keith, Bruce Johnson, Meadow Williams, Vic Morrow, Frank Parker, Gloria Delaney, Jack Klugman, Andy Keuhn, Margaret Salas, Bill Osco, Tura Satana, Kirk Fogg, George O'Hanlon, Phil Benjamin, Cindy Eilbacher, James Millhollin, Tamar Cooper, J. Pat O'Malley, Jack Grapes, Lenka Novak, Dave Wiley, Gina Gallegos, Dabbs Greer, John Lawrence, Marcia Wallace, Victoria Pearman, Ray Rappa, Chris Trainor, Miles O'Keefe, Rick Hurst, Gwen Humble, Larry Block, Sid Clute, Ogden Talbot, Sondra Theodore, Kent Scov, Beau Kaprell, Barbara Bingham, Ricardo Brown, Pamela Hartley, George Reynolds, Gary Burghoff, Alyscia Maxwell, Ray Vitte, Berlinda Tolbert, Jo DeWinter, Lev Mailer, Bill Robards, Pat Cranshaw, Bud Harris, Tom Nordell, Gary Shafer, Hal Shafer, Ted Lange, Jerry and David Zucker, Bud and Teressa Botham, Jim Abrahams, Ted Hartley, Dina Merrill, Jack Lukes, Samira Elkhoury, Jenny Bang, Bob Basso, Ramon Bieri, William Bronder, Stanley Brock, Tony and Bill Patri, Carmen Zapata, Nelson Alderman, James Woods, Helen Barkan,

Steve Carlson, Carolyn Conwell, Marie Dehn, Jill Jaress, Ann Quelyn, Bob Balhatchet, Henry Beckman, Groucho Marx, Stan Laurel, Oliver Hardy, and Jesus Christ. To my cousin, Lindy Heidt, who was always my fan and encouraged me; thanks, Lindy, wherever you may be. All of these fine folks, some of whom are no longer with us, helped shape my thinking; I shared with each of them and I love them all.

A very special thanks to Judy Hollowell of West Los Angeles for her tireless efforts during the final proof-reading, and to Chuck Essegian for his advice and direction, and especially for asking his very intuitive, insightful, and brilliant wife, Holly, to look at the first draft, which she did thoroughly. Her wisdom, encouraging words, and constructive comments helped me greatly in this work's completion.

My account of the days and events I've written of is based on my journal notes and recollections of some thirty plus years. Please forgive me if I've forgotten something, or someone I loved...

CHAPTER ONE

Tell Me About Yourself

I wish I had a nickel for every time I was asked how I became a casting director. "Tell me about yourself" always seemed to be the first question posed by directors and producers to the artist being interviewed. I'll try and give the reader some insights and explain the why and how that personally drew me to casting as a vocation.

I grew up at the back door of Metro Goldwyn Mayer. We lived in Culver City, a suburb of Los Angeles, California, when I was born. My parents had purchased a new home a few blocks west of Metro Goldwyn Mayer Studios. While walking home with my chums from nearby La Ballona Elementary School, we were always drawn to stop and watch the filming, looking through the cracks of the old wooden fence around the perimeter of the MGM lot. Sometimes I was even able to sneak onto the lot. Often, my cherubic face and never-ending inquisitiveness softened some grip and I was invited in, to get closer to the actors, the camera, and the excitement. This was a fun, amazing, and exciting thing I was seeing. I remember thinking to myself, I want this fun. My friends having already disappeared, I would always be the very last to leave and finally go home, often late, sure to get a scolding—or worse, the belt. Being part of this world was what I wanted from this, my earliest recollection, and many times I would hear about this same dream as I cast shows and interviewed the many people I did for all those years.

The amazing invention of television entered our home in about 1947. I remember some of the radio programs, but we had ceased gathering around it as much and were now hovering around the very small round screen of this new innovation. I remember mimicking the different accents, or dialects, and personalities I was learning from the television set when I was in kindergarten. I kept my good buddy Chuck Eskridge laughing. Our teacher, Mrs. Bell, laughed too, but told me to keep the antics and behavior I was acquiring from it out of the classroom.

My father worked as an auto mechanic in the MGM garage. He was a personable and charming fellow, as well as a remarkable and brilliant mechanical technician. Superstar Clark Gable took notice of my father's special skills and became mesmerized by them. My mother told me Mr. Gable would come into the garage and my dad would spend time explaining how something worked. He respected and admired my dad. At day's end, he would often walk out onto Culver Boulevard with my dad and jump into the rear seat of our very small 1937 Ford, and toss my brother, Irv, and me around when my mother had come to pick up my dad. My dad told us that on more than one occasion Clark Gable said to him that he would give up all of what he had for a son; that my dad was a very lucky man. John Clark Gable, his only son, would be born years later, after Mr. Gable's passing. Sometimes, when we were on the way back from dropping my dad off for work, Mr. Gable would cruise up

JIMMY garners tips from actor Timothy Carey. Often compared to Brando, he replies, "I feel within myself expressions just as valid."

*Mike,
your veracity
is only exceeded
by your tenacity
Timothy*

James Dean, Tim Carey on the set of *East of Eden*.

next to my mother's car and invite us to race him down Culver Boulevard to the beach. My mom said she would laugh and wave to him as he sped off and she turned to go to our house on Commonwealth Avenue.

Mr. Gable had several cars and motorcycles in the MGM garage. One morning he instructed my father that he didn't want anyone but him to work on them. As the story was told to me, shortly thereafter, the shop foreman at the garage found my father working on one of Mr. Gable's cars and fired him on the spot. He was told to collect his time and to get his things immediately from the garage. My dad tried to explain what Mr. Gable had said, but was again told "get your time and exit the lot." He did so and went home. My mom said about an hour later the phone rang and my dad was summoned back to work. Mr. Gable had come into the garage looking for my dad, who had been trying to fix a problem on one of his cars. When Mr. Gable learned of what had happened, that my dad had been sent home, he became furious with the foreman and had the foreman fired. My dad had felt sorry for the foreman, but always said he had a wife and kids to consider first over politics and emotion.

When I was about nine, my brother Irv and I met a young actor at the still uncompleted Veteran's Memorial Park, just to the south of the MGM studios on Culver Boulevard. His name was Timothy Carey, and later he was in *Paths of Glory* (Kubrick), *One-eyed Jacks* (Brando), *East of Eden* (Kazan, with James Dean), and *The Killing Of A Chinese Bookie* (Cassavetes), just to name a few. Mr. Carey lived not far from the park and used it as a grand stage to read and study Stanislavski and other acting material. He would act for my brother and me, giving us our first acting lessons, his impressions of what the art was really about. Even then I knew this man was very different, but I liked what he was talking about. He compared it to "pretend" play, and said that in acting one could be completely different, with very different voices and accents and characters. This really got my attention. My brother and I started bringing him food, apples and whatever we could find from our rather modest pantry. One day I brought Tim Carey a couple of oranges. After listening to another short lecture he gave while he ate them, and with a newfound enthusiasm for the art of acting, I propelled myself to the MGM casting office on Washington Boulevard and asked—demanded—to be seen. I was told that casting director Al Trescone didn't have time to see me, and I wouldn't be seen anyway unless I had an agent. What's an agent? I thought. I then went up the street to RKO Pictures and met with the same rejection. My first attempt at being discovered and stardom had gone totally unnoticed. How could they not recognize this raw talent? Tim Carey would ask.

Typically, I was probably the kid that didn't get enough attention at home. I was becoming the funny kid in class and elsewhere, with more daring and off-the-wall antics, looking for the laughs and the attention these brought. I was often called into the principal's office for being this developing jokester. I did impressions of all the greats of the day: Bogart, Stan Laurel, John Wayne, Peter Lorre, Barry Fitzgerald. I had become famous on campus doing Barry Fitzgerald's brother,

Arthur Shields, from his long-running series of commercials for Gallo wine. It was a regular thing for me
to visit the dean of boys, but more serious to be summoned to the principal's office. What was it this time? I
would ask myself. Probably the Stan Laurel impression
I had done as I was passing out corrected papers. I got
the laughs; now I'm going to pay for being disruptive.
Mr. Drayton Marsh would always say I had great talent and was funny, that my fellow students liked me,
and that the teachers loved me. But he would ask why
I didn't work harder, keep quiet with my voices, learn
something I could take with me into the real world. My
response was always something like, "Well, sir, Stan and
Ollie and Uncle Miltie and Red Skelton and Sid Caesar
and Hank Penny and Pinky Lee and Arthur Shields are
in the real world and doing okay." Sometimes I changed
the order, depending on which comedian I thought was
important in the world, or left one or two out. But he
recognized that, at an early age, I knew what was important to me: people who could make you laugh.

On one occasion in the seventh grade, I was quite at
a loss to explain what I had done when I was instructed
to report to the principal's office. At this meeting something felt different. Mr. Marsh actually laughed and
smiled, and seemed to loosen up some as he explained
that his request to see me on this occasion was for a
far different reason. He said that Four Star Television
had called and asked him to select a few students from
the student body to work in an up-and-coming television show. He said he could select anyone, the very best
of the academic students, but had decided to choose

young people who might gain the most from the experience, and he thought I might be one that would. This was my very first casting experience. He said I was right for the part and he wanted me to do a good job. I would work in *The Ralph Bunch Story*, with the fine actor James Edwards in the title role, and then would be called back to work in *The Jackie Jensen Story*, also for Four Star. In *The Jackie Jensen Story*, I worked alongside another fine actor, young Gregory Walcott.

After this, my first acting experience, my mother and father bought me an inexpensive Argus camera for Christmas. I say inexpensive because I think it cost thirty-five dollars, an expensive gift for the average family, especially our family. But nothing was too good for Raye and Vernon's sons. The Argus was very different and had some viewfinder features that made taking pictures interesting and exciting. I started shooting everything that moved and didn't move. I wrote a story—a script, if you will—and cast the kids in the neighborhood as the players and took stills of them to illustrate it. It was an action piece and I was meticulous about the staging, camera angles, and makeup. Finally my photographs were assembled in a photo album. The story I typed on a separate page, underneath each corresponding photograph. The moms of Commonwealth Avenue loved it and the kids on the block, for a time, called me "director."

My best friend in those days was Paul Ostoja. Together, Paul and I were trouble. He was as inventive as I was daring, and vice versa. We played off each other like two well-attuned improvisational actors. My mother especially never approved of my hanging with "the Stoge," as he became known.

When I was eleven, my mother opened her own beauty salon, and on a busy Friday night or Saturday afternoon, when the shop was abuzz, it was showtime. It became my first stage for really playing to an audience. I could and would do anything for laughs, especially from the hair-roller-adorned and hair-dryer-filled-to-capacity house. My mom and her customers would laugh as I delivered my latest routines and impressions. She would then throw a brush at me, and I would exit on the laughs and the brush. My mom was a great straight man for me. I discovered that it was truly heaven to hear a group laugh. I was now on my way to stardom, with what I had done in those TV shows—on my way, for sure, I thought, and so did my mom's customers. And how could they be wrong, with their hair being put up in those pompadours?

Paul and I were now expanding our mischief to experimentation in Paul's father's bar and getting cigarettes from a local vending machine. We would then return to my backyard tree house and smoke until one of us would vomit what we had siphoned from his dad's bar.

When I was about fourteen, my brother Irv had multiple "junker" cars (at least that's what dear old Mom called them) parked around the house. Dinner conversation always would come to focus on the time that they would be forever gone from my mother's view. Some were parked in the driveway, some on the street. Our older cousins, Tony and Billy Patri, thought they were pretty cool. There were two things Paul and I dreamed of doing most, and driving a hot-rod Ford junker was the second one. The car Paul and I liked best was parked in front of our house. It was a 1940 Mercury convertible, primer gray in color. It was truly "bitchin'." We'd often sit in it and choke on cigarettes until we'd puke while pretending to be driving with our favorite centerfold. The Mercury didn't have a motor in it, but most people wouldn't know just by looking at it.

One day when nobody was home, I got the daring notion to push it into the middle of the street and ask someone for a push, under the pretense that it wouldn't start. Our ploy: we'd say the carburetor was flooded. Then we'd get a mechanic from the nearby car dealership to push us, as they used Commonwealth Avenue to test cars. At first, they always seemed more than happy to give us a swift and thrilling push to the end of the block. When it hadn't started immediately, they'd take off and resume testing their vehicle. They would tell us if we hadn't gotten it started by the time they returned, they'd give us another push and try it again. We're onto something here, we thought, what a thrill.

But then it started happening; the same mechanics kept coming out testing cars. On one occasion, one stopped pushing, got out, and started looking at the slightly elevated front end of our 1940 Mercury dream car. He began to walk up to the front and said he wanted to open the hood to see what the problem with the carburetor was, and mumbled something about why wouldn't it start. Previously, I'd been able to head off any inquiries with, "I think it just needs to sit a few minutes; I've flooded the carburetor," at which point they'd always return to their vehicle, wave, and disappear. Then we'd push it around so that it was headed back home, and wait for the next mechanic or Good Samaritan. On this occasion, before I could stop him, he had the hood open and saw that it was missing the very important flathead V8 motor. He started laughing when he realized what we were up to and pushed us again to the end of the street. On his return, he smiled, moved up slowly to our bumper and gave us another swift push back in front of my house. We did this for a few more days, taking turns with the thrill of steering and driving, but the word was out. All the mechanics knew what we were up to; we couldn't get a push anymore. We would have to wait for a Good Samaritan to come along.

Over an hour passed, we waited and waited. I think we smoked at least two packs of L&Ms. It was Paul's turn to steer when we looked back and saw this elderly woman, who appeared to us to be no less than a hundred and fifty years old, pulling up to push us. She waved as if she knew what she was doing, then banged into us several times in an effort to line up bumper to bumper. Paul went and explained to her about the push. When he returned, we started joking and laughing because we thought she might die at the wheel and then we'd be in real trouble. It had become our custom that whoever was driving would go and instruct the pusher to give a good push and then back off, and we'd pop the clutch to get it started. In 1956, most everyone understood what popping the clutch meant, but this old lady was driving a DeSoto with an automatic transmission and probably had long ago forgotten about clutches, among other things. During Paul's explanation of our alleged problems, I heard her repeatedly saying, "Okay, I understand, pop your crotch, pop your crotch." At least that's what it sounded like she was saying.

When Paul came back we started laughing and then we started moving, but she didn't get it. This old lady just kept pushing us. She banged into us continually, and continued banging us out onto Culver Boulevard and then east up to MGM Studios, where Paul finally had to slam on the brakes to stop her. We both got out this time and calmly explained that we wanted to turn our car around in the opposite direction and then we could try it again—slowly. She nodded and seemed to understand. At this point, we really didn't care about popping anything; we just wanted to get my brother's car back before he got home. She nodded again. Then, she started turning her DeSoto around as we pushed the Mercury into position. When we got back in the car, I realized it was my turn to steer. So we were changing places by climbing over each other when she slammed into us again, yelling out her window, "Pop your crotch! Pop your crotch!" Fortunately, I grabbed the steering wheel just as we were about to veer into a collision with the curb. She accelerated us quickly in the direction of home, but was pushing us too fast. Coming around the corner at Commonwealth Avenue I tried to brake to slow us some, but she just kept slamming and pushing. I almost sideswiped a car parked on the opposite side of the street. When we were almost in front of my house I fiercely applied the brakes, and we all came to a screeching halt, further imbedding her DeSoto into my brother's Mercury. Paul was shaking and already puffing on an L&M when she finally disengaged. She pulled up alongside, smiled, and grumbled something about us not knowing how to drive. I calmly explained that she was right, saying, "We don't have driver's licenses, and the car doesn't have a motor in it, or a battery." Her response was, "Well, it's probably flooded," and then, "You didn't pop you crotch." She then smiled and waved, and the Mother of Time drove off. Unfortunately, I think this was when Paul really got the smoking habit. He was definitely very nervous, and smoking more and enjoying it less.

The next day was Saturday. Everyone in my family had left early, and Paul and I were up to our usual mischief. We had snagged enough nickel bottles to buy cigarettes to send us puking for days. We then returned to our dream car, where I convinced Paul that we should interview the pusher possibilities more thoroughly, so we could cruise longer. It was several L&Ms later that we interviewed our first new pusher. I did the talking first this time, to pre-qualify the pusher and make sure he wasn't some sort of deranged serial pusher like the demented demon who had tried to take us to Hell the day before. I don't think Paul had fully recovered. He was smoking like a fiend now, definitely suffering from some sort of post-lunatic-pusher syndrome. I interviewed and then lined up our bumpers. This guy was a mellow chap. I explained that we needed a swift push to pop the clutch, and for him to back off when he got us up to speed.

And a lovely push it was, a long moment of aloneness, cruising. When the pusher came alongside, I said, "It's probably flooded, we'll wait a while." I thanked him and waved, and he drove off.

But this time, instead of stopping and turning around at the corner I turned right, going west, as Horace Greeley had advised young men to do, and we were most definitely daring, adventurous young men. Paul and I both craved an even longer, faster, and lasting ride on the big, smooth highway of Sepulveda Boulevard, and there it was. We decided we would go just the mile or so south to La Ballona Creek and then turn around and come back. We waited and smoked, we smoked and waited. Then it came. It was Paul's turn, and he was out interviewing and explaining to a young guy in a hot-rod V8 Chevy truck. Yeah, good one, I thought. He got us onto to Sepulveda heading south in one fast and smooth thrust of his hot-rod Chevy. He then gently touched bumpers and launched us very quickly to about fifty miles per hour, backed off, and Paul pretended to be popping as we cruised to La Ballona Creek, a faster and much swifter ride, for sure. We were hooked. There would be no turning back, at least not immediately. Just a little farther, we would say, just one more push. We took pushes that day for some thirty plus miles south on Sepulveda Boulevard, all the way to the Los Coyotes diagonal traffic circle in Long Beach before turning around to return home. The difference on this voyage was that our little secret about not having a motor was discovered multiple times. Another guy in a big truck noticed the front end sitting high and popped the hood before Paul or I could stop him with our little act. He started laughing, and he and his girlfriend pushed us for about ten miles of the return trip to Culver City. Another amazing thing was that the police never noticed us. We saw them, but fortunately they were all too busy to bother with us. We were parked in front of my house, puffing and coughing on L&Ms late Saturday afternoon, and nobody was the wiser. But this would be our last adventure; the past two days had scared us.

My parents and my brother learned of our escapades, and my parents then forbid me to have any further contact with Paul. They also decided I should be sent to military school; that I needed discipline and was borderline incorrigible. My parents were baffled by my behavior. Maybe I had seen *Rebel Without a Cause* one too many times, or maybe I was going crazy. Whatever the rationale, they became convinced I was headed straight for reform school, and would probably bypass jail and go straight to Hell. They did some research of private schools that offered hard "head-thumping" discipline and, after meeting and interviewing all possibilities, decided on John Brown Military Academy in San Diego. For about a half an hour in my new role of yearling or plebe at this prestigious military academy, I thought perhaps I should make my parents truly proud and pursue a military career and become an army general. I would go to West Point and perhaps learn to fight wars and conquer countries. But my dear mom was right; I didn't have a serious bone in my body.

Upon my return to civilian life and public school, after a stint of even wilder behavior and nearly being expelled, I had a million stories of what life could be like for those aspiring young rebels that didn't have a cause. I became very popular on campus as the kid who had seen the truth and was truly changing direction. Everyone wanted to help me and hear of my experiences, but nothing would change the fact that I had lost almost a full school year with my antics this time. It was only after some hard-fought negotiations that I was allowed to return to my ninth grade class and wasn't set back fully to the second grade, where some suggested I would fit in better. To my good fortune, as I re-entered public education I became acquainted with a young chap at Culver Jr. High School by the name of Douglas Campbell. Doug had a completely different mind-set and a very different perspective. Doug was directed and motivated for success, and he had set very distinct goals for himself. He had very definite plans for the future. Doug loved football, and wanted most to be the quarterback of the high school football team and bang all the cheerleaders. I could relate to the latter. But he also wanted to get good grades and go to college. Doug began coaching me to work a little harder and become a more accomplished student, and to set goals for my life. Unfortunately, I was never inspired in school to excel beyond the gratification of trying hard to find something funny to do or say. Doug's vision of the future, that included the possibility of banging those cheerleaders, finally got my attention. Acting, literature, photography, and business law classes were of most interest to me, but even in classes I truly enjoyed I only scraped by.

In spite of my newfound popularity and my new friendship with Doug, Paul Ostoja and I were still hanging out, much to the adamant disapproval of our parents, and we were looking for other adventures. As we entered our sophomore year, we discovered all the wonderful nearby MGM exterior sets on lot 3—the lake, the boats, the canoes—that on any given evening of the week were left behind with all the props nearby for the next day's shooting. We discovered that this lot was where the original *Mutiny on the Bounty*, starring Charles Laughton, was shot. Like two young pirates we had to find her, and there she sat on the lake, the *Bounty*, with very little security in the late '50s, only one guard. At about midnight he would take a walk around the premises, pick his nose, fart, and talk to himself a lot, and then return to his office, where he probably did the same thing. Paul and I would explore and act out our fantasies on those sets instead of going to the library. Then we made the mistake of telling a couple of our close chums about our newest adventure, and were being hounded to share it. We knew the layout best, so we started leading small groups of kids into MGM's lot 3 for fifty cents a head, but we lost control. The word quickly spread, and soon the place was crawling with kids and we weren't making a dime. Visiting MGM lot 3 became the ever-so-trendy thing to do. Kids were coming from as far away as San Diego and Bakersfield; it started to get ugly. The yachts on the lake were being vandalized, with all the gauges being stolen, probably to end up in somebody's hot rod. The Culver City Police were stepping up patrols in and around the perimeter of lot 3, and one suddenly had to be very careful about entering or exiting the premises.

On one Friday night, I had told my parents I was staying over at another friend's house, and Paul had done the same. We entered MGM lot 3 when we saw the last group of grips and laborers leave at just after six p.m. At about eleven p.m., there were hordes of kids breaching the fences, and Paul and I got separated. Another good buddy, Mickey Martin, son of a captain with the Culver City Police Department, came climbing over the fence and he joined me on the excursion. There were so many kids; they were everywhere, sneaking about in the shadows. Some had quietly taken to the canoes and were starting to row from one end of the lake to the other. I thought it was very risky, but finally we couldn't resist any longer. Mick and I jumped into a canoe and engaged in the competitive paddling. Then canoes started bumping into each other, and then began crashing into each other. "The Stoge" suddenly came crashing into me from the side, breaking the quiet of the night with his crazy hyena laugh, previously heard only on Friday nights at the Culver movie theater when you least expected it. It quickly escalated and got very rambunctious, with canoes sinking and listing. Then, all of a sudden bright lights came up all around the lake, and there were police just about everywhere. In the commotion, Mick and I jumped in the lake and swam in the direction of darkness, where we were able to escape by stepping into the shadows. Through the fence, we could see numerous positions on the outside of the lot where police lights were now flashing. We managed to get over a back fence farthest away from the activity, on the Baldwin Hills side. We had moved down to Overland Avenue, just south of Jefferson, when another good buddy, Dick Astle, saw us. He drove up to us and said that the police were thicker than flies, and for us to quickly get in the trunk of his very fast '50 Oldsmobile. We got in, soaking wet and shivering with cold, and when Dick moved back into the lane, over a loudspeaker we heard, "Pull over! Pull over to the curb!" Mick and I could see a glimmer of the red lights flashing and could clearly hear the police radio; we were done for.

As the policeman approached Dick started talking. He wasn't too scared, as his dad was a very prominent attorney in Culver City and already had gotten him out of a scrape or two. We heard him telling the policeman that he had been to a movie and then to his girlfriend's house, playing Parcheesi and drinking cocoa with his girlfriend and her family, and had lost track of time. "If you know what I mean," he added. "They're all Parcheesi and cocoa addicts, I think. You can't leave until you've had your fill of Mom's cocoa." It was almost three thirty a.m. I don't think the policeman believed him. We heard him ask for his driver's license, and mumble something about who his father was. He then directed Dick to get out and open the trunk of the car. We heard Dick getting out and approaching the rear of the vehicle, keys jingling, and then inserting them into the lock. He was just a turn away from opening the trunk when the policeman's radio sounded with an emergency call. I heard him say, "Okay, Astle, go home now! I've got an emergency." He then sped off. Dick turned the latch and we played dead for a beat until we all started laughing and acknowledging our unbelievable luck to each other. He had the key in the latch, no less. Everything we said to each other on the way home that night was cocoa enhanced; we laughed for some time after that at Dick's story, and would have stories to tell for a long time to come.

For me, the adventures at MGM were now over. The reality of even worse trouble had finally gotten my attention; this would be my last visit to MGM lot 3. It wasn't that we were bad kids. We all came from good homes and had been taught resolutely the difference between right and wrong, but we were all taught to be creative and independent thinkers as well. Therein, perhaps, was the conflict. Mickey, Dick, and I once got suspended from high school for three weeks for singing "Down By The Old Mill Stream" in the boys shower, and we sounded damn good. The dean of boys said we were insubordinate; that we had been told not to sing in the shower. I could never understand why we weren't sent to choir or made to perform for the entire student body. That would have been the worst kind of punishment. But it was three weeks' suspension for singing in the shower. It was definitely a different time.

In high school I was fairly popular with everyone by maintaining my neutrality between those that were referred to as "socialites" and those that were tagged "hodads," the latter term coined by my very inventive friend Paul Ostoja. Paul was always coming up with clever, trendy labels for things. There's no way to authenticate and confirm this remarkable deed, but I know it's true.

I had begun to calm down some, but I still couldn't resist adding a verbal comment to any zany observation for the laughs. I was anything for the laughs, and my quest for knee-slapping laughter hadn't diminished. I had to have those cherished moments that the kids talked about at lunch. It would be music to my ears when they talked of something I had said or done weeks, months, even years later. My often-disruptive personality would sometimes be just the item to give a teacher the incentive to give me a class grade that my parents considered unacceptable.

I had gone to some of the school plays and thought the drama department was absolutely dreadful. I became enticed instead to go out for "B" football, to get close to the cutest girls in school, those much-desired cheerleaders. One of those young beauties was Patti Lauderback, who would go on to appear in most of the American International Frankie Avalon and An-nette Funicello beach-and-bikini genre films of the day. She was always a regular supporting cast member, a bikini dancer—and what a bikini dancer she was. I was a fairly good athlete, but because of my lean build I always seemed to get hammered early and taken out of the game. Doug Campbell and I became football workout partners, where we would practice our football-handling skills until after dark almost every night during the season. Doug had made first string varsity quarterback and had developed quite a good throwing arm. I loved football, but I should have joined the drama department and learned to channel that performance energy on stage.

In my senior year, after thirteen years of school, I was being considered for and voted on as the "Best Sense of Humor" honor in the yearbook. It was rumored that I was a sure thing to win, but from out of nowhere came the forgotten glitch. Some bean counter at the board of education had discovered that I didn't have enough unit credits to be a graduating senior. My lost semester at military school had caught up with me and bitten me squarely on the buttocks. There wasn't any way I could make up the deficit before the school term ended. I would be denied graduating with my class, and thereby denied this most coveted and prestigious honor. I was crushed. I was beside myself, devastated, seemingly beyond repair. All the teenage sex my girlfriend could give me in her mom and dad's rocking mobile home was of little or no help in distracting me. For two whole weeks, three or four times a day, she tried to distract me. Nothing seemed to help. Then, my classmates started coming up to me and saying they knew who the real winner was. Even Steve Zagorin, the kid who received the honor, said I should have received the accolade. I didn't believe him. But when Patti Lauderback signed my yearbook, hugged and kissed me, and indicated that she lived in other than a rocking mobile home, I began to get over it.

I would enter Santa Monica City College in the fall with my class, make up the deficit and get my diploma; Doug would become the quarterback for Santa Monica City College; and that summer we would learn to be very successful vacuum-cleaner salesmen. It was a natural thing for me, as I wasn't much concerned with making an ass out of myself. I was just naturally wilder, and this selling thing was kind of halfway between the acting performance and making a wild ass of oneself. I just had to learn the script of the canned presentation and believe in the product, as the first sale has to be to oneself. I had to know and learn and love the product as the actor knows his character, inside and out. After attending sales-training classes I caught on fast. The sales meetings consisted of high-spirited, very stimulating presentation stories from successful salesmen. Then, they would cut us loose in the early afternoon with scheduled appointments to sell "dirt suckers" in Orange County, California. Doug was somewhat more reserved than I. He was more methodical, analytical, and cerebral than my wild off-the-wall nature. But by coaching each other incessantly he was loosening some, taking more risks, and soon was making an ass out of himself, too. We started having fun with it as soon as we got the script committed to memory and out of our hands. Several weeks passed, and we had started to make some fairly decent money selling those amazing "dirt sucker" machines, as we called them. We were rocking and rolling in money for a couple of nineteen-year-olds, and I was second in sales volume to only one other salesman of the entire sales force.

We started to meet regularly in a local coffee shop, where Doug met Wanda. He tried for some time during that summer, but Wanda wouldn't. Me? I had met a beautiful young woman named Mona, and Mona would—loudly. The last time I was with Mona, afterward she informed me that she was separated, and that she thought her husband was outside. That's when I inquired as to the location of the rear exit. She informed me that there wasn't a back exit in their small apartment, only a front door. A husband and no rear exit. To this day, I think what followed was probably my best performance ever. I was immediately up and dressed in a flash. I assembled and toted my vacuum cleaner box and all the attachments out on the front steps, in full view of a very large man standing out front—my only option. Loudly, I commended her on her attempts at being a better homemaker for her husband and her future little ones, and said that she had learned the equipment and cleaned well. I could see her husband moving about nervously, which made me very nervous. I continued selling, and reassured her through the door opening that she could afford the unit, and if she wanted me to come back and give her good husband a demonstration I'd be happy to do so. I then added that I thought I could get my manager to throw in the attachments at no extra charge, as gesture of community goodwill for the young couple. I was learning a lot about selling and performance. Very lucky indeed, and who thinks about back doors and husbands when one is young and stupid? was Doug's only observation.

There were about sixty people at the sales meetings each day and it was mandatory that everyone attend. We were there to get fired up and take our enthusiasm and product knowledge out and sell with it. It was at the beginning of one such sales meeting that I learned another lesson I have carried with me to this day. Bill Smith, who was vice president of the company, had summoned me to his office. He asked me to sit down, gave this great ear-to-ear smile, and said, "Mike, I'm afraid I'm going to have to let you go." He continued with,

"I've watched you, Mike. You never smile and you share very little, only what you have to share, and some of the newer salespeople are twice your age. You come in, you and Doug, and you keep to yourselves—your private clique." Doug didn't have to sweat anything; his dad was the president of the company. This was the first time anyone had ever suggested I was a snob, or had to direct me to smile and be more personable and fun. I confessed to Bill Smith that perhaps it was because of my youth; in that, because of the other sales agents being older, I had felt somewhat shy and insecure at times. Then Bill Smith said, "I know you're smiling and performing for Mr. and Mrs. Buyer, I see it in your outstanding sales. You're making lots of good sales, but you're not smiling at the other salespeople here at the meetings. You need to smile at them, Mike, because they need your assurance that they can be as good a salesman as you, and you need to teach them how you're doing it. Forget about this age thing. You need to open up to them and give them a sample of your performance, because it's your great, honest performance the people are buying, as well as this great equipment we offer." He looked me straight in eye as he continued his mentoring and said, "When you smile at them and share with them the little nuances, the things you do to keep and hold the attention of the buyer; when you show them by example of your personal performance, it's going to make you an even more spectacular and powerful presenter."

And then he said, "I heard that you want to be an actor. I wanted to be an actor once. The actor and the salesman are similar, in that they are both salesmen of sorts; they both must continually hone their craft. Real growth is only accomplished by continued practice and the sharing of knowledge with each other. Think of over-acting and over-selling as the over-inflated balloon; it will eventually pop and destroy the illusion. To keep the balloon from over-inflating and popping, it must be given just the right amount of air. Or, simply put, you must always know your limits so that you deliver a real performance and it doesn't over-inflate and pop. So here are some balloons; go pop some for the boys out there and tell them this story. Remember, the actor must first learn about what it is to be bad so that he can gauge what it is to be good. And above all, Mike, remember it's like the song, 'When You're Smiling, the Whole World Smiles With You.' Smile and share, Mike; smile and share and go practice, knowing limits, and pop some balloons." Man, I came out his office shaking everybody's hand, like I was running for office, smiling and sharing with a large balloon in my mouth. A little tidbit of wisdom I've never forgotten and I've employed it in everything I've done since that day.

At month's end, to reward ourselves, I talked Doug Campbell into going skydiving with me and making a sports parachute jump at Lake Elsinore, California. I haven't heard the end of it to this day. Every so often, for my benefit, he still kneels down, kisses the ground and says, "I love you, Mike made me leave you, I'll never leave you again." We had quite an adventure that summer.

CHAPTER TWO

From the Mailroom to the Casting
Department at 20th Century Fox Film Corp.

B obbi Parsons, a personnel director at Fox and good friend of my brother Irv's, had suggested that I come by the lot and apply for an opening in the mailroom; that it would be a good place for me to work while I took college classes at night. She explained that the mailroom had traditionally been the start for a great many people who had distinguished themselves within the industry, and that it would be an opportunity to observe the business, meet people, and explore all the other very interesting and creative departments. I had gone to a party at Bobbi's house one evening, and little did anyone know that she had put a tape recorder behind the shower curtain in the bathroom. Anyone (or any group) that visited the bathroom and talked to each other or to himself or herself after having drinks was recorded. Under those conditions, I could do some of my best work with my best voices and impressions of the day, and I did. As the evening wore on, and with the consumption of more cocktails, my visits to the bathroom became constant, as did my antics. A few days later my brother told me what Bobbi had done, and that she said she had some very funny stuff of me in the bathroom practicing different voices. Bobbi thought I was a natural for the business and destined for certain stardom. She arranged an interview for me and I was hired.

The dispatcher in the mailroom was Carl Joy. Carl would shoot a circling fly out of the air with a rubber band, splattering it on the window directly in front of the mail boys as they sorted the mail. There were fly stains and fly body parts all over the windows until some observant member of the janitorial department cleaned them. Very impressive shooting. Carl would shoot, we'd hear the splatter, and then he'd tell us we'd get the same if our mail routes were late. Carl and I became very good friends under the fastidious and meticulous verbiage master and mail department supervisor, Mr. Bill Papahristos. I loved this lot and was instantly mesmerized by the show business energy. Carl had spent some time in the Navy and I had just completed a six-month active reserve enlistment in the Marine Corps. Both were serious experiences in the early '60s, with the conflict in Southeast Asia heating up every day. I was still in the active reserves, well trained and ready for possible call-up. Most of the mail boys didn't have this experience; most were connected to wealth and power within the industry and were trying to find a direction for their lives. Carl and I were connected to nobody. I was reminded by Bill Papahristos to smile and be cordial and helpful to anyone I met on the lot. He informed us that you just didn't know who was connected to whom, and how a simple kindness to someone might help open a door to some sought-after job in some much-desired department. It was the "be kind and kiss everyone's ass on your way up, because the same people will be there on your way down" philosophy. Mr. Papahristos was right; I would learn that those same people will catch you, if and when you slip and fall, if they like you. They'll support you and push you back if you haven't stepped all over them on your climb up. If you have, they'll let you just lie there, and ultimately die there. It was very good advice.

One afternoon I was on a "special" delivery to producer Arron Rosenberg's office. Mr. Rosenberg was in the midst of production with the Marlon Brando film, *Morituri*, currently shooting. I was chatting for a minute with Tillie, Mr. Rosenberg's loveable elderly secretary, when the master himself walked out of Mr. Rosenberg's office. It was Marlon Brando. I couldn't believe it. I know Tillie wanted me to have a thrill, so she called to Mr. Brando as he was leaving and introduced me to him. He stepped back and shook my hand, and we chatted for about half a minute. He was very gracious. "*One-Eyed Jacks* is still one of my all-time favorite western films," I managed to blurt out, like any nervous fan would. I loved that movie; the story, the acting, the direction. It was the only film ever directed by Mr. Brando, and my pal Tim Carey had a great villain role in it. The musical score from the film is truly beautiful; I still listen to it today. I was in awe of actors of his caliber, and I couldn't wait to get back to the mailroom and tell everybody I had met Marlon Brando. The hand that had shaken Marlon Brando's hand would be famous for a few days.

Marilyn Monroe had passed fairly recently and there were some still grieving broken hearts to be felt around Fox, her lot. In the mailroom you were privy to all kinds of stories, rumors, and juicy gossip. We also got firsthand information on jobs that were opening up in various departments. I had been on the lot approximately one year when Carl Joy was offered a position in the extra casting office. The head of the casting department at that time was Owen McLean. Under Mr. McLean was Cliff Gould, who headed up the very busy 20th Century Fox Television casting department, soon to have more than ten shows. When Cliff Gould left casting to write, Jack Baur came aboard, and finally replaced Owen McLean when he retired. I too, had moved into another department for the bigger paycheck, but was still very actively eyeballing the more creative job opportunities on the lot. I was studying acting privately, taking classes in photography and other courses at night, but hungered to be closer to the real movers and shakers, the decision makers on the lot. At the time my needs were comparatively simple. I had some expenses, consisting mostly of transportation costs, acting classes, college tuition, and dating coeds. I could still live at home for as long as necessary—and that might become necessary, as I wanted desperately to continue studying acting and quality teachers of the craft were expensive. Tim Carey had said that, for the most part, anybody who was anybody came out of the New York theater, or had at least had been trained there. I would continue studying locally for a while longer, but New York would become my focus. I would go to New York and study.

One day Carl Joy called me and told me over lunch that his office might be expanding soon, with the addition of another person to the extra casting staff, and asked if I would be interested if that happened. At once, I said that I would. I thought this would be perfect; I could meet all the casting directors, I would be closer, and I would be discovered right under their feet. I'd always had above-average knowledge of actors and actresses, brought about by my older brother Doyle's keen awareness, as he had always seemed to know the name of every actor and I was impressed with that. This would be a natural. I interviewed for the job in extra casting and just a few days later I was hired as the third person in the office—low man on the old totem pole, the gopher; go for this, go for that.

At that time, an older gentleman was the head of the extra casting office at Fox. It was me, Carl, and the older and fatter-than-almost-anyone gentleman for about six months. This older gentleman was a fairly happy and upbeat chap, but an absolute control freak; he and I would butt heads many times. He had to give his approval for almost everything anyone did within his view—no independent thinking here. He was constantly looking over my paperwork and putting his initials, with a little squiggle under them, on everything. It was like, don't flush that paper; it hasn't been initialed by the fatman. Everything had his initials on it. Very controlling and very insecure, he drove us crazy. If someone came into the office to visit, he would have to know the nature of his or her business, and sometimes would use his large heavyset frame to muscle you away and himself into the center of the conversation. Nobody dared to say anything to him because he was the boss, but he often was intrusive and very rude.

Theatrical agents—Hal Gefsky, Larry Kubik, Phil Gittleman, Bill Haber, Hal Shafer, David Samuals, Ed Sotto, Ron Meyer, Don Gerler, George Ingersol,

Walter Kohner, Freda Granite, Ivan Green, Thelma White, Pat Amaral, Herman Zimmerman, Julian Olenick, Bill Meiklejohn, Lew Sherrell, Mary Ellen White, Jack Weiner, Billie Green, Nina Vine, Kurt Frings, Len Kaplan, Maury Caulder, Alex Brewis, Budd and David Moss, Coralie Jr., Bill Robards, Norah Sanders, Ray Sackheim, Lou Deuser, Ted Wilk, Lou Irwin, Mike Rosen, Meyer Mishkin, Velvet Amber, Toni Kelman, Sam Armstrong, Bob Thorson, Sid Gold, Glen Shaw, Bill Barnes, Larry Rosen, Dale Garrick, Ruth Blumenthal, Howard Rubin, Carlos Alvarado, Maurine Oliver, Jack Wormser, Mary Grady, Abby Greshler, Leon Lance and many more that came to sell their wares to the casting directors down the hall—were invited to come into our office to use the only phone available for visiting agents. Often the casting directors would escort them down to us if they didn't know where the guest phone was.

I had become friends with Joe Scully, a casting director in the expanding feature film and television casting departments. In the days ahead, Joe began to rely on me more and more, and requested me to assist him on various tasks. He went to Cliff Gould and asked if he could ask the extra casting supervisor if he could formally borrow me to assist him in running down film on actors, or with interviews. At first, it would be the popular *Peyton Place*, starring Ryan O'Neal and Mia Farrow, that I would work on for Joe. (Ted Hartley, who played the town minister on *Peyton Place*, is currently the president of RKO Pictures). My assistance would become a regular request for Joe Scully; it was a gentle request initially, if the extra casting office could spare me. Joe was denied his help request often, and not because the extra casting office was busy, either; the fatman wouldn't let me go without his ego being stroked first. I would soon become consumed with these other responsibilities and with the excitement of these other duties.

In 1965, there weren't videocassettes or the Internet to view an artist's most recent work on. Somebody had to order or borrow a film from a production company, view it in a projection room, and hope to find a suitable professional-looking scene or a moment a director, producer, or casting director could look at to judge the actor's work, quality, or range. If one didn't find the right scene, Joe Scully or his secretary or whoever would have to call the agent or the artist and get another suggestion of what to further view. These duties were now mine. My assisting Joe Scully and some of the other casting directors—Phil Benjamin, Larry Stewart, Mike McLean, Bill Kenny, David Graham, and later Richard Wolke—afforded me little time for my regular extra casting duties. Joe D'Agosta had recently joined the staff, and Ross Brown had been hired for the pilot season but would stay longer; all called on me for assistance. It drove the fatman crazy. He didn't have any control over any of the decisions I was making away from his office. I wasn't trying to hide anything from him, but he was on me continually to know exactly what I had been doing; what actors I was looking at film on and for what project. I had designed a form to simplify the casting department's requisitions and for the return of borrowed films by the Fox printing department. The supervisor started coming over to my desk and putting his initials on these documents, which he really had nothing to do with. I still worked under his supervision, and this very controlling and insecure side of his personality was very unpleasant. Frustrated, I started going over to Carl's desk and putting my initials on Carl's paperwork, with a little squiggle under them. When I would come back from the projection room, I would find that Carl had played the same prank on me, writing "C.J." on everything he could on my rickety old desk.

Joe Scully would become extremely busy with *Peyton Place* and his upcoming feature assignments. He and Joe D'Agosta couldn't stand dealing with the situation any longer, and went to Jack Baur and requested that I be given assistant status. The request for me to be officially promoted to assistant casting director was denied; I was told that the department had no budget for it. This was at a time when casting people didn't receive screen credit at Fox, either, and advancing through the ranks from lowly casting clerk, a position under union jurisdiction, to independent contractor as a casting assistant would prove to be impossible. I didn't get the lofty title, but I would no longer be under the extra casting department's jurisdiction. I would move to a corner of the office, with my own phones, my own duties, and would work exclusively for the feature and television casting departments, where the real action was—and no more initials.

The next four plus years I would be groomed and trained. I observed all aspects of casting, SAG contracts and negotiations, and what sparked my interest most—the visual side of film production, acting, and telling the story. I went to casting meetings, and at noon every day I was asked to view "dailies" or "rushes," as they were called in those days, of everything that was being shot under the Fox banner. I would spend hours upon hours looking at films each day. Some days, if I had nothing to do I watched whatever I liked out of the vast Fox film archives. My knowledge of the filmmaking process as a whole—who was doing what, and who might be future names—was vastly improving and growing.

Joe Scully had discovered motorcycle-riding Steven Oliver as an addition to the *Peyton Place* cast, and he was fast becoming the rave sensation, offbeat bad-boy; perhaps the new James Dean. Steven was a wonderful talent and extremely charismatic, with the James Dean look and rebel persona. He could charm and sell anyone anything. Tall, lean, muscular, and handsome, he brought it all in front of the camera. He seemed destined for superstardom. Joe sent me to deliver script revisions to his dressing room a few times, and we would chat. When he would come to see Joe in the "New Ad," he would cut through the extra casting office to the hall and then down to Joe's office. He would often stop and shoot the breeze with us for a few minutes.

Steven dropped by one day and we began talking about flying small aircraft, and he said that he wanted to learn to fly. I casually mentioned that my first two times of flying had been in a Cessna 172, but that I hadn't landed with the plane. I explained that I had completed two sport parachute skydiving jumps at Lake Elsinore, California. Steven said he'd always wanted to make a jump and asked what it was like. I told him it was a very difficult experience to describe, but that simply put it was euphoric and a surrealistic sensation, to say the very least. He then asked what I was doing on the following Saturday. I said I had no plans for anything special. He said, "You do now; we're going out and make a jump." We exchanged phone numbers and he asked that I call him with what he needed to bring, and that he'd pick me up early Saturday morning. We spoke a couple more times that week and he got even more psyched up for the jump.

Saturday morning arrived and there came Steve on his motorcycle. I never thought to ask how we'd get to the desert; I thought he had a car. I suggested we could take my car; he declined, and said that his ride would be part of the adventure. It was a little kiss and a wave to my beautiful wife, Dottie, and we were off. I felt certain I would die that day, as the ride to the jump center at Lake Elsinore, California, was at full throttle all the way. At a stop for gas, he confessed to me that Fox had forbidden him to ride the bike anymore; that he was only to ride during filming. Steven Oliver was definitely the rebel of his day. I don't scare easily, but that day I was praying we'd return okay.

We arrived at about ten thirty a.m. and went through several hours of jump school instruction. Everyone there knew who Steve was, as *Peyton Place* was the hit show of the day, but he received no special treatment. I had to complete jump school again, since too much time had elapsed since my previous jumps. At the conclusion of jump school we suited up and boarded a larger Cessna jump aircraft that held up to ten other jumpers. It seemed we reached altitude fairly quickly. We were at just over five thousand feet and the jumpmaster asked who wanted to go first. I had been the first out on my other jumps, so I nodded acceptance of the honor. I then gave a thumbs-up to Steve and stepped out of the aircraft, placing my left foot on the step and then my right foot onto the rubber front tire. The pilot had cut the engine, so all I felt was the windblast and all I could hear were the surrealistic sounds the wind made as it hummed around me. I leaned into the strut and pushed off into the wind current, lifting my body level as I let go and sailed away. The rapture came over me again for a moment; an absolutely awesome and exhilarating experience. Steve shared the same sensation. The jumpmaster and the more experienced jumpers aboard then soared with the plane up to 7,500 feet to make their jumps. An invigorating, thrilling feat, to say the least—I was hooked again, as was Steve. We couldn't stop talking about it.

But I was confronted with an even greater fear on the trek back to Los Angeles. It was late afternoon before we finally started the return trip. Approximately an hour on the road and we experienced what Steve thought was the reoccurrence of a minor ignition problem. We pulled off the freeway onto the shoulder, but he didn't have what he needed in his tools to fix the problem. We were still in a fairly rural area, but thought we had seen a house a short distance behind us. We attempted to hide the bike as best we could and began walking back over a hill to where we thought we had seen the house. Then, over another rise we saw this beautiful home off in the distance that suddenly looked like an oasis. As we got closer, we realized it was a very large home and rather upscale. There were a number of new, expensive cars in the drive, very well-manicured grounds, and beautiful flowers all about the perimeter of the landscaping. Slightly hidden from the highway, it was a distance of about a mile and a half to this very lush and green setting. It seemed somewhat bizarre that this incredible home was just sitting there by itself.

As we approached the porch, a young girl was already opening the door saying to her parents, "Mom, Dad, it's Steven Oliver—Steven Oliver from *Peyton Place*." We were already in the house when her parents came into the room. I then introduced myself, as Steve was well-known to them all. Steve explained that his motorcycle had an electrical problem he thought he could fix temporarily if he had a short piece of electrical wire, and then he could get the bike to the shop in the morning. We talked show business for a little bit before these kind, wonderful folks said they were just sitting down to dinner, and that they would be honored if we would join them, and then they could drive us back to the bike with all the wire we needed. We shared a marvelous meal that evening with a family of angels (I think they were), and then they drove us back to the bike and within moments Steve had it running. It had gotten dark and cold so we shook hands, exchanged invitations a second time for them to come to the lot and visit us, waved, and we were off. Over the years, Steve and I would often reminisce about our sport parachute jump. I think what we remembered most about our adventure that quiet Saturday afternoon was the uplifting, positive conversation we shared over a wonderful salad, a pasta and meat dish to die for, and the kindness and sheer goodness of some truly loving folks we met along a highway.

Mike McLean had a door that entered our office, a back exit from his office, and he often would escape from his office through our office to miss the assembly of agents and actors that would be trying to see him on any given day. His good buddy, James Brolin, whom Mike had convinced his father to sign as a contract player, often came through our office to meet with him through his rear exit. Sometimes, he'd come in and plop down and sit for a while, and we'd enter into long conversations about acting, life, and the universe; down to earth, I thought. Larry Stewart, Irwin Allen's casting director on *Voyage To The Bottom Of The Sea*—or *Voyage to the Bottom of the Ratings*, as we called it—and *Lost in Space* also often wandered down and attempted to entertain us with some amazing stories of his exploits and accomplishments. The company was very busy, but it seemed there was always time to converse with people as they sat on our old casting couch. It was a continuous hotbed of activity, and a central gathering place of rumors of what was happening on the lot and around the city. Visitors to the office were the people from behind the scenes that would stray by—mostly assistant directors, extras, and stuntmen. Carl's good buddy from high school, Richard Lang, son of film director Walter Lang, was amid the constant flow, as he was a first assistant director at Fox. Anyone visiting would come in and sit down on the couch, and everyone in the room would conduct a collective conversation with that guest. Over the years I made a personal observation; that is, I came to believe that most studio employees, no matter what their field of expertise, had hidden desires to step in front of the camera, be discovered, and act. I think this theory applies especially to the people working on the set daily. When "action" is called by the director and all is quiet, some have nothing to do but watch, listen, and dream.

Extra talent visitors to the office would make the long walk on the east side of the new administration building to the north side, where our offices were located, to the extra casting's open windows in order to scout for work. The "New Ad" was built in the late '30s or early '40s. But it was still called the "New Ad" in the early '60s because there was still the "old ad," the original administration building built on the Fox lot at the extreme northwest corner. Sometimes, the office would take on the appearance of a circus from the myriad of characters that would drop by to sell their wares, sign contracts, or pick up extra work vouchers for the various shows shooting on stage. On any given day, it might include heavyweight contender Al Bain, who fought Two-Ton Tony Gelento and whose persona was mirrored precisely by Anthony Quinn for the 1962 version of *Requiem For A Heavyweight*; to little person Billy Curtis, whom Clint Eastwood appointed town sheriff in *High Plains Drifter*; to Dave Sharpe, Paul Stader, Chuck Hicks, Vince Deadrick, Dick Dial, Carey Lofton, Bud Ekins, the Eppers (Gary, Tony, and Stephanie), Dean Smith, Donna Garrett (stunt double for Raquel Welch on *Fantastic Voyage*), Bill and Chuck Couch, Gary McLarty, Paul Nuckles, Chuck Roberson, Gil Perkins, George Fisher,

Glen Wilder, George Sawaya, Gene and Mike Lebell, Hal Needham, Dick Ziker, Dar Robinson, Denver Mattson, and many, many more that were either extras or stunt people who were regulars to the office.

This would include my cousin, Lindy Heidt. Lindy was an actor, and he would also stray by for a visit. He had acquired some supporting credits over the years, but mostly was hired to laugh. Cousin Lindy was like one of those little laugh contraptions that when you press a button it goes through a complete laugh cycle, from the beginning chuckle to a gradual infectious crescendo of a hysterical cackle. My mom always said one day the vein on his forehead would burst and my cousin Lindy would die of laughing. He was always wonderful to sit near at family funerals.

One cousin Lindy tale: One afternoon, I was leaving the casting office to go over to UCLA and sign up for an evening class. Lindy was visiting and said he would drive me. I tried to decline the invitation. I had seen his bigger-than-normal personality all my young life and sometimes I'd shy away from it. I was doing my best "I want to be alone" act. When we got out to the parking lot, he chuckled, waved, and pointed, indicating that his buddy Howard would drive us over in his big black limousine, which had come closer. Lindy opened the door, bumped me in, laughed, and said, in his best gangster dialect, "Come on, kid, we're taking you for a ride." And then came the laugh that had made him famous—in our family, at least. When we arrived at very near the campus entrance in crowded Westwood, I heard him say, "Howard, give Mike the Red Carpet

Treatment." I had an idea what that might mean and I started to bolt, but it was too late. As I opened the door, pushing past laughing Lindy, loudspeakers sounded the roar of a trumpet's fanfare. Howard had rolled out a red carpet, extending up and onto the sidewalk area. Needless to say, I was beet-red embarrassed, but for a beat I worked the passing pedestrians like I was Steve McQueen playing the same unexpected moment. I nodded and smiled to a few curious kids as I quickly disappeared into the mass of students passing by. I could hear cousin Lindy still cackling when the limo was out of sight. Oh, how I dreaded the ride back to Fox.

One afternoon, stuntman Tony Epper came by extra casting, sat down on the infamous "casting couch," and shared the details of a story we'd only heard rumors about. He had been working as a stuntman on a film in Montana that co-starred his pal, Bill Smith. Tony Epper had the reputation among the most rugged stuntmen as being one very tough hombre, six foot five and two hundred fifteen pounds of hard body. For that matter, most the Eppers were stunt people and as hard as coffin nails. Bill Smith was a "name" television star of the day and was like a bull himself at six foot three and two hundred twenty pounds; extremely strong physically, and having won local Hollywood/Los Angeles arm-wrestling championship competitions several years in a row. The film they were shooting in this small Montana cowboy town was for another production company. Tony said that after the day's shoot he and Bill would wander up the street to the only local saloon for a couple of beers.

A few days had passed and they had found themselves there again, and on this occasion about three beers deep, some local asked if they were part of the "queers" from the Hollywood movie company shooting in town, and then had laughed to his neighbor. Tony Epper said that they lost count of the maybe ten to twelve or more cowboy-assholes that they punched out onto the street; that he and his colleague Mr. Smith tried to teach those old boys some manners at first, but then realized the only thing they really understood was a knuckle sandwich. They proceeded to divide and conquer and take no prisoners. They cleaned the place out after feeding them a snack. I'm sure it was the last time those cowboys asked that question.

A number of big-budget films were being planned, including *Hello, Dolly!* and *Star, Patton, Butch Cassidy and the Sundance Kid, Valley of the Dolls, Stagecoach,* and *Von Ryan's Express,* starring old blue eyes, Frank Sinatra. *The Sound of Music* was the first project I would work on with Robert Wise; later, *The Sand Pebbles,* starring Steve McQueen, which he would also direct. The Albert Finney and Audrey Hepburn film *Two for the Road* and *Bedazzled,* starring Peter Cook and Dudley Moore, were readying to start shooting in Europe for Stanley Donen Productions. With nearly ten television shows in production and more pilots slated, Twentieth Century Fox was growing very busy—very busy indeed.

I had been doing my newly created duties for about a year when former baseball great Chuck Essegian joined the expanding staff of the television casting department. They didn't have office space to accommodate his position, so he was given space next to me at the agent's phone station. His persona was that of the strong, silent type; that is, until you got to know him. We all made friends with Chuck quickly. He was extremely likeable, a man's man, a former major league baseball player who hit two home runs during the 1959 World Series as a Dodger, now sitting right next to me in the extra casting office. I tried to find out what was happening in the department. Instinct told me he was connected to somebody, and I felt I was suddenly being passed over and that he might be assigned a show to cast before me. I was slightly annoyed and resentful at first, to say the least.

After a few days we began interacting more, exchanging simple observations. I knew he had kids, since he diligently called home every few hours to check on his family. I could relate to his concerns for his family. That year, I had met the beautiful young Dottie Fisher, fallen in love, and one weekend we surprised everyone by dodging the big wedding, finding a minister and getting married. We both wanted kids, a huge family. I just happened to overhear things that got my attention about Chuck's family and who he really was. A straight-A student at Stanford, I would learn, graduating pre-medicine while working full time forty plus hours a week in a restaurant. I knew about the home runs, but how did his experience relate to casting shows? I was the casting protégé, studying acting and earning my stripes within the department. What could he possibly know about acting and actors? How can this guy adapt? I thought.

He was a baseball player. What could he possibly know about the casting process?

Funny thing; as Chuck revealed his inner self to me over the next months, he would have been the first to say that he didn't really want to cast anything that wouldn't catch a trout. In the days that followed, I detailed the elements of my responsibilities to him and he asked if he could tag along and watch some films. Then, he started to hang with me on a regular basis, since his duties hadn't been clearly defined. Some days I'd have to run down tons of film on talent for both TV and film projects, and we'd be away from the offices for most of the day. We'd talk life, business, show business, and sometimes play chess with the film projectionists. From Chuck's perspective, the casting process was just knowing the actors, and knowing what you like and what a producer and director likes and needs. It was just simple business, a choice, an apple or an orange, and then analyzing the variables. Chuck Essegian was fairly reserved with most people, but if he knew you and liked you, his shirt would come off his back if you needed it, literally. He became a mentor to me, whether he realized it or not. I soon began to value his judgment, interpretations, and evaluations of just about everything. He taught me that the best method for understanding and acquiring solutions for simple problem solving was to approach the problem by concentrating on and analyzing its specific weaknesses; that it's assessing what is coming at you and then stepping into it, taking your best swing. Sometimes you are successful and sometimes not, but you keep working to be a better "hitter";

no matter what the pitch is, you adapt and keep working to get up to bat. Chuck had great respect and admiration for Ted Williams. He would say that Ted Williams was the first at practice and the last to leave the field. "Take this hard-work ethic into whatever you do, Mike," he said to me one day. My neophyte resentment would change to great respect and deep gratitude for what I would learn.

Some time later it was disclosed to me that fellow Stanford alumnus Richard Zanuck had brought Chuck into the fold at Fox, as they had been close friends while students. Richard Zanuck was now president of the television wing and his father, Darryl, was CEO of 20th Century Fox Film Corp. Both had seen Chuck's All-American football performances at Stanford and were big fans and friends of this whole, extremely intelligent, and still accomplishing person. They had offered to groom him to be a producer, and production was of great interest to him, but first he would learn casting. As we all got to know Chuck better we discovered he didn't much care for self-important egotistical types. He wasn't easily impressed with any of the big-shot casting directors that would often visit our office with grandiose stories of how they single-handedly saved the day or the show. Most were filled with pomp and self-importance, the exception being Joe D'Agosta, who had a normal perception of himself. When the important types did come down to our office for nothing more than telling us how wonderful they were, Chuck would disappear. Sometimes he bolted for the door. After a while I could tell exactly who would send him out first.

Larry Stewart had a million stories, and he seemed to derive enormous gratification from taking several weekly breaks and sharing them with us. He had accomplished a great deal, including being the very first president of the Academy of Television Arts and Sciences. He'd produced and directed television, but some of his stories seemed somewhat embellished, to say the least. I think Larry was always trying to impress Chuck especially, as he always seemed to direct his opening remarks to him, looking for a reaction. Most times, however, when Larry would enter, Chuck would look at me and whisper, "Walter Mitty," and then get up and exit the office as fast as Larry had entered. One thing truly amazed Chuck Essegian and me with regard to Larry Stewart and his bigger-than-life/boastful view of his personal accomplishments. In 1973, after we all had left the Fox lot, Larry Stewart created, wrote, and directed the hit television show *Thrill Seekers* for NBC, hosted by Chuck Connors. The show focused on people and their various above-average, thrill-seeking, larger-than-life adventures; perhaps the very first "reality show." I thought it was another great example of the "He becomes what he dwells upon" adage, and Larry Stewart was always doing exactly that, dwelling on bigger-than-life ideas and stories, practicing and presenting, and trying to get up to bat. Finally he did exactly that, again.

Chuck Essegian loved musicals and photography, and he was always sharing some tidbit of wisdom of both with me. Sometimes, we'd sneak into recording sessions on the lot during the scoring of films, and sit in the back and enjoy the melodious works until the musicians would go on a break. If I had a musical to run down Chuck was always right there with me. I had begun working with Phil Benjamin on *Guide for a Married Man*, a film that would star nonstop funnyman Walter Matthau and Robert Morse, to be supported by a huge cameo cast of everyone famous. Gene Kelly was signed to a multiple-picture directing deal, with *Guide* to be the first and the extravaganza *Hello, Dolly!* to follow. I had met with him several times as we began the process of viewing films to consider the talent suggestions made by Phil Benjamin, to determine the ones that would take a meeting, but whose status had risen above being asked to read and audition for a role.

Chuck and I had gone to a projection room and were watching the musical *South Pacific*, for a totally different film project than Mr. Kelly's. Most of the projection rooms in the editorial building were elegant, with posh leather seats, phones, and other amenities; a smaller version of the big-screen commercial theaters, seating maybe forty people at the most. The screen went from a foot or so above floor level to just below the ceiling, which was probably no higher than twelve feet. Chuck and I would always start by asking who had the popcorn and then the clowning around would begin. I mean, we were the only ones in the theater, we could do and say what we wanted, and like a couple of big kids we always did exactly that. We were well past some of the big dance numbers, and as usual were adding a lot of our own absurd dialogue and laughing our brains out when one of us would say something really funny. Finally, in a kind of laugh stupor and at Chuck's continual coaxing, I had gotten up and was dancing about in front of the screen during another big dance number, attempting to dance up the projection room wall. Chuck was on the floor, laughing hysterically at my attempts to join the people on screen in the dance and ascend the wall. I was blinded by the bright projection light in my eyes and I couldn't hear much better. I was doing my best Donald O'Connor impression when I realized Chuck had stopped laughing and was maybe talking to someone, probably the projectionist, I didn't care; I continued.

Then, a voice said to me, "Very good, Mike! Good! Keep going!" as if it was an audition. Recognizing the voice, I immediately stopped. The person who had seen me dancing and clowning was the star of *Singin' in the Rain*, Gene Kelly, and the master had encouraged me to dance on. I was clowning around, and had never, ever thought of myself as a dancer—maybe an improvisational clown dancer, but never a real dancer. Chuck and Gene were old acquaintances; they had met when Chuck was a Dodger. He later told me that Mr. Kelly was a straight-up, great guy, and that he loved athletics of any kind but especially was a fan of baseball. Mr. Kelly had come into the wrong projection room that day, and as he left he again encouraged lowly me to dance on. He said, "Mike, come by and let me see what you can do." He then said something about being in the wrong projection room and again told me to keep it up, "Keep practicing, Mike," and left the room. Chuck was laughing again, saying, "Let me see you do that again, go up the wall again." I made another attempt. I never forgot Gene Kelly's encouraging words that day. Later, I would think that Gene Kelly had been clowning around as well, to a much larger audience, and in the process had enjoyed his life immensely and made a great many people very joyful and happy. What a wonderful and lucky gift for him, and especially us.

Carl Joy would soon move up to into a supervisory capacity, as this older chap was to retire in the not-too-distant future. Carl was his favorite and was being groomed for that position. On one very quiet afternoon, I played an impromptu prank on our former supervisor that Carl and I still chuckle about to this day. The fatman often would come back from lunch, put his feet up on his desk, prop a newspaper up across his lap, hiding his face, and take a little siesta. On this occasion it was just the fatman, Carl, and me on a warm, sleepy afternoon. Carl sat right next to his chubby highness, facing in the same direction, and facing me across the room. I looked across and noticed fatty nodding off and blowing his ritually placed newspaper up and down. I looked at Carl and nodded, gesturing for him to look in his majesty's direction, trying to get Carl to look at him blowing the newspaper. Carl was trying his best not to look at me or be involved in any mischief I might come up with. I knew I could break Carl up; he'd laugh at anything I did, but usually had to be coaxed from the reserved side of his personality before he would let loose. If something was funny, he'd laugh, but the more restrained side of Carl was trying to be in control here. I turned, grabbed some newspaper, propped my feet up on my desk, and mirrored the exact movements of the plump one. I did about two minutes of what I thought he looked like, very quietly, across the room. I nodded; I puffed the newspaper up. I could see Carl was becoming amused by my antics. He was smiling, shaking his head and saying quietly, "You're crazy, Mike," and then looking down and away, trying hard not to look at me. Then, all of a sudden he couldn't control it any longer. My silent mischief had pulled him in and he suddenly burst and exploded into laughter, breaking the quiet of warm siesta time. He couldn't stop, and it jarred the fatman awake.

His focus went immediately to Carl, as I had gone back quickly to looking busy, feet off my desk, absorbed diligently in my work. Carl was still laughing uncontrollably and the supervisor was thinking that maybe Carl was laughing at him. Carl was almost blathering, trying to explain, with tears coming out of his eyes and saying, "Oh, it was Mike. Mike, he was doing something really funny," as he continued to laugh. I was playing it very serious, saying, "What, Carl? What was I doing? What, Carl?" The fatman went quietly back to his work and I to mine. Carl was still giggling and babbling, trying to explain something of the funny things he had observed me doing. I continued with the denial. "What? What did I do?" The more I played it straight, the more Carl realized how it must have looked to the boss and the more he would laugh. The fatman was looking at Carl as if he had gone completely insane, while Carl continued to slip deeper into the laugh hole he was digging for himself. It was with every bit of my trained actor's control that I was finally able to exit the room, as I was really having great difficulty maintaining my composure.

I gave Carl one last look, with another, "What, Carl? What did I do?" I shook my head and stepped into the hallway, and then bolted for the men's room, where I let loose one huge, hysterical knee-slapping chuckle.

Dave Sharpe and Dean Smith were probably the very best horsemen of their individual eras. Dave Sharpe had been an early cowboy western star when he was younger, in the silent film days. Somewhere in his mid to late sixties when I came into casting, he was known for being an exceptionally agile athlete. Now white-headed, he still had handsome-leading-man good looks, was fit and strong, and the consensus of opinion was that he could still do any stunt. I had always loved horses, and recently in my film viewing I had seen some footage of Dean Smith doing one of those seemingly impossible Dave Sharpe jumps onto the lead horse of a stagecoach, where he worked his way back to the rear and fought with the bad guy, or the good guy. I've always respected the artists who would attempt to do their own stunts. Steve McQueen and Burt Reynolds were just two that often would have to be convinced that someone else should come in and take over when it was getting too dangerous.

I'd seen Dean do horse work for numerous television and western genre films, among them Fox's remake of the classic *Stagecoach*. Dean's incredible skills and the possibility of learning to ride that well intrigued me—mesmerized me. I learned that he had a few people that he instructed in some regularly scheduled classes on the weekend. He came by the office to sign a stunt contract one afternoon and I asked him about his classes, and he invited me to come out to his ranch to participate. I went out a couple times, but mostly observed, in awe, this amazing athlete Dean Smith working with his horse. He was absolutely gifted and a true delight to watch, but I could never manage to find the time to get back out there and stay with it. However, I was confident if I had ever gotten a role that required riding skills I surely would have known one end of the horse from the other, thanks to Dean Smith.

In my quest to learn stunt work, get a regular workout, and become an all-around, versatile actor, I took some boxing lessons from Denver Mattson at Paul Stader's 3rd Street gym in Santa Monica before it was a trendy walking street. Denver was a fairly large-framed chap, well-known and experienced in staging fight scenes, and a good guy to have in your corner at the bar. This was considerably more to my liking, as I had been taught to punch a speed bag and box at an early age by my older brother, Doyle. Paul Stader, who owned the 3rd Street gym, was Irwin Allen's stunt coordinator on *Voyage to the Bottom of the Sea*, and was considered and revered as the premier and favorite water-specialty man around. He had done a multitude of high falls into water. He was Errol Flynn's stunt double, and you can bet that just about any high fall from the top of the mast of a sailing ship in all those swashbuckler films Errol Flynn starred in, and any other high fall in a film of that era, was Paul Stader's work. I also took a few classes with Paul at his gym, and he gave me some pointers and showed me a couple of moves to guide you directly at a target, so that you will land right and not hurt yourself by either landing forward on your face or on your back; all very interesting and an absolutely grueling workout.

With the increased production schedule and the projected future projects slated, Carl Joy added two more to his staff, totaling four. Chuck and I made it six people in the large single-room office. One young guy that joined the department was Bruce Maidy. Bruce was a terrific young man, good-looking, extremely intelligent, and a very good singer, very talented and charismatic. I think I may have been a wee bit envious and jealous of Bruce, as he was trying to do some things I hadn't mastered—like sing, for one. You could set your clock by Bruce; he was very meticulous and detail obsessed, so it seemed. Bruce would come back from lunch at precisely the same time every day and ritually retrieve a Baby Ruth or some other tasty sweet from the stash in his very neat desk and begin the unwrapping process. Then, he would sit and eat and savor, very slowly, his after-lunch treat. He was the kid at the other end of the sandbox who was eating food in front of everyone that didn't have food. It drove Carl and me crazy. I once told Carl I was going to go to Bruce's desk, grab his candy bar from its precisely placed position there on an opened wrapper, and eat it like a candy bar was meant to be eaten—in one bite; a chewing, gulping, single bite—and then burp at Bruce. Carl laughed and told me to shut up and sit down. I would wonder how anybody could be so organized as to have a candy treat in his or her desk for after lunch. I'd eat them on the way to my desk; I could never get them into my desk, much less eat them slowly. I was also envious of his neatness and methodical way of doing things, and it started to freak me out. I just had to mess with this neat new kid.

Carl was the new department head, since the whale had finally beached himself into retirement, and I had no fear—none whatsoever. I started by playing practical jokes; unbeknownst to Bruce, his pledging our office fraternity had only just begun. I had recently acquired several different composite photographs of this positively homely, if not outrageously ugly man who wanted to be considered for acting work and had submitted his photos to the casting office. These had gotten to me by way of Pamela Hartley, Joe Scully's secretary from down the hall. It would appear that she had become lightheaded, very near queasiness, and nearly lost her breakfast after opening the morning mail and seeing the photo of this most unfortunate fellow. I had passed her desk at precisely the moment of the opening and had witnessed her young face and pretty complexion going almost pale. I managed to revive and save her by intervening and pushing the photos of this poor chap back into their envelope, out of her view. She then caught her breath, thanked me, and asked me to see that the contents of the envelope were never again viewed by anyone. She said they should be immediately destroyed by fire. When I left Joe's office with my assignments, she again instructed me, "By fire, Mike." As I stepped into the hallway and headed back to my office, I reached in and took a look for myself. Ugly, yes; this guy was so ugly Don Rickles would have been nice to him.

At once, it occurred to me that I might have a use for ugly. There were several small pictures on the back of each composite of the actor doing different things and in different poses, such as the holding the face with a hand under the chin shot or the talking on the phone shot. Frankly, I have never understood either of those poses. "Oh, he can talk on the phone, let's get this guy!" This guy looked scary, sinister, and ugly. I took my favorite ugly shot from the back of one of the composites and had a supply of copies made in the Fox print shop. I returned to the office and slyly put the originals and the copies in my desk, waited for Bruce to leave the office for lunch, and then went to work. I showed Carl the supply of ugly guy copies I had obtained from those marvelous chaps in the printing department. Carl was up now, looking on and cackling like he'd just been released from a mental hospital by mistake. I then began the careful cutting-out process—an ugly guy cutout about one inch in diameter. I then locked the doors and sent Carl to the window on lookout, and opened Bruce's desk drawer and removed the candy bar on the very top. I carefully unwrapped it and placed the ugly guy on the top, caressing the Milky Way, I believe it was. Oh, he might want the Fifth Avenue or the Clark Bar or the Mars Bar. I would have to do them all. I started putting the ugly guy on everything that was Bruce's. At one point, I even took the dial out of the center of the phone and put the ugly guy in. Early one morning, I booby-trapped the stall where Bruce would always do his regular morning ugly. I thought it appropriate, ugly on ugly, so I rolled out all the butt-wipe and placed several cutouts of the ugly guy at different intervals two or three layers from the top. I even put him on the side mirror of his car for his ride home. Just when Bruce thought it was safe, I'd give him the ugly guy. Ugly guy terror went on for weeks. Carl often would curl over laughing when nobody was around but me, him, and the ugly guy. It was always the same: Bruce would pull open his desk drawer, take out a candy bar he thought hadn't been tampered with and then begin the unwrapping. As he unwrapped, he'd be looking around the room at Carl and me, and then we'd hear him slam it into the metal trash can, making a loud thud. I had the "What did I do?" look perfected by now.

One Friday afternoon, Carl had stopped at a newsstand to get the trade papers and had bought a copy of the *Los Angeles Free Press*. Friday's *Free Press* would become a new source of cutouts other than the ugly guy, as our ugly guy supply was almost gone. Carl was becoming even more deviously involved. He had discovered this new source, with cheesy pictures of male and female body parts to cut out and torment Bruce with. It would be the selection and removal of the just-right body part from the newspaper to place on Bruce's goody. I let Carl have his fun with this one. Like a couple of little demented children, we'd open a candy bar and rewrap it with a cutout of a naked man, and place it back in his desk drawer. We had gotten down to the last copies of the ugly guy supply—no more copies, but I could make more since I still had the originals hidden in my desk. We felt a naked ugly man or a sleazy fat woman, or body parts thereof, would be a nice change for Bruce's pledging to our casting fraternity. We were diversifying; we now had choice in our terror/torment portfolio.

Then casting department office administrator (Susan Macintosh) came in to inform us of other changes; that the entire casting department was to be remodeled. Rambling she said that Carl's office was to be immediately painted, carpeted, and also would get new desks, with the painting to commence that coming weekend. Most times we could barely understand her heavy Scottish accent, so we paid little attention to her, as usual, and we certainly didn't believe any of the "new desks" part of her announcement, as we'd heard it all numerous times before. Our desks and office furnishings had been in the office since the dawn of time, and management seemed somewhat frugal on such matters, to say the least. It was said that when God rested on the seventh day, he had rested at my rickety old desk where, among other things, etched into the wood top was "God sat here and rested." We were instructed to be ready for the office remodeling by throwing out old outdated files, production schedules, and any other junk clutter. In the days that followed we all discarded and threw out. I had taken some items to my car, but the ugly guy still remained hidden in my desk. There would be still time to find him a new home.

I had returned from the projection room that afternoon and fly-shooting-ace Carl immediately shot me with a rubber band, hitting me smack in the middle of my forehead. After a few beats of playing "You shot me in the eye! I'm blind, I'm blind! I can't see," I straightened up and told them that I had just passed Paul Newman and Robert Redford in the projection building hallway. "Me, Butch, and the Sundance Kid,"

I said, and Carl shot me again. This time he hit me on the ear and it really stung. I was really hurt now and I had to return Carl's fire. Carl's sudden urge to attack me for no apparent reason would erupt into the mother of all rubber band wars. I think what triggered that first rubber band shot heard round the office was instigated by my making light of Carl's devoured sweater collar and his shoe(s) earlier that morning. Let me back up some. Carl had come to work that morning wearing black slacks and a nicely pressed button-down shirt with a very fashionable paisley tie, over which he wore what had been a handsome black alpaca sweater—handsome but for the chewed-up and fraying collar. On his feet was at least one chewed-up expensive Italian shoe. I asked him where he was buying his clothes and applauded his nice choice, and asked if he was trying to start a new style; perhaps the torn and ripped look by designer Peppy? Carl avoided my query and asked to be left alone, but I couldn't resist pestering him further. I then tugged at some of the dangling sweater material hanging from his collar and he pulled away, saying, "Don't do that," and it unraveled and frayed even further. I laughed and said, "Oh, sorry, let me give you back your sweater," and handed him a small ball of yarn. Carl had recently gotten married and had purchased a dog from a champion line, with champion-line papers, no less. Peppy the champion was his name, and Peppy was eating Carl's clothes and everything in his and his pretty bride's home. Carl took me by his house at lunchtime one afternoon to check on Peppy and all the legs on his new Danish Modern living room furniture (wedding gifts) had been gnawed off—and I mean all the legs, off! The new television was resting at a slant and ready to fall, since the stand was dangling on three legs. Peppy would always have a light meal of Carl's shoes to start, then select a few nice sweaters and chew on the collars. No one really knew why he would chew just the collars of these expensive garments. Carl's bride was going insane from it. The marriage was doomed, as it was suspected that Peppy had possibly chewed more of Carl's things than met the eye. I asked Carl why they hadn't kept him tied and restrained in the yard until possibly he could be obedience trained or shot dead. Carl explained that they were renting and weren't allowed pets. They had to keep him hidden and confined to the house, which was proving to be disastrous. Carl motioned for me to follow him; he wanted to show me something. We walked into the backyard. As though with a chainsaw, all of the plants, shrubs, trees, and anything growing had been visited and territorialized by Peppy, the living chainsaw, and gnawed off level with the ground. I couldn't believe my eyes. Everything living and growing, without exaggeration, had been toppled.

When I walked into the office that afternoon and took Carl's first rubber band shot to the forehead, food-fight mentality kicked in, but there was no food. Deadeye Carl was blasting me with rubber-bands shots like a machine gun. I lunged for a large unopened box of rubber bands and commenced return fire. For a while it was a very intense rubber band fight. Every rubber band in the office had been used and was on the floor—hundreds, they were everywhere—so there was plenty of ammo. Rubber bands covered everything. Then the course of the battle changed when Carl came and took my top desk drawer out and dumped it upside down on the top of my desk; the battle escalated and took a new direction. I charged Carl and beat him with the rolled-up production schedules that hadn't been thrown out yet until they broke and flew apart. The room was a mess, but this was only the beginning of the war. I had captured Carl's desk, and I pushed the top contents onto the floor with a growl, looking for a reaction. We were now trying to outdo each other. He raced to my desk and did exactly the same thing. I then took the top drawer out of his desk and slung it hard to a corner. It became a seek-and-destroy frenzy. Carl seemed demented, more demented than anyone had ever seen him before. He was laughing as he countered my every move from the other side of the room. He was at my desk, laughing his demented head-of-the-extra-casting-department laugh as he continued to fire rubber band missiles at me. Bruce and the other clerks answered the phones, and moved when the chaos of their supervisor's destructive path approached their position. Carl then went to the executive hallway entrance, the door of which now read: Carl Joy – Extra Casting. He locked it, for fear that Susan Macintosh would come in and say something we could understand. He then turned to my desk, where he removed the remaining drawers and proceeded to turn my desk completely upside down. John Burnside, an extra chap and buddy, stopped by to look for work for the next day, but nothing stopped the affray. "We're kind of busy, John, be right with you,"

I said, as I turned Carl's desk upside down. John Burnside entered from the outer office entrance, sat down on the couch, and watched the remainder of the battle, saying occasionally to whomever, "Oh, good one." The room looked like a small war had taken place, and we were exhausted; sweating and laughing hysterically, with a verbal replay of who had really won. The room was an absolute mess. Allegedly, we were to get remodeled, with new desks, so we didn't much care that the room was in slight disarray.

The next workday morning, which was a Monday, brought a big surprise. At about nine thirty a.m. when I arrived, I noticed carpet remnants on the exterior entrance of the office. What none of us expected was not only that they had painted and put down carpeting, but also there were handsome new and expensive-looking Danish Modern desks at all the workstations—five new desks. The office looked newer, larger, brighter, and much more elegant and distinguished than anyone could have imagined. It was night-and-day different from how it had looked when we closed up shop Friday afternoon, the day of the great rubber-band war. The paint, carpet, and desks had come in over the weekend. Carl, Bruce, and I were amazed by how nice it looked and how quickly it had been done. We all thought it would be done in stages, with the new desks being the last change. The department was very busy that morning, as we had several new films and television productions scheduled to start that week. *Che Guevara* was shooting on location at the Fox Malibu ranch and *Butch Cassidy* was winding down. Mondays were always the start day of new films. Carl and his staff had been there since before dawn, checking in extra talent for all the shows currently shooting. I asked Carl about the location of the old desks, since I hadn't seen them outside. He said he didn't know where they were. Carl seemed detached and very busy. Nevertheless, I prodded further and quietly explained that our ugly guy was hidden in my desk. I advised Carl that I wasn't worried and I could retrieve him if we could find the location of where they had taken my old desk. Carl was suddenly more than concerned. We guessed they were somewhere close outside, so we went out and looked again. No desks anywhere in sight. Carl was instantly on the phone, and was informed that the old desks had been transported to the North Lot (now Century City). No problem, I thought. We'd just go there, find our desks, and retrieve the ugly guy. Carl dropped what he was doing and told his staff that he had misplaced an important document that he thought was still in his old desk, and that he was going to the North Lot to retrieve it. He then called what was referred to as a "Rover," which was like an on-the-lot taxicab that would take an employee where he had to go in a hurry. We jumped in the Rover and raced to the North Lot location where the desks had been taken. What we didn't know was that desks from all over the lot had been taken there. Probably more than two hundred old wooden desks were stacked in a huge pile to be dismantled. All the offices on the lot that needed new desks had gotten them that weekend. Both Carl and I were dressed in suits and ties, but for well over an hour we climbed, fell, pulled, and tugged to locate my old desk with the ugly guy in it. We felt compelled to find him; we missed his ugly face, and the thought of Bruce never having to see him again drove us way beyond sanity and the simple quest to search. There we were, two junior executives on a very busy Monday morning, searching for the proverbial ugly guy needle-in-the-haystack so that we might continue tormenting a good friend. Finally, dirty and sweaty in our business suits and having exhausted all efforts to locate my desk, we gave up. We couldn't find the ugly guy and we were devastated. Our personal fun with the ugly guy would be lost forever. It seemed like an old and dear friend, who just happened to be ugly and that we always had got a chuckle from, had passed on; we had gone to the funeral and paid our respects. He was gone now; let him rest in peace, buried in my rickety old desk. Rest in peace, ugly guy, we said as we boarded another Rover back to the office. In the days ahead we tried with other ugly guys, naked men, or naked fat women, but it just wasn't the same. Ugly man terror was over. We finally confessed our sins to Bruce Maidy and affirmed his admittance to our fraternity by taking him to lunch and buying him a nice box of assorted candy bars.

Joe D'Agosta gave me my very first opportunity to cast a role. I was pumped and ready. He was casting a film entitled *Way Way Out* that starred Jerry Lewis and was being produced under the Fox banner and co-produced by Lewis's production company. A futuristic comedy, its theme revolved around Russia and America competing for moon space. I was doing my usual duties and had read the script, and had casually suggested to Joe that he should get Joe Karbo to play the role of the first car salesman on the moon. In the early sixties, pitchman Karbo, later to become a talk-show host and marketing guru, was very popular. For many years he had been the spokesperson for a local Los Angeles-based automobile dealership. Everybody knew Joe Karbo. Joe Karbo then created the first all-night TV talk show, *The All Night Show*, where he and his wife, Kitty, interviewed countless celebrity guests—Sammy Davis Jr., Dinah Shore, and Frank Sinatra, to name a few—into the wee hours of the morning. Joe D'Agosta's reaction to my idea of Karbo was that maybe Karbo wasn't well-known nationally; maybe he was just a local hero. He said he would run the idea by the producer, Malcolm Stewart, to see what he thought. He asked me to call Karbo's agent, check out his availability for our shoot dates, and get some money "quotes" for any recent jobs he had completed. Joe got back to me the next morning, said that Malcolm liked the idea and had given him the go-ahead, and that I should set and hire Joe Karbo for the car salesman role if he was within our budget. I was ecstatic; I thought it was a dazzling choice, a brilliant inspiration, my first casting. It would be the first time that I would negotiate and hire an actor with an agent. I was very excited with my ex-panding responsibilities. I got a price from his agent of what they wanted for the approximate days we needed him. I checked the accuracy of those quotes with the pro-duction companies submitted, and they were correct. He was established at his quoted price, and was within our budget. I relayed the information to Joe D. and he again gave me the go-ahead to set him. I then started negotiating with Joe Karbo's agent. I had heard Joe D. and Joe Scully negotiate hundreds of times, and I did exactly what they had taught me: always offer less than what was in the budget, and a good casting person always has backups. "Tell them you have a good backup and you'll go in that direction, if we can't buy the talent for what's in the budget," Joe D'Agosta had said. The agent wanted big dollars for the days we needed him, but finally accepted my final offer, which was less than I could have spent. I had skirmished diligently in an effort to save a few dollars and I won. I had saved the company some money, and I was proud. I put a hold on Joe Karbo for the approximate start date and gathered his personal information for his contract, to be drafted by Joe's secretary. I had arrived. I was onstage the day Joe Karbo worked. I introduced myself and talked with him for quite a while; what a nice man. He told me that early on he had studied at Pasadena Playhouse, and that acting was his first love. In his scene, he pitched the futuristic-looking automobiles, selling them to a television audience on the moon. He finished working, was dismissed, left the stage, and left the lot.

The following day, it was well after six p.m. when I finally returned to my office from the projection room. I had a message on my desk that Joe wanted to see me. He was always in his office until well after seven p.m., so I headed down the hall to his office. I knocked and entered, and when he saw me he began laughing almost hysterically, and started telling me what he had learned and what had happened after lunch that afternoon. He said that Jerry Lewis had heard that Joe Karbo had worked a scene in his movie, and was very upset. He had come down to the casting department after lunch, seething. He had announced to all that he would shut down production if any additional talent was hired without his personal approval. Joe D'Agosta was still laughing when he explained that Jerry Lewis had once been invited as a guest on Karbo's late night/early morning talk show and hadn't shown up. Karbo and his wife, Kitty, then proceeded to poke fun at Jerry Lewis all night long, since they had no guest or backup guest replacement scheduled. They had little to talk about that didn't come full cycle back to Lewis's no-show. My first casting assignment had met with a huge ego. Joe D'Agosta was a very compassionate and understanding human being. He knew I would feel responsible and upset when I heard about it the next day, and wanted me to hear it from him first. He then asked, "Are you sure you want to be a lowly casting director, Mike?" He added, "It's a no-thank-you job and it's never easy; don't worry about it." He broke into his infectious laugh again and said, "Jerry Lewis just makes me laugh; he's a funny guy." Then we were both laughing and pouring drinks from his office bar.

The next week I had arranged to shuttle several actors selected by Phil Benjamin to location, to have them read for a role for director Richard Fleischer on *Che Guevara*. Mr. Fleischer had requested that I accompany the talent so that I could read with the actors. I had assembled the talent at the "casting corner," which was the northwest corner of the "New Ad," just steps away from the back door to the extra casting entrance. While I waited for the arrival of the talent at the corner and for the transportation to arrive, I had noticed a small aircraft flying unusually low over us more than once. Transportation finally arrived and provided a "stretch" sedan to take us to the location where they were shooting, at the Fox Ranch in Malibu. We had boarded and departed for the location, and were still on the lot when not more than a couple of minutes later we heard on the studio car radio that a plane had just slammed into the "New Ad" administration building. We then tuned in to a local AM station, and news reports were just coming in as we continued through the North Lot and onto Olympic Boulevard. Preliminary news reports confirmed that it had happened just minutes before. We were concerned about people on the ground; my wife was on the second floor in the legal department of the "New Ad." When I got to the location, I immediately tried to get through to her, with no success. I then called Carl, and he said that the plane had struck just feet from where we had been assembled only moments before, and that there were wreckage and body parts everywhere. He said that no people on the ground or in the building had been injured, but the legal department had taken a direct hit and everybody was shook up. I told him I had seen the plane buzzing the lot just moments before we pulled away from the "casting corner," but thought nothing of it. Carl said that apparently the pilot had buzzed again, coming in lower, and couldn't pull up fast enough, and had lost control and slammed into the west side of the building. It was messy at the "casting corner," to say the least. I asked Carl to call up to the legal department while I was on hold and see if he could find out anything about my wife, Dottie. He came back on the line and said that he had gotten through to her and had her on the other line. He said she had been more concerned about me, because she knew where I was and what I was doing. I sent my love to her and told Carl to tell her I would try and get through to her again after the readings were concluded. Carl came back on the line with, "If you'd just been a few minutes later in leaving, Mike." The big "what if" question would resonate in my thoughts. I was surer than ever that life was truly a gift, and that a person has but one chance to live the gift to its fullest. I had met my wonderful wife, Dottie, just outside the casting offices, almost at the spot where the plane went down. Later that day, I was finally able to get through to her and was relieved to hear her voice, and to know that this beautiful young woman was okay. Somehow, life would become more precious for both of us, with a new found perspective.

The studio would go through some restructuring and changes in the months to follow. Doug Cramer and staff had moved into the younger Zanuck's job, as Richard had moved over when his father stepped down when under attack from shareholders. Chuck Essegian would move to the Fox Western Avenue lot to take over the casting of *Daniel Boone*, starring Fess Parker, for the remaining seasons. Doug Cramer's assistant, Tom Miller, had become more and more reliant upon my opinions about who I thought might become the future stars and leads, if you will, of tomorrow. Carl Joy's department was pretty much the same, but extremely busy with *The Boston Strangler* having started production. The only real change to come was absolutely amazing. Peppy, Carl's dog, had been sold, obedience trained, and had won his fifteenth straight contest, and the money was starting to roll in for the new owner. Peppy would win every contest he entered; however, it was too late to save Carl's marriage. Carl was still chewed up from the whole experience, absolutely beside himself at Peppy's success, and still wearing his chewed-up expensive Italian shoes. Like so many people, Peppy the chainsaw dog just needed some education and direction.

Tom Miller came by one day and asked me to help Doug Cramer with a little gag they wanted to pull on the industry as a whole. Mr. Cramer was married to *Los Angeles Times* columnist Joyce Haber. Doug and Tom knew I acted, had done theater, and was continuing to study. I had told Tom I was studying improvisation and enjoyed it immensely. Doug called me to his office and asked me to act out a fictitious character they had created for Joyce Haber's column. For the interview, and especially the *Times* photographer, I would be Harry Lee Bowers, screenwriter. I was always writing as well, so this would be a natural. I would rely on my improvisational training to bring this character to life for just a few minutes for the benefit of the camera. It came off without a hitch, and on Sunday, January 28, 1968, Joyce Haber's made-up spoof appeared in her regular column in the *Los Angeles Times.* Suddenly, everyone on the Fox lot thought I was somebody else—incognito, perhaps—working in casting but presumably writing a script, as this made-up character was a screenwriter. Big shots on the lot were kissing my butt since everyone thought I was tantamount to George Plimpton. It would be Andy Warhol's fame, but only two minutes of it; the remaining moments would come later.

Other changes came about when Joe D'Agosta was offered a position with Desilu to do all shows produced; *Star Trek*, *Mission Impossible*, and several other pilots slated to start. Joe and I had become tennis, jogging, and workout pals also, and for a couple of minutes there had been discussion of my going with him to Desilu as his assistant, but he chose longtime theater associate Gary Shafer instead. I understood; Gary was older and maybe more experienced, but I felt another slight letdown. At the end of that season there was a rumor that Desilu was about to be acquired by Paramount. Doug Cramer was offered the head of television production post and signed a pact to take over the reins. Tom Miller would move also, again to be Doug Cramer's assistant, but only for a short while before going into production on his own. They wooed Bill Kenny away from Fox, and Tom Miller suggested that I be his assistant at the new Paramount Television Casting Department. I was ecstatic about the possibilities of the move, but out of loyalty I went to Jack Baur and explained that I had received a very good offer to go to Paramount, to cast a new show in the fall. Jack Baur said they had nothing at the moment to offer me to stay. Then, like a father, he advised me to go and jump on the opportunity; that he appreciated my loyalty, but that I should not hesitate. I told him that I just hated to leave the lot; I loved the lot, and after nearly five years it was like home. Jack said there'd be other lots to love and he pushed me from the casting nest.

In 1970, my good friend Chuck Essegian decided there wasn't much real future in casting and, with the Zanucks having left the Fox lot, even less chance that he would be assigned a Fox project as a producer. He entered law school, where the amazing Mr. Essegian obtained his law degree in record time, and has been happily practicing law ever since. He once told me that it was extremely interesting work, and invited me to visit him in court anytime, but said that if I did, I shouldn't attempt to dance up any courtroom walls.

CHAPTER THREE

Paramount and turning out as a Casting Director

Jack Baur was right; Paramount, too, was a wonderful place of make-believe and storytelling magic, a beautiful lot. It was the early part of 1969 that Bill Kenney moved first to a small suite of basement offices that had been remodeled especially for our arrival. They overlooked a small park-like setting on the Gower side of the lot, and had been Joe D'Agosta's offices. The master casting director, Joe D'Agosta, had been terminated after his contribution at then Desilu. He had cast all the *Star Trek* episodes and was waiting for renewal, but it never came; some jerk at the network pulled the plug because of a slight ratings slump, or to make room on the schedule for something more contemporary, something not quite so far out. Joe D'Agosta's keen insight had given *Star Trek* a dazzling look of strong talent that helped keep the science-fiction saga renewed for its short life, but this time renewal did not come. Bill Kenney also took his former secretary, Betty Pollakoff, with him from 20th Century Fox. Betty was extremely efficient and very knowledgeable of the casting process. When I arrived a short time later, I would occupy a small office just up the hall, not far from Bill and Betty's location. Bill disclosed to me that my friends in the front office, Doug Cramer and Tom Miller, wanted to hire a more seasoned casting director for the pilot season. and the newcomer would be housed in the larger office at the end of the suite. Bill was a straight-up guy, and advised me to be patient and I would be moved up soon; that Doug Cramer thought I was highly capable and worthy of promotion.

Paramount Television had a strong schedule, with the return of *Mission Impossible* and *Mannix*. The new shows slated for the fall lineup included *Love American Style*, *The Brady Bunch*, and *The Odd Couple* to start production, and with the pilot season scheduled, including *Barefoot in the Park*, it was going to be an exciting and very busy season. Bill immediately affixed his attention to *Mission Impossible* and *Mannix*, and was consumed by what was already in production, but he also burnt the midnight oil preparing for *Love American Style*. I would spend my first months at Paramount assisting Bill on everything, but mostly culling through the tons of submissions of young comedic-type actors for *Love*, for what were called the comedy "Blackouts." The Blackouts were bridging material between the segment and the commercial. Most were comprised of very short comedic moments that could be inserted where they would work best, usually at the opening or closing of a segment. I was a little miffed when Jim Merrick joined the staff to take over on *Mission Impossible*, but I would be patient.

Not long after he joined the casting department, and after a comparatively short time at the helm, rumors quickly spread that Bill Kenney also would soon be

replaced as department head; that a new person, someone older, was being considered for the post. Bill Kenney
was an exquisite and extremely knowledgeable casting
director, as clever as Joe D'Agosta was, but for whatever
reasons he, too, would be downgraded and then finally
replaced. *Love American Style* was an extremely stressful
show to cast, as there was a cadre of Paramount executives and their assistants to have to please. And then ABC
had its own group of young network jerks and directors of this and that, who always thought they had better ideas; very seldom was there unanimous agreement
on any casting suggestions. Bill was constantly checking
with the network powers that be to formulate some sort
of unified approval before he could even talk realistically about anyone with the producers of the show. And
then, when he did talk to the producers of the show,
they often would have conflicting and very dissimilar
ideas and concepts of the roles in question. Bill, Betty
Pollikoff, I were constantly checking availabilities of actors, and then at the last minute everything could and
would change, with a change in an episode's shooting
schedule. All too often the producers would choose to
wait and shoot an episode at a later date, or even an earlier date, to accommodate the schedule of some name
actor/superstar who had warmed to doing the show.
Anything and everything happened on *Love*, just too
many damn opinions, too many jerks, too many chiefs
and not enough Indians.

In forming administrations, new producers join a
company or new people come on staff at a network and

request or suggest casting people they've worked with in the past, or have heard of. It's just that simple. It can be a very hot kitchen, and if you can't take the heat or if you cross someone's ego, you can be replaced and gone for whatever reason on a whim. *Love* was an extremely perilous post for even the very best; they would have fired God.

Prior to these casting changes being implemented and being anything more than rumor, Bill Kenney sent me on a wonderfully delightful assignment I shall never forget. On *Love*, it was customary to send with the script a bottle of something very nice, accompanied by flowers, as an enticement to charm the big-name actors into considering the possibility of doing the show (and television). Bill had used dear Spring Byington on *Batman* at Fox, and we all loved her; the world loved her. She was probably best remembered as the lead in the television series *December Bride* in the early '50s, but she had over a hundred supporting lead credits in big films. She was definitely on the A-list. Ms. Byington was getting on in years, and Bill thought it best that I should personally deliver the script with the flowers and a nice bottle of expensive sherry. I picked up the sherry, and went by the florist and selected an arrangement of flowers, and then I was off to Spring Byington's house. She greeted me at the door, as cute and as sweet as she had been in *The Good Old Summertime*. That sweet, wholesome appearance and smile, everybody's mother (grandmother now); her persona exuded warmth, love, and goodness. I never knew either of my grandmothers and that's where I was, at Grandma's house. I handed her the flowers and explained that the sherry had been sent as a gift as well. I went on to say that everyone thought she would be wonderful in the role for *Love*. The producers wanted her, casting wanted her, the cadre of Paramount and ABC executives wanted her—that everyone was in agreement, which rarely occurred on *Love American Style*. Spring said, "Oh, isn't that nice," thanked me again for the flowers, and set them on a table where she continued to arrange them. She then returned to me and said, "Well, Mike, why don't we have a taste of this excellent sherry?" She disappeared for a moment and returned with a couple of sherry glasses. She asked me to open the bottle. I opened it and poured, and then she poured, and then she poured again. We laughed, she giggled, and we seemed to really like each other. We talked career, show business, current movies, and politics, and then I poured again. I told her of my experiences; that I was studying acting, singing, and doing theater, and working out with stunt people. I told her I was enjoying casting but really wanted to act and perform. Her face brightened as she encouraged me. She said excitedly that it was a wonderful dream; that life was indeed a short play; that I was in the wings preparing to go on. Then she became even more philosophical, saying that it was truly more rewarding to feed the soul than the stomach; that growth of the soul advances all human endeavor; that the rewards of a wonderful meal are fleeting, but the food of artistic expression nurtures all of the human spirit and can endure all tests of time. She then chuckled and asked me if I was hungry, if I wanted a bite to eat; the other kind of food, she said.

I was in awe after consuming her meanings; I thanked her and told her I'd had a big lunch, and that I wouldn't need food anymore, ever. We hadn't spoken a word about the *Love American Style* script, just this personal chatting about life for well over an hour, and the sherry was gone. Spring smiled and excused herself for only a couple beats, returned with another bottle of sherry, and we poured again. She drank a little and then said for me to help myself while she went off and read the very short script (a fifteen-minute episode), and she would give me an answer straightaway. I told her I thought it was a swell idea, doing my best Stan Laurel. She smiled and said, "That's very good," and disappeared. I was feeling fairly relaxed if not a wee bit tipsy. In fact, I was feeling awfully good and fast becoming a big admirer of sherry. Maybe ten minutes rolled by and I was still sitting by myself. I poured again; as I was sure I had the sale, I would celebrate success. Another ten minutes, another pour, and then I was up and looking around my new friend's home to stretch my (now wobbly) legs. When Spring returned and picked up her glass of sherry, she said, "A toast to you, Mike. Live your dreams." We drank again and laughed again, and then she said that it was a lovely thing for them to think of her for the role, but that she felt it just wasn't something she wanted to do; it was a little too risqué. I said maybe they could rewrite it and change something. She smiled and shook her head. She thanked me again for the lovely flowers and the sherry, and especially the conversation, said maybe next time, and invited me back for another visit when

I was in the neighborhood. I felt as if I wanted to curl up on Grandma's couch, but directed myself toward the entrance and thanked her for her time, the wonderful conversation, all that she had given the world as an artist, and especially her words of encouragement. We hugged each other and I stepped into to the bright sun of the afternoon totally buzzed. I drove a very short distance and then decided to walk to a nearby coffee shop for something to eat and some coffee, and call to give Bill Kenney the bad news. I always intended to get back for another visit but just never seemed to find the time. Spring Byington passed away in September 1971.

Word that Millie Gusse had been commissioned as the new head of casting for Paramount Television had officially been delivered to the department. Late in the afternoon, Doug Cramer called me and requested that I come to his office to meet Millie and escort her back to our offices; that Bill Kenney had already been informed of the change. During the next few days she would rely on me for a great many things. First, she called me and requested that I accompany her to inspect the first-floor offices of the DeMille Building that had been designated as a possible new site for the television casting department. The next morning we walked through the offices together and she openly asked for my opinions and listened attentively to my thoughts and suggestions. I knew she was trying to win me over, but I also felt sincerity and honesty coming from this woman who was also old enough to be my grandmother. Bill Kenney would stay for a while and continue to cast *Love American Style* under Millie's supervision, but he, too, would soon move on to other offerings. She immediately set the tone for the department, and among other things she informed me that she wanted no people on staff, secretaries or otherwise, that aspired to act. Under a veil of the most clandestine secrecy, I would continue to study and do theater around town under noms de plume; Harry Lee Bowers, among others.

Millie Gusse had created the reputation for herself of being "one tough old broad." I had heard agents say this numerous times even before her arrival. Millie liked it—the tough part, that is—she told me over drinks one afternoon. The tough part of her reputation scared the weak and meek and undetermined away; they would give up and thus not waste her time. She said, "So, for the most part all that is left is the very strong, the very talented, the cream of the crop." Then, smiling, she added, "But there are always exceptions." I would later learn that her rule worked because she didn't take all the theatrical agents seriously and she didn't see or hold court with every agent, only the upper echelon, on a regular basis. If there were people out there who had slipped through the cracks and were being represented by the middle- or lower-echelon theatrical agents, she had her staff to filter them out and bring those exceptions to her attention. I also learned that Millie Gusse liked her Scotch and soda at lunch and then again from her private office bar, which was usually open after five p.m. If I wasn't in readings on a show, Millie would always summon me to pour cocktails about that time of day. When I poured, she would always say to me, "Now don't slug me, Mike, don't slug me," which I would learn was my cue that she wanted a good stiff one first. She'd always take a mouthful and say, "Ah, Mike, you slugged me." She'd nearly finish the glass taking that first sip, and request another with, "Only don't slug me this time, Mike." On her next drinks she'd often loosen up and take me under her wing; teach me and tell me things like I was her twenty-seven-year-old son.

In spite of what we learned about Millie, and what was said of her behind her back in the seasons to come, I always liked her and respected her for her good business sense and tactics. For a while, I got great satisfaction out of slugging her because of what had seemed an injustice that had happened to Bill Kenney, but she began to grow on me and I warmed to her. As my own dear father had said, I, too, had to adjust and think of my family first, and not be concerned with company policy. Millie would teach us all a great deal about negotiating and paying close attention to the exact details of contracts, specifically the Screen Actors Guild contract, and to get everything in writing, even among the very best of friends. She encouraged us all to be frugal; that it was honorable to save the company's money because you just didn't know when knowledge of that specific attribute might save your own job. Millie was very frugal, and not just in business; she was plain tight in everything she did. I heard an agent once say, "If Millie were to have accidentally sat on a piece of coal and it were to have gotten lodged there, up her butt, in two weeks it would be a diamond." This very uncouth analogy—that Millie Gusse was tight with a buck, company interests, and especially with her own personal money—was a complete understatement. Millie Gusse had the first dollar she ever made and it would be a sure bet that it wouldn't be found in her mattress—probably in blue-chip stocks or gold—and she was still making more money from those first dollars she had earned. That agent also said for the staff not to expect much at Christmas, and not to expect her to buy lunch anytime soon unless she put it on an expense account. "You'll never see her with cash; green, or even coins." He was right. Those years I worked with Millie, I never once saw her have any ready cash. If she paid, it would be charged to an expense account.

Under Millie Gusse, I would almost immediately turn out and be given the official title of casting director. First assignments: *The Odd Couple* and *The Brady Bunch.* I honestly wasn't really very excited about my *Brady Bunch* assignment. It seemed to be such mediocre drivel, destined for a short life. An even more saccharin version of *Ozzie and Harriet* or *Leave It To Beaver*, without the off-the-wall low-key comedy. I wanted to be where the real action was, and from my perspective *The Brady Bunch* seemed extremely prehistoric even then. I had met Robert Reed before production began while having some lunch in the bar of Nickodel's restaurant. Nickodel's was very close, a few yards from my office door out the front gate, and was famous for the very best Caesar salad. Papa Brady and I would become drinking buddies during the years I was at Paramount, and when at one point I explained I wasn't that kind of guy, we still remained drinking buddies. He was an honest actor and an honest man. I would think that perhaps Robert Reed's discomfort with doing this show was not far off base. We both shared the opinion that it was dreadful stuff—dull, old-hat formula comedy. After reading the first ten or so scripts that had come into my office at the beginning of the season, I took to scanning the drivel for scenes where any guest characters would appear; that's all I had to do. I never really had much knowledge of what was happening in the stories; it was just such drivel to read. The paperboy at the front gate could have cast *The Brady Bunch*. Whenever I would speak of my assignments at Paramount Television to anyone, I would detail anything other than *The Brady Bunch*, *The Odd Couple*, or the *Love* Blackouts, and never say a word about *The Brady Bunch* out of sheer embarrassment. If asked, I would finally acknowledge it. There is status among casting directors and this was, without a doubt, a distinction of a lower standing. I had tenure at Paramount and on Millie's staff and felt I was as good as anyone on anyone's staff, but I was still the youngest with probably the least amount of real casting experience, and the more desired Paramount television casting assignments went to the older staff members.

Sherwood Schwartz, creator and executive producer of *The Brady Bunch* was a true prince of a gentleman and a grand mentor to all. I loved the guy, but I wanted more than half-hour, milquetoast, goody-two-shoes, saccharin themes to cast. Shortly after pre-production began, another writer/producer named Howard Leeds joined Sherwood's staff as producer. Sherwood's focus would lean more to the creative aspects of story and script development than to that of day-to-day production. Howard was younger and more hip, and I was hopeful that he would be able to shape a more realistic story line and more believable characters. I know he often fought a battle or two in an effort to do so, and sometimes won some ground. I would forge ahead positively on my assignment, never divulging my innermost feelings to anyone. I would diligently try and attract to *The Brady Bunch* those actors and personalities that I could bring to it. I would always try, if possible, to suggest and hire solid, recognizable names and faces, but there were always a lot of actors that simply could care less about doing a half-hour sitcom, even if it was a wonderful role on the hit show *The Brady Bunch*. Some actors just didn't want to do television, much less that show, or that kind of show. At the risk of constantly being negative, it's very difficult to explain this to some producers. They don't understand when you tell them that the artist they met socially, or an old friend, or their star neighbor who happens to be with the same agent, just didn't want to do *The Brady Bunch*. Howard Leeds got it, but Sherwood Schwartz was one of those producers who just didn't understand this.

After five seasons *The Brady Bunch* would join Sherwood Schwartz's only other television creation, *Gilligan's Island*, both to be acclaimed two of the most successful shows ever produced. It just goes to show you, what do I know? Reality exists in the conversation, remember? Dreadful and drivel; my words, my reality, my conversation. The bottom line: *The Brady Bunch* was, and is, very entertaining to the pre-pubescent viewer and made a great many folks awfully rich, and who is it that's laughing all the way to the bank?

I had greater expectations of working with the newly evolving writing team Belson and Marshall, and what their many creations would deliver. They were younger and hip; their kind of comedy and show concepts seemed more avant-garde, off-the-wall wacky and contemporary. There were feature films they were writing and I was hopeful that I would be assigned something there as well. I wanted more meaningful casting assignments that would assemble the very best talents on both sides of the camera. My assignments with the sitcoms would be a piece of cake compared to what I had already experienced on *Love American Style*. I had interviewed all of what Hollywood and New York could offer that could do comedy. Most had improvisational or stand-up comedy training. In addition, I had observed numerous local workshops and classes, including Harvey Lembeck's and Danny Goldman's, where I found a great many that were considered. I had always felt confident with my knowledge of the more established actor talent pools, but after those first months I felt even more secure that I was ready to cast anything. But comedy shows would become my forte and my passion.

Ramsey King also had joined Millie's staff, initially assigned *Mannix* and *The Immortal.* He would be stationed at the more serious end of the suite—the dramatic end, Millie's end—where no one laughed, except Mary Prange after lunch at Nickodell's. *The Immortal* was the one about the guy that couldn't die, but he did—those jerks at the network again. Former agent Mike Rosen also would join Millie's growing staff to cast *Love American Style* and *Barefoot In The Park.* Mike's office would be next to mine. We had an adjoining door that connected our offices so we became good networking associates with the constant sharing of information and casting suggestions back and forth when the door was left open. Soon we became known as Hanky and the Rose, or Mike One and Mike Two, bestowed upon us by the nickname-adorning Mary Prange, whose loose lips sank more than ships after her usual luncheon. Mike Two had been a theatrical agent since college at his father's office, the Larry Rosen Agency, and he had a very different perspective that was often beneficial. For the most part I knew more actors, but Mike had more experience in more complex contract negotiations, and was more focused on issues concerning the bottom line. Betty Martin came in later to take over on *Barefoot In The Park,* as *Love* would prove to be enough for Mike—or any one casting director, for that matter. Eddie Morse also would join the staff later when the pilot season began. Eddie had held the exalted position as head of casting for Paramount Motion Pictures and had the reputation of being strict, very formal, and aloof. It was an act, the same tough act that Millie Gusse used, but Eddie was more of a showman—a salesman of talent, an actor—but mostly a very crafty and shrewd businessman and dealmaker. I would come to believe that these were important ingredients of what it took to be a very good casting director—salesmanship and showmanship—and, of course, having an excellent working knowledge of the talent pool. But I wanted to take it to the next level. I wanted more than relying on choices of "the tried and the true" lists. I wanted to direct performance and bring out the very best of the artist, and be the complete casting person.

We had moved into our new offices in the DeMille building just in time for me to get settled in as both *The Brady Bunch* and *The Odd Couple* were gearing up to begin production. I would have a first meeting with the newly assigned producer of *The Odd Couple,* Jerry Davis. Jerry was a very dapper, stylish, slim, and handsome guy in his late forties; another very hip and capable writer/producer. Tony Randall and Jack Klugman, having never met previously, would meet for the first time at the meeting that afternoon. No pilot episode had been shot; it was simply cast with these two as the centerpiece. On the day of the meeting Tony Randall arrived first; on time, gentle, intelligent, well-dressed, and with a very suave demeanor. Jack Klugman was late, sloppy in dress, and seemingly disoriented, saying that half of his luggage and belongings were still at the airport while shaking Tony's hand for the first time. My theory concerning their initial behavior at the meeting was, they were both two of the finest actors, Method actors, like Brando and Olivier. They became their characters immediately when they decided to accept the offer and were cast in their roles. Oscar Madison was the pizza-stuffing, beer-guzzling slob, but a respected, intelligent sportswriter who might enter a meeting slightly disheveled and saying that half his luggage was still at the airport. Felix Unger was an anal-retentive hypochondriac, a dusting-the-lens-constantly photographer who is also highly sensitive, very intelligent, dapper, suave, and elegant. What Jerry Davis and I observed at that meeting was perhaps the beginning of character development and performance, which really began when they first read Neil Simon's words and thought, "I want to do that role someday," or saw Matthau and Lemon in the movie. I think actors are very much like little kids, they can't wait to play and pretend. They can't wait to act and try on their new characters. As Stanislavski suggested for character exercises, Jack Klugman and Tony Randall brought as much possible to the surface that was like their roles that day and left what wasn't like their roles out of sight. Performance began at that first meeting. Wonderful casting by someone. I was never quite sure from where the notion of Klugman and Randall evolved, but it was a brilliant casting idea. Those jerks at the network aren't all bad, sometimes.

The publicity department offices were just across the hall from my office, and were the only offices on the first floor of the DeMille building that weren't a part of casting. Jim Denyer, the director of publicity, would come across and shoot darts with me almost every day. That is, when we weren't terribly busy and I wasn't slugging Millie. But there's always time for a quick game and I could get back to slugging Millie. The office of his secretary, the lovely Suzanne Gordon, was almost directly across the hall from that of my secretary, the lovely Sandy Thayer. We were all like a big, happy family there. Sandy was extremely efficient; a beautiful young woman with a very happy personality and a great sense of humor. Suzanne and Sandy shared one other thing in common; they both had infectious laughs. Apart from Tony Randall's visits, and other scheduled actor interview business, some of the comedy writers (mostly Harvey Miller and Billy Idelson) would wander over and sit with Sandy. I think they were in the midst of writer's block or writer's break, or both—possibly it was Sandy break. But they would always proceed to get Sandy laughing. Soon Suzanne would be laughing from across the hall, chiming in comments since she could overhear everything in Sandy's office. I think some of the writers wanted to date Sandy, but mostly I think they were warming up and testing material on her. I would come to believe that comedy writers were frustrated stand-up comedians. They were always testing material on anyone—Sandy for the big laughs, and then to see if they got to the back row of the theater, over to Suzanne, which they always did. We were all full of laughter at the front part of the building, a distinct difference from that of Millie's drama end of the suite. There, it was definitely more reserved and serious—unless, of course, as I said previously, it was after lunch and Mary Prange had returned. She had become known for an outburst of cackling occasionally; well, perhaps more than occasionally. I can still see her covering her mouth with both hands, eyes bulging, looking toward Millie's door entrance and sheepishly uttering "Oops!"

In spite of this complete difference in the office decorum, I always thought it fitting and necessary that we at the comedy end of the casting suite should develop a keener sense for the absurd and the ridiculous, as we were exposed to it on a constant daily basis. Additionally, I was a guy that had an inventive comedy sense. Casting comedy shows and being exposed to the continuous off-the-wall absurd elements of comedy all around was bound to have some wacky effect. We laughed a lot and developed a more abstract perception; funny was our work, our business. At Millie's end it was very different; unless, of course, it was after lunch.

In the months to come I would give Mike Rosen the benefit of my vast comedy-actor files and lists and he would, in turn, introduce me to at least one actor that I didn't know. One day he had overheard me talking to an agent about a character in one of my shows and he suggested I meet character actor Richard Collier. Richard had done a lot of television and film work (*Blazing Saddles*), and almost as many commercials, which just goes to prove that no matter how good a casting director is,

THE PRINCE GEORGE HOTEL

IS A FRIENDLY HOTEL

WON'T YOU COME THERE WHEN YOU ARE IN TOWN.

THE PRINCE GEORGE HOTEL, WHERE THE SERVICE

IS SWELL, WHEN YOU SLUMBER THERE'S HARDLY

A SOUND.

AND SHOULD YOU WANT TO PLAY, FORGET YOUR

CARES, THE PRINCE GEORGE HOTEL IS JUST A

COUPLE OF MINUTES FROM ANYWHERE.

CONVENIENT IT'S GREAT, 14 EAST 28TH,

NEW YORK CITY'S, IT'S A PITY IF YOU PASS

US BY

WITH A THOUSAND ROOMS TO CHOOSE FROM

THE FRIENDLY PRINCE GEORGE HOTEL.

no one can know everyone. He further explained that you have to give Richard a little extra time to get to an interview because he didn't drive his car much; he rode a bicycle all over town for interviews, and to work. When he and his wife traveled around the city they rode a bicycle built for two. I ran into them once in Santa Monica, out enjoying the day, and then I started running into Richard Collier everywhere. Once, I was driving through an extremely remote part of Los Angeles and I turned a corner and there he was, pedaling along. I couldn't believe he was there. It started happening so often that people suggested it was more than mere coincidence; that we had some sort of mystic psychic connection. It happened so many times, in so many bizarre places, I lost count. I once asked Mike if he knew where Richard might be. I explained that his agent didn't know where he was and I had a possible interview for him on one of my shows that afternoon. Mike laughed and said, "Go for a drive, you'll find him." Once, I hired Richard for a day-player role that was going to shoot at the end of the following week, and we decided to mail his script to him because we knew he biked around and he lived in far-off Marina Del Rey. We thought it just easier to mail it than having him pick it up. That evening I drove to the Valley to see a play I was covering and was motoring along some obscure street in North Hollywood, and there ahead of me was Richard Collier. I looked over on my passenger seat and on top of the pile of my daily homework was the script to Richard I had forgotten to put in the mailbox. When I approached him, I simply rolled down the window, honked, and handed the script to him as I passed. We both laughed and were amazed. I pulled over and we chatted a few minutes before we both continued our journeys.

Tony Randall often would visit Suzanne Gordon across the hall about publicity matters, and on one occasion we were all chatting when she mentioned to him that I was studying voice and aspired to be a singer. From that time on Tony, would come by and share opera with us both, and encouraged me to continue studying and singing. At times he would invite me by to share tapes of different opera singers that were his favorites. One evening I watched him on the *Tonight Show* with Johnny Carson, where he sang an early radio commercial ad for the Prince George Hotel, which highlighted its many sumptuous features and amenities. He sang the entire song. I was in awe. He was hysterical; I laughed my brains out. I had to have the words so I could sing it to my little sons. I asked him for them when he came the next day, and Suzanne Gordon typed them out for me as he slowly sang the song in a private encore performance. I'm proud to say that I can still sing it almost as well as Tony.

Sometime later, on a visit to the office of associate producer Tony Marshall (Garry and Penny's wonderful father; I liked him a lot), I made a comment about the grand job the artist had done of Tony and Jack in a charcoal drawing for the cover of *TV Guide*. Tony Marshall said, "Oh, you like it? It's yours; it's a copy, take it." I did and thanked him for the gift, and took it back to

my office. I put it at the end of my desk, leaning against the wall. Tony Randall popped by a few days later and I saw him chatting with Suzanne across the hall. I took the drawing to him immediately and asked him to give me an autograph. He said he would, gladly. He smiled and said in his best baritone voice, "I'm going to write something you'll really like, Mike." He wrote "To Mike, thanks for suggesting me for the part." He smiled even bigger and handed it back to me. At the time I thought it was pretty cool, but I found I would always have to explain to anyone that read the inscription that I hadn't really thought of him; that Mr. Randall had written it in jest. It was Tony Randall's way of sharing and saying he liked you. This pleased me most because I had always respected his talent enormously, and worked very hard on *The Odd Couple* to bring talent to the show that would make people laugh and that Tony and Jack would want to work with again. Jack Klugman would write on the same drawing "Mike, thanks for all the help." Jack Klugman hadn't warmed to me as Tony had; he always seemed cold and distant. But my feelings changed one day when I took my bright, cherub-faced three-year-old son Christopher to visit Tony Randall on the set. Jack, upon seeing him enter the stage, immediately broke and tore away from rehearsal, and literally dropped to the floor like Chris was his own child. His body language mirrored Chris's; it was clear he loved children and was a bit of a child himself. He got down to Chris's level, laughed and frolicked with him, and gave him his uninterrupted, undivided, childlike attention. Then, everyone joined in and showered Chris with attention and affection, calling out his name from every direction, almost as if they'd never seen a child before. It was a big-time day for a little boy. And then it was a little child's voice saying, "Bye, Jack, see you next time." You could almost see the tears well up in Jack Klugman's eyes when my little son Chris waddled off the set. I liked Jack Klugman a lot when I saw that.

At Paramount it was just a little thing to me, but because of the early desire I shared with all struggling actors, I developed an inner root-for-the-underdog actor who was always knocking at my door. I informed my very capable and efficient secretaries there—first Mary Prange, then Diane Perkins, then Sandy Thayer—that if anyone called, with or without representation, and asked to see me, to always schedule them for a general interview. I had already grown to resent the heavy-handed push of the big agencies that controlled all the big-name talents. I felt I could always get their people, the so-called "tried and the true," those on the A-list. The B-list, and even the C-list, was easy. I knew those actors before I ever professionally entered the field, when I was in high school, and I loved those actors. Any casting people worth their salt knew those actors. It was finding the new ones before anyone knew them that I considered the real challenge for the hardworking casting director. There's less danger and it's always safer for one's career to hire the more established artist; the blue-chip choice means less risk. It was very daring and risky to find unknown talent from the small agency lists, from the not-so-impressive lists, or considering an actor that had no agent and even hiring them. When you did this, you were possibly putting your reputation and maybe your job on the line. If you make a mistake in judgment and the actor shows up on the set and he's terrible, it's the casting director's fault.

In television especially, most directors don't have time to direct performance. They want to know you and what you're going to do with the material before you ever get to the stage; they don't like surprises. And it's not just the producers and director that have to be pleased. It's also the studio hierarchy and the network that bring out the axes when they see something they don't like. This happened when I had suggested one of my then favorite child actors, Clint Howard, to play Tony Randall's young son on *The Odd Couple*. We had gone through the usual selection process, suggestion lists, meetings and readings; we saw every cute kid in town that was right for the role. Clint was the best actor; the funniest and the most animated, I thought, and Millie backed me up. I sold him hard and he got the part. Jerry Davis and the director loved his performance, but when Doug Cramer viewed him in the same dailies, he hated him. It wasn't his performance he hated, it was the way he looked. Doug Cramer came down on Millie Gusse, and Millie came down hard on the entire casting director staff. We were instructed to always suggest attractive people for guest star roles on all Paramount shows—no exceptions. If Mr. Cramer had loved Clint Howard as much as the rest of us did, or if Clint Howard had become an immediate exciting new star, or perhaps had received an Emmy or Oscar nomination for his work somewhere, the credit and recognition for excellent creative insight would have gone elsewhere. It would have been absorbed by someone other than the creative casting person that most likely first thought of him. Casting doesn't hear much unless things go wrong. The accolades for excellence go to producers and directors, and camera and lighting, and sound and wardrobe. Perhaps even the studio head is thanked and mentioned in somebody's acceptance speech, for having provided an exceptional creative environment where one could engender a brilliant choice. But the process of casting itself gets no special rewards. The perception that the casting process is part of management and not part of that wonderful creative environment is a misconception that is long overdue for reexamination by the Academies, the Screen Actors Guild, the Golden Globes, and other award presentation entities. Everybody gets a prize except the person who most often had the first vision of the selected actors playing together and brought them to the stage. Thus, it's my opinion that the casting person, and what he can bring to a piece, is as important to a production as any contribution made by anyone. I may write this more than once in these pages.

Another battle I found myself involved in was for Charlie Martin Smith. Through the constant persistence of small-office agent Bob Thorson, I had met this talented young man, and had read him and affirmed that he was indeed a possibility. I had been casting a supporting role on *The Brady Bunch* with some difficulty. We just hadn't found the exact quality the director and the producers wanted in the character. The talent we wanted on the first list wasn't available or simply had no interest in doing the show. Charlie had come in, and had met and read for Sherwood, Howard, and the director, and they loved him. Charlie wasn't a Screen Actors Guild member as of yet. At that time, it was very difficult to get someone new into the Guild without a possible fine levied against the production company. In theory, the Guild could fine a production company if it could prove that actors, already members of the Guild, could have played the role being cast. We interviewed everyone available and took the position that, because it was the role of a young person and young people are constantly changing, there were not many around precisely like Charlie to choose from. I convinced Millie that we had little choice but to risk being fined. The producers wanted him and the work dates were approaching. She met with Charlie and then authorized me to sign his application to join the Screen Actors Guild and work on *The Brady Bunch*. The bottom line—the final choice in casting is the creative selection of the director. The director doesn't care about or want to hear about restrictions, he just wants to add his touches to the piece. Therefore, in going beyond the Guild, the so-called professional ranks of membership, we had to insulate ourselves by compiling evidence that we had interviewed an adequate number of available Guild members for the role in question and were unable to find those unique qualities the director was looking for. What determined that one was professional was having a Guild membership card. If not a Guild member, the artist wasn't considered professional because he was not a member of the Guild, and couldn't interview for professional work or get professional theatrical representation because he was not a member of the Guild. It's the old Catch–22 of the dog chasing its tail. In Charlie's case, he started working on *American Graffiti* for George Lucas almost immediately after he worked for me, and I don't think he looked back. He was very professional indeed when he starred later in a favorite of mine, *Never Cry Wolf*. I don't think he stayed long with Bob Thorson, either. It's simple economics; the artist is rushed, wined, and dined by the bigger office that handles the whole package—the director, the producer, and the writer. With those kinds of connections the actor can most assuredly get more serious exposure. The fact of the matter is, the theatrical agent acts as a kind of filter as the proverbial cream always rises to the top, or we're judged by the representative company we keep. If you have a top agent, it's an affirmation of "I've arrived and I'm damn good." More often than not, the better, more capable and experienced artist finally lands with the big office, top representation. Remember the Millie Gusse theory here: some casting people only want to deal with the top offices because it's safe—very safe. The smaller office initially opens doors, but the economics of the system will finally lure the prospective super-talents of tomorrow away to the bigger offices. The bigger office has more connections, so ultimately when a newcomer, who is represented by a smaller office and begins to win out and get jobs, the bigger agent is trained to find out why. If he doesn't, he'll soon be replaced. Using their business-connection clout, they will either obtain information directly from the producer of the show, who might be their client, or obtain the daily call sheets from some source to find out who's getting those missed important jobs. When the big office learns that talent is still represented by the lowly agent, the power-rush for the hot actor/talent commences. It's always nice to see the new discovery take the little agent with him or her to the top, but it seldom happens. Also, the artist's ego can become inflated, creating a monster of sorts, with the focus on self-centered, self-serving, self-absorbed egotism and the sole belief in only his or her fan mail.

Over the years I've personally been promised many things by people on the way up who are huge today—moguls, multimillionaires, maybe billionaires—and not so much as a lunch bought at The Cheesecake Factory or a Christmas card sent. How quickly they forget that you helped roll the dice in their favor. Mr. Allen's insincerity in Hollywood again. It's not that they owe anyone anything. The company that employed or engaged me for my creative expertise paid me a salary; nobody owed me anything. Personally, though, I think if I had made a ton of money as a result of someone going to bat for me, and not only helping me get my foot in the door but helping me keep it there, so that the world would recognize what they had seen in me, I might have bought them a malt at Johnny Rocket's once in a while. Accountants and the quest for greatness distort and especially fog memories of what really happens. It's this Fred Allen truism of the artist clawing and devouring their way to the top that I always disliked most.

Sometimes, success immediately changes people, and the hidden me-me-me, self-centered, cut-you-off-on-the-freeway persona rears its ugly head.

On the other hand, there were a great many stars that were always very caring and generous. Elvis Presley, Dean Martin, Frank Sinatra, Kirk Douglas, and Paul Newman, to name a few, never forgot their beginnings and shared with the people that helped them during their early days, and continued this practice well into their working careers. How many Cadillacs did Elvis give away as gifts? I suppose these artists realized they couldn't take any of the material world with them at their departure. They simply gave back out of their own pocket, without some financial planner's direction to do so, because it made them feel good. Kirk Douglas still gives back to the world through numerous peace-centered causes. The many times Frank Sinatra pulled some financially strapped pal or his widow and family out of some hole, he did it his way. And as I put the final touches on this work, the talented, generous, and giving Paul Newman has passed, but he will never die. I'm proud that I worked on *Butch Cassidy* and saw him up close, and he smiled at me. He was a godsend; a role model for how to do it right; the "do it the right way" side of the "how to break into show business" spectrum I wrote of earlier.

There were so many unforgettable moments when I was at Paramount, and so many unforgettable people. I got very efficient at finding talent that seemingly had started to fade from memory and had begun to fall through the cracks. I would do it numerous times; that is, find and

locate that special someone that had escaped back to Podunk and was working at jobs other than acting. I really
don't know why I pursued them; I guess I didn't want to
let go of the past and wanted to see them work again.

I grew up on *Dobie Gillis* and had become a huge fan
of Dwayne Hickman. I was a fan of his brother Daryl
also; whom many said was a much better actor. But one
thing I learned early was that no two performances are
the same, and Dwayne brought to a character what his
brother and no other actor could have. I had thought of
Dwayne for something and was unable to get a contact
number on him from SAG membership. I was told me
he was working for a casino in Las Vegas; that he held
some sort of talent-booking position similar to that of a
casting director. I learned of the casino and made contact with him, and I started calling him every time I saw
something he was right for. He was elated at my persistence. We talked of him coming back to town and having a career again, maybe a possible series somewhere,
more movie work. I encouraged him to think about it,
saying that I considered it a huge waste for him to stay
in Vegas. The next time we spoke, he called me and
expressed his halfhearted contentment there. I invited
him to come by and say hello the next week, and said
that I had something I could bring him to read for, if he
were there. That next week he read and we hired him.
In effect it kind of jump-started his acting career. He
moved back to Los Angeles, gave up the Vegas gig and
started to work again. A few days later, Dwayne came by
my office to say thanks. We were chatting, and the conversation drifted to the making of *Cat Ballou*, the 1965

comedy western classic that Dwayne had co-starred in with Lee Marvin, Jane Fonda, Nat King Cole, and Stubby Kaye, among others. Dwayne told me the following amazing story. He said it was a location shoot for a number of days running. A stretch sedan was sent to pick up him, Lee Marvin, and some of the other cast members very early in the morning and take them to the rural location, to start filming at first light. He said it was a long distance to the location site, so everyone would get into the stretch, lie down, curl up, and go back to sleep for maybe a couple of hours. Dwayne said he entered the stretch sedan, greeted everyone as usual, and went back to sleep. He said he was sound asleep when he was startled awake by a loud explosion. He immediately popped up to see that it was daybreak, and gazed over the next seat to where Lee Marvin was sitting. Lee had a drink in one hand and a smoking .45 automatic in the other, dangling out the window. He saw Dwayne looking and he pointed back at the passing field. Dwayne said he looked back in the direction Lee Marvin was pointing and saw a poor cow go down on its knees, then slump over and die. Lee Marvin turned to Dwayne and said, "Nice shot, huh?" It was a well-known fact that former Marine Lee Marvin liked to shoot his automatic and also take an occasional drink when he was on location. Dwayne laughed when telling me this Lee Marvin tale, and said the production company had to go back later and settle up with the unhappy cattle owner, big-time.

Another amusing incident occurred on an episode of *The Odd Couple.* The episode revolved around a Gene Autry cowboy-hero-type character and his sidekick. I had brought in a wonderful character actor by the name of Pat Cranshaw for the sidekick role. We had cast old-time great Dub Taylor as the Gene Autry character. Dub had actually played alongside Gene Autry as Gene's sidekick, Cannonball, in a number of the early Autry western films. Pat Cranshaw was white-haired and looked older, much like Gabby Hayes, who played older when in fact he was younger. At the end of the readings, I was walking back to my office with Pat when he asked me if I thought he got the part. I told him he had read really well, but that Belson and Marshall thought he was a little young; that maybe he was too handsome, too distinguished, and they wanted an older craggy-character look. Pat said that he could look older and funnier-looking, more character. Somewhat skeptical, I stopped walking and said, "How? Show me now." He reached in and removed his dentures, which immediately brought his chin up underneath his nose—a drastic change in appearance, to say the least. He looked very different and funny-looking, a complete loss of the distinguished look. I then directed him to turn around and told him we're going back up to Belson and Marshall. It had been just a few minutes since we left Belson and Marshall's office. I gave a tap at the door and entered, and explained that I wanted them to see something. I waved Pat in and he simply looked at them, chin up to his nose, for half a beat. Both Jerry Belson and Garry Marshall broke into laughter, and Garry started mumbling in that New York drawl, "Hire him, give him the job. He needs some teeth, but tell him to leave them in the glass next to his bed when he works. This is the look we want."

Another artist I met at Paramount that had an enchanting effect on me was Liv Von Lindenland, *Playboy* magazine's 1972 Playmate of the Year. Absolutely one of the most beautiful, sensuous, sexy, and intelligent young women I had met to date in my twenty-seven years. Tan and slim, and without a doubt a figure that was second to none, absolutely gorgeous, with this deep, raspy Swedish accent. I fell in like the moment we met. She captured my heart; I was completely infatuated with her. I was suddenly finding the job very difficult and wonderful at the same time. Liv and I were to become very good friends. She would always call me, from wherever she was in the world, and ask me if I was still married. At the time I was, and still in love with my wife and working hard to focus on that relationship, but Liv Von Lindenland would be a major fantasy of mine for a long while to come. Years later she called me, very excited, and told me of a chap she had met and fallen in love with. My heart sank like a rock. I didn't really want to hear about it, but I listened. I haven't heard from her since; she's living somewhere in Europe, I presume, and I hope living happily ever after.

There were hundreds of talented people I interviewed for general interviews on *Love American Style*. One of the most memorable was with the then complete unknown, Penny Marshall. At the time we met, I honestly didn't have a clue she was the sister of Garry Marshall. I had begun working with Garry Marshall and Jerry Belson on *The Odd Couple*, but I hadn't noticed the similar brother-sister characteristics. I thought Penny was so special and so funny; she had me on the floor, laughing, for days after she left. I tried to get Paramount to consider putting her under term contract, specifically for the next series of Blackouts, to no avail. Personally, I've always been attracted to offbeat, intellectual, sexy, witty, abstract-observing, low-key types, and Penny Marshall had all those qualities. I would learn later who her older brother was.

I also spent a lot of time attending as many plays around town as I possibly could. I went anywhere and everywhere to see anyone who called and invited me to see his or her performance. When I saw someone dazzling I wrote a note to Millie Gusse, with copies to Doug Cramer, and at weekly department meetings I would share my finds with the department. One afternoon I had poured drinks for Millie and myself, and slugged us both, as it had been a terrible day. She asked me if I would attend a play that evening that she had been invited to and could not attend. She informed me that tickets would be at the box office for me. After I called home and checked on my wife and my sons (Doyle, our second gift, had come along and joined his big brother, Chris), I finished up my work and left the office at about seven p.m. There was a restaurant-bar across from the theater, so I took an upcoming *Odd Couple* script into the bar area to read while I ate. Just after eight p.m., I had finished the food and the script, had settled my bill, and I made my exit and crossed the street to the theater. I entered the foyer and noticed that the entire theater was going through renovation, with an added second-level balcony area still unfinished and in rough stages of construction. There was

a small table at the balcony entrance the theater attendant was working from and had placed all the tickets.
After he checked my name from his list, he indicated
that I could sit anywhere; that they hadn't attached any
specific seat designations as of yet. I was curious and
chose to sit up in the new balcony, away from the crowd.
I was asked to be careful; that the planking was still unfinished and uneven in areas of the second-level floor.
I sat down in the middle, in the rear, to avoid any actors that might want to give me the rush with a picture
and a resume. Sometimes, I just wanted some quiet time
without the hustle, and this was one of those times. The
theater had started to quickly fill up, with several groups
moving close to where I had settled. A young woman
came at the head of another group of people, and she
broke away and sat next to me. I thought, here we go;
she knows who I am, probably has a picture and resume
in her purse. She said hello and we started chatting. She
said she had a girlfriend in the cast; that she wasn't an
actress and worked in a totally unrelated field, but loved
theater. She asked if I was an actor. We shook hands,
but still hadn't exchanged names yet, or much else. She
was very cute and I felt a strong, keen kinship—more
instant "like," I think. I hadn't finished smiling and saying hello when she said that she thought the seats we
were sitting in were reserved for family and/or friends
of the cast. In jest, I jumped up and said that I could sit
elsewhere. "I can move over there, or over there." She
laughed and replied, "Oh, no," but it was too late. I had
taken not more than two steps out of my seat when my
shoe caught on the edge of the uneven planking and I

went airborne, head-first, over the side of the balcony wall, a good distance to the floor. In the nanosecond on the way down I managed to turn my body in this unexpected flight by doing precisely what high-fall stuntman Paul Stader had once told me to do. I came down and landed—feet first, no less—exactly in the center of the theater attendant's little table, crushing it flat to the floor, tickets and lists going everywhere. The attendant didn't know what to do. I was standing on his table and suddenly in the midst of a number of people that were being checked in for the evening's performance. The attendant was shocked as he asked, "My God, are you all right?" Surprised myself that I was perfectly okay, I answered that I was fine, but his table might need some attention. I was a little embarrassed and hesitated for a moment before returning to my seat in the balcony. It crossed my thoughts to escape into the night and go home, but I had to report back to Millie. I gathered my wits, again apologized to the attendant for the little table, and waved to my new friend who was now peering over at me from above. I headed back up to return to my seat, and as I did, I got some spontaneous applause from the seated audience. I turned to them and said with a smile that it was all part of the show, thanked them, and then gave them some applause in return. I sat down next to my new friend, and with a big forced smile told her that I was a stuntman and had done the fall for her benefit but unfortunately had misjudged the poor attendant's table at the bottom. She then offered her name. "I'm Paul Stader," I said, and shook her hand again. I was going to tell her I was kidding around by giving her the great stuntman's name, but the curtain rose and it got very quiet. By the end of first act I had observed enough of the actor I had been sent to see. Between acts, I excused myself to the restroom and finally escaped into the night, and went home to my little ones without further embarrassment. I think Mr. Stader, and especially my wife, would have been proud of my moves that evening. The next day I gave Millie Gusse the anticipated report without any references to my spectacular high fall.

I always felt live theater was the very best way to find new talent, with the New York-trained actor being the most highly regarded. You get a chance to view the actor working, and if you like what you see, you add his name to those constantly changing casting lists. Additionally, in the quest to find those next stars of tomorrow, most studio casting departments reserved a time period during the week for theatrical agents to discuss or remind the casting directors of their specific stable of artists and their new finds. While at Paramount, it was Tuesday from nine a.m. to eleven thirty a.m. On that specific "Agents' Day," I always tried hard to give every agent an audience. I would listen to all conversations concerning the business of talent, especially during this time. Personalities sometimes clashed when I'd stick to a schedule and make some of the young and self-important agents from the bigger offices, who had just taken a meeting with Millie and who just happened to drop in on me, wait their turn from a sign-in list. A pissed-off William Morris agent once told me that they represented 75 percent of all the talent—not just the actors, but the writers, directors, and producers. In the same breath, he then tried to force me to consider an absolutely absurd idea for an upcoming role on *The Odd Couple*, no doubt an artist who was unhappy and threatening to leave his office if the interviews and jobs didn't start coming. I would always listen, but always voted for who I thought could play the part the very best, regardless of agent representation or other internal pressures. In retrospect, if I had played politics I might have gotten more referrals for jobs from those top agents. They want to keep you working if you're buying their product consistently, and happily suggest you for openings when they hear of them. They want to have you in their back pocket and own you, if they can. It was very risky playing that kind of politics. My loyalties and first allegiance was always to my employers; after all, they paid me a salary to protect their interests.

The notion of my having a kind of "open door" policy at Paramount, beyond the regular weekly Agents' Day, was spawned by my attempt to see Al Trescone at MGM way back when. Through an agent's suggestion and persistence, for what was referred to as a "general interview," I would set appointment times for exactly that—a first meeting, for general reasons, to get to know the work of an artist and make an assessment of where he or she might be used immediately or for possible future projects. I had met and interviewed a very young Jodie Foster this way. I liked this very bright kid; we talked for a long time, and I thought if she stayed with it she was destined for great things. We considered her for a *Brady Bunch* episode, but for whatever reasons chose someone else. I always tried to give everyone and anyone my ear and it worked a great many times, by finding a new and exciting someone who would work for less money, keeping budgets down, and also finding a new face, "a find," like Charlie Martin Smith.

Millie had enforced the practice of checking most recent employment "quotes" at other production companies, to be certain that an artist had earned what his agent had quoted his salary demands to be. If I had an approved budget of a thousand dollars for a day-player role, I would always attempt to save some of the budget by exploring who exactly on my suggestion list might work for a little less. Those being considered might range in price anywhere from SAG scale, or minimum, to my budgeted money. All staff casting directors had to comply with this to satisfy Millie's directive, except when it was an established name artist. But if it was someone making the transition to "guest star" status and wasn't established at what was termed "top of the show," or the maximum a show would pay for a guest-starring role, Millie would encourage us to fight for every dollar if we were considering someone that wasn't established at "top of the show." If this were the case, upon making the deal the artist might be offered less, say five hundred dollars less, for the required time needed, but on his quote, the information given out to other studios, it would boldly state to quote "top of the show." This way, we saved some money and got our first choice for the role and the actor got a higher quote. Most times this tactic would work. But sometimes agents, knowing full well that a role was an important one, a "guest star" role in important scenes opposite other big-name actors on the A-list, would stick to their guns and demand the billing and the money that the role commanded, whether the artist was established or not. I started to do this on a regular basis; that is, always describing to agent representation that there was far less money than was actually allocated. In jest one day, I told my agent buddy Dan Multhrope we had only SAG scale, or minimum, to pay for a role in an upcoming episode. The word quickly spread around town that I was paying only SAG minimum, and the nickname "Minimum Mike" was born. I didn't mind. Millie smiled big when she learned of my new nickname. Suddenly, I found a lot of really good actors that would work for scale, plus the 10 percent agents' commission of course, that I could put in roles when budgets were truly tight. Frugal Millie Gusse was so proud.

My office was a corner one that had windows on two sides, and it was said that Cecil B. DeMille's huge desk had been moved into my office and remained there (yeah, right). Mr. DeMille, Samuel Goldwyn, and Jesse Lasky had founded the Lasky Film Company in 1913, which became RKO, Desilu, and then Paramount, but I doubt if his desk could have survived. The view from my office window on the north side was the Western Street, where countless exteriors of western films had been shot, including *High Noon. Bonanza* was still shooting there, and on occasion I would run into Michael Landon at the studio gym, the exterior of which was an old building, and it was a few steps from my office on the Western Street. Michael Landon was a genuine,

down-to-earth chap who loved to exercise daily, especially to box. I overheard him talking about an article in
the newspaper one day that had moved him. He seemed
honestly concerned about the human condition; as he
openly expressed compassion concerning the article,
he seemed to care about people. One noontime I had
been punching the speed bag and he said something to
me about someone he had been waiting for that hadn't
shown up, and then invited me to come into the ring
and spar a couple rounds. I accepted and we touched
gloves for a while and broke a good sweat until he got
a phone call. I was happy he got the call. He was a very
good boxer and was quickly wearing me down. I only
saw him a couple more times after that.

John Wayne's Batjac Productions was upstairs from
casting. I would often see Mr. Wayne out of my north
window as I sat at my desk. He would saunter up the
walkway that led to the stairs up to his suite of offices,
walking that famous walk. If I looked out and he saw
me, he would always wave and give that big smile. One
day, after half a dozen or so waves, I ran outside and
introduced myself, and expressed my gratitude for his
many great and entertaining films. He immediately
asked which I liked best. I told him I thought he and the
late, great Montgomery Clift in *Red River* was probably
my favorite, but because I was a former U.S. Marine, *The
Sands of Iwo Jima* was a very close second and a favorite
of every Marine I ever knew. From then on, when I saw
John Wayne out of my office window he would give me
the big smile and a little two-finger salute instead of a
wave.

One quiet afternoon I was at my desk, reading a script and jotting down some preliminary casting ideas for the next *Odd Couple* episode, and I looked out my east window and saw a man drop over the very high wall about fifteen yards from our office entrance. He was dressed like a worker, wearing a workman's cap, bib overalls, a tool belt, and a small satchel with what appeared to be an oil canister protruding from the opening. When he landed, he looked about and then gathered the things he had dropped over and started moving quickly up the street. For an instant I thought perhaps he was a worker. Nah; having scaled a few high studio fences myself, I decided to investigate further. I shot out the side entrance of the DeMille building like Cecil himself had hollered "action!" and called out to the infiltrator, "Hold it right there, you're under arrest!" I then smiled and laughed and motioned him over to my office. I suspected that he might have been an actor that wasn't sitting by the phone waiting for his agent to call. We returned to my office, where he confessed that he was indeed an actor and that his name was Ken Sylk. I told him who I was, and that it was my job as well to keep an eye on the east fence for infiltrators attempting to breach Millie Gusse's bar. He confessed he'd heard about her and her bar, and said that he could use a drink. I told him to settle down and explain what he was doing jumping over the wall, and asked him what he had in the little oil can. After a long, thoughtful beat (he milked it), he replied, "I can't tell you that, Mike." I had fallen into his trap, and asked why he couldn't tell me. He informed me that he lubricated hinges on doors with the contents of the can. The contents were a family secret, and if he divulged the ingredients, then perhaps I would go out and get the same can and ingredients, and he would be out of a job. It was a great monologue and presentation. I was sold, again. I'd heard it before but with other twists, for what is acting but to change things? I laughed, and he continued to explain his approach for meeting people that could possibly hire him. He said that what he would do, after gaining access to a studio lot, was find what looked like a producer's office and/or recognizable names, or show names, on any signs of the interior buildings. He would then make a selection, enter, and start oiling door hinges, looking for the action; that is, recognizable producers and/or directors that might be interested in meeting an interesting and inventive storytelling artist. Ken went on to recount that when Mike Nichols and Larry Turman were having a casting meeting in New York for *The Graduate*, and hadn't fully decided on Dustin Hoffman yet, he showed up with his oil can and started oiling hinges in Larry Turman's office. He said Mike Nichols immediately approached him and told him to stop; that he couldn't do it at that time, and demanded to know what he was doing. Mr. Nichols stated firmly they were in the midst of a private meeting and wanted no interruptions. Ken said that he calmly explained that he didn't work for the studio; that he was an independent contractor, and if they didn't want the hinges oiled it was okay by him, since he would still get paid. Ken said he started putting his tools and oil can away, and as I had done, Mike Nichols had asked about to the contents of the oil can. Ken gave him the same "Hey, I can't tell you that" response. He said Mike Nichols smiled and asked, "And why is that?" Ken gave him the same answer he had given me. "I tell you what I got in this can and you go out and get a can, he goes out (he pointed to Larry Turman) and gets a can, and pretty soon there's a bunch of folks out there doing this work and I'm out of a job. What's in this can is a trade secret." He said Mike Nichols and Larry Turman were both smiling by then. Larry Turman asked, "You've got to be an actor, am I right?" Ken said he then confessed to them that he was. Larry Turman and Mike Nichols praised his efforts and his moxie inventiveness, but said they were still very busy. Ken offered that he had heard what they were looking for and thought he was right for the lead role in *The Graduate*. He said that after a moment of looking over his resume, which he had produced from his tool bag, and a moment of quiet discussion betwixt themselves, Ken said they agreed that maybe he might be a possibility. They gave him some material and asked him to return in a few days to read. When Ken told me this story, he said of all the people they had considered it came down to just him and Dustin Hoffman as finalists. I, too, read Ken that afternoon and found that he was a very good actor and also very different, as the young Dustin Hoffman was different, but similar in quality. When he left that day I wasn't about to stop him on his journey, I thought him to be quite harmless. He gathered up his things, shook my hand, asked for directions to Millie Gusse's bar, and walked off smiling and making drinking gestures. I had found another way of finding interesting talent.

Many years later I would run into Ken at my alma mater, the 20th Century Fox lot, and he would tell me of his good fortune that Fox had optioned for him to write an original screenplay based on his oil-can marketing tactics.

Still another unexpected incident occurred just a few days later. It was late in the day on what had been a very hot, hectic afternoon. I had gone out to my producer's office to retrieve script changes that would add as many as one or two characters to the next *Odd Couple* episode that was currently in rehearsal and on the stage. I was in a bit of a panic, to say the least. I was late getting back, and Sandy had already shown my next general interview appointment into my office to wait, as Sandy's office waiting area had the overflow actors waiting for *Mannix* readings at Ramsey King's office. I usually had several general meetings scheduled throughout the week and would do my best to spend a little time with each one. On this day and at this time I was frantic, as I had other problems that were surfacing on *The Brady Bunch*, with rumors that Robert Reed hated the next scheduled script and wasn't going to do it. But this wasn't the first time I had expected a production shutdown or a change in shooting schedule over this issue. I went to Sandy with *The Odd Couple* changes, and she explained that because of the overflow she had let my afternoon appointment, a young woman, go directly to my office and wait for me there. When I entered my office, I was more focused on retrieving information of the added character(s) and getting that information out to the responsible agents, and continuing to check actors' availability for the roles I might need if we switched *Brady Bunch* scripts. It was not a good day for meeting someone new and/or for being especially cordial. I said hello and introduced myself to her as I briskly walked to my desk. I explained briefly and asked that she give me a few minutes to make some calls to catch up. She said she wasn't in a rush, and as I directed my energies to requesting Sandy to call a number of agents, she said, in a rather sexy tone, "I'm a nudist. It's so hot, would you mind if I took off my clothes?" Most of the time that office was abuzz with jokesters saying all sorts of absurd and off-the-wall things, so I paid little attention, only half hearing what she had said. I was more focused on other items of concern. I replied, without even looking at her, "I don't mind, but I have to make these calls." I never looked in her direction again until I was finished. Then it occurred to me what she had said. I gazed in her direction again, where she was completely naked and sitting on the proverbial "casting couch." She asked, "Do you like?" as she moved her hands over her more-than-ample breasts. I could feel beads of perspiration begin to form on my forehead. I was maybe going into shock as the term centerfold came to mind. I suddenly imagined Millie Gusse trotting off to go to a meeting with Doug Cramer and gazing in to see a naked lady sitting across from me. Nervously, I instructed her to see how quickly she could get back into her dress before we got into trouble. She replied, in a very sexy tone, "I like trouble." As I almost lunged to shut my office door,

I told her that I didn't. A very uncomfortable feeling came over me, as in passing my nostrils filled with her very strong, sexy, almost titillating scent, which I hadn't paid much attention to upon entering. Now, with the door closed, it seemed very thick. I quickly and nervously returned to the safety of being behind my desk. I now wondered if any of the talent wandering about the hall had seen her sitting there naked. She had been doing a lot of sexy eyeballing as she slowly finished getting dressed. I then crossed again, took a deep breath and opened my office door. Like I wasn't already nervous and stressed enough that afternoon; I didn't need this. We talked for a few minutes, mostly about being a nudist. She confessed she was an exhibitionist and thought nudity was a natural thing; that she liked to tease, and that wearing clothes was unnatural. I nervously looked at her resume and was surprised that she had done quite a lot of good-quality New York theater study, experience, and work. I decided that I should give her some material to read, or sides (pages from a script), and then asked her to take a walk and look at them for a few minutes.

I concluded my calling and got caught up by getting approval to hire the talent for the additional *Odd Couple* roles to start in the morning. After a cool drink and the air conditioner on high for about ten minutes, I called her back in and she read for me. First, a rather serious dramatic scene, and I was really quite surprised. She was very good; totally different from the sexy person she had portrayed while getting dressed. I then asked her to read a funny character cold; that is, without looking at it for more than a minute or so, and with only a brief explanation of the story. Again, I thought she was really quite excellent. She was different, and created a very dissimilar character and quality for herself. She had obvious good looks, so I decided to run her up to the administration building and let her meet Belson and Marshall, and maybe over to meet Howard Leeds and Sherwood Schwartz. Howard and Sherwood weren't available, so we turned and entered the administration building on our way to Belson and Marshall's suite of offices. The legal department was on the first floor, and as we passed through the hallway I noticed old friend Marvin Katz, an attorney who my wife had worked for when I was at Fox, sitting behind his desk with his door open. Marvin was a great guy, with a great sense of humor. He was on the phone, but he waved for us to enter and I ushered my new discovery into his office. Suddenly, my new friend jumped out of her dress and twirled around. Marvin continued talking on the phone, eyes bulging, and just as quickly she dressed and we made an exit without Marvin saying a word. Marvin laughed hysterically later as he explained that he had been on the phone with a judge, trying to talk his way out of a traffic ticket when we walked into his office and she twirled her beautiful body. He laughed and said he had become so distracted he lost his concentration and his presentation to expunge the violation from the record failed.

Casting Directors Reveal . . .
TV Hopefuls Will Bribe, Lie, Scheme — Anything to Get Into a Hit Show

In desperate attempts to break into the big time, actors and actresses use everything from bribery, lies and sex to wild and wacky schemes to land even the tiniest roles on top-rated TV shows, reveal Hollywood casting directors.

"Most actors and actresses are desperate for any parts in major TV series," declared Michael Hanks, casting director of "CHiPs" and "Lucan."

And Joel Thurm, casting director for "Starsky & Hutch," marveled: "There are a lot of people who would give anything to be on the show."

In a series of exclusive in-

By CHARLES PARMITER

terviews, top TV casting directors revealed:

• How one eager performer jumped over the fence of a studio and started oiling every door he came to with an oilcan until he reached the office of a producer he wanted to see.

• The time an ambitious actor had himself delivered in a wooden crate to a producer's office and popped out with resume and picture in hand.

• An attempt by an aspiring entertainer to use a 4-foot-long submarine sandwich to get a part.

• How offers of cold cash and sex are used to try to get roles.

"I have had offers of sex from actresses. It happens all the time in this business," said Hanks.

He added he has also been offered kickbacks from an agent who "was trying to get a continuous flow of his clients some work."

Hanks — who says he turned down all these outrageous offers — recalled the actor who leaped over a studio fence and began oiling door hinges until he got to the office of a producer he wanted to see.

"The producer asked what he was doing, and he said, 'I'm really an actor and I'd really like to read for this role.'"

He was allowed to read, but didn't land the part.

Joel Thurm recalled one actor who offered himself to a producer as sort of a package deal. He came boxed in a crate.

The crate was opened with a crowbar and, recalled Thurm, "Out popped this actor with a coat and tie and with his picture and resume in his hand.

"He said, 'I just wanted to meet you.' The producer said, 'You _____,' and he walked back into his office. He wouldn't see him."

One actor offered a casting director a really huge 4-foot-long submarine sandwich. "But he did not get the part. We thanked him for the sandwich, though. It fed the whole office building," said Bob Hoffman, casting director for TV's "Happy Days" and for "Laverne & Shirley."

Some performers — desperate for a break in the Hollywood jungle — resort to out-and-out lies. Patti Hayes, casting director for "Battlestar Galactica" and "The Eddie Capra Mysteries," declared: "Actors are very often trying to pull the wool over my eyes. When I tell a (bitpart) actor to leave me his picture and resume . . . I would say that 60 percent of the time you cannot believe those credits (on the resume)."

One time Hayes brought an aspiring actress to read for a producer — who got to see more than he ever bargained for.

As soon as the actress met the producer, "she proceeded to lay out props —" and take off her clothes," recalled Hayes. "I was sitting there going. 'What!' I couldn't wait to get her out of there, I was so embarrassed!

"It's very sad in a way that people have to reach that level of desperation. I am amazed that they will do these things."

November 1978, an actress twirls again.

Belson and Marshall had told me that we should always be on the lookout for beautiful people, and if I met someone exciting and different to bring him or her by, and if they could break away for a moment they would, and they did. In fact, they called the entire male staff, all the writers and assistants, and my new discovery twirled. Ten comedy writers and a naked girl created a very a funny distraction for all of us on that warm afternoon. After several minutes of spontaneous one-liners and the laughs that followed, we were dismissed. I would hire her for a small role on an upcoming episode. I noticed in the weeks and months to follow that her name would emerge in the end credits of other shows around town. In the seasons that followed I would occasionally see her name in *TV Guide*, and so it seemed she was still twirling. Ken Sylk had his oilcan and she twirled—both seemed to get attention.

Just to the south of the administration building, out the doors of the Bronson Street entrance at the corner of Marathon Street, was another wonderful restaurant called O'Blaths that catered mostly to a show-business crowd. It was probably not more that ten yards from what was then the main Paramount entrance. It had a counter, and if you wanted to eat quickly and needed to get off the lot for a while, it was a good choice. I had gone there just for those reasons, and except for one seat at the counter, a few steps from the busy cashier, the place was packed and noisy. I raced for the empty seat next to the wall, and as I sat down everyone in the room seemed to become immediately quiet and looked toward me. The room had gone from lunchtime chatter and clinking to completely silent, with not a fork or a glass or a sound of any kind. Everyone in the place was gazing in my direction. More than slightly self-conscious, I stared back at the crowd staring at me, thinking, what the hell are they looking at? I peered back, smiled, and grabbed a menu. With the crowd still staring and the room dead silent, I turned and gazed further behind me to the cashier, and paying his check was Marlon Brando. He was still on the lot finishing up *The Godfather*. For that moment, which seemed like an eternity, I felt it—the awe, the quiet respect and observance of the huge megastar presence. Amazing, every eye was on him. When he was about halfway out the door he turned, smiled to the lunchtime crowd, mumbled something, and gave a little wave of gratitude and then disappeared. The crowd immediately started talking and the utensil sounds began again as the name Brando reverberated around the room. It was another unforgettable and indelible moment, the likes of which never occurred again in my experience.

Millie Gusse also assigned me the task of putting out a breakdown synopsis of all the scripts currently being cast so that agents could get them when they visited on Agents' Day, more low-man-on-the-totem-pole-dirt work. I slightly resented this task it, as it was time-consuming to read all the scripts: *Mannix, Mission Impossible, Love, Barefoot in the Park*, and my shows, *The Brady Bunch* and *The Odd Couple*. It was like doing multiple book reports every week. But I decided to have some fun with it. I'd inject some off-the-wall absurd humor here and there to get a chuckle out of agents visiting to retrieve them.

I'd write a brief story outline and a complete character summary. Among the many agents that would visit on Agents' Day was Norah Sanders. Norah would come by and bring her actor son, Gary Marsh, to visit whomever he could. I liked Norah and I remember explaining to Gary about my breakdowns. He was amused and laughed aloud at some of my script and character summaries. Gary thought it was funny and an interesting thing that I did. A short time later, I heard through his mom that he was providing this service for the entire industry and had some clients. I never really thought he had a snowball's chance for survival. The major studios and networks traditionally hadn't allowed someone from the outside to come in and read their scripts, and have access to their story ideas—a huge hurdle. I never thought it would work, but Gary had a vision and tenacity. He persevered and fought the uphill fight. He believed in the idea and he won, like a hard-charging Marine. He found a niche and filled it with a very good service to the industry. Breakdown Services was born.

Wally Amos was another success story that evolved while I was at Paramount. Wally was a real gentleman; extremely intelligent, class all the way, a warm and honest man, personable and charming to everyone in his path. He had been with William Morris as an agent and then became a personal manager. Everybody liked Wally Amos. Wally was a happy person and you looked forward to a smiling time when you saw him coming. When he would visit casting, he would bring with him a bag of his homemade chocolate chip cookies, still warm, baked fresh that morning in his home. He would always give Sandy and me a supply and then work his way back to Millie's domain. I don't think he ever really got to Millie in person on his cookie runs, but he took care of all the staff at that end of the suite and he always left a few for her. They were really good cookies; they tasted like Mom had just made them. As he would hand them out, someone would inevitably say how good they were and that he should open his own cookie business. I don't think anyone thought it was really viable, since at the time most of the folks making cookies were the big conglomerate companies. I personally thought it was highly remote that his idea would ever become popular. But everyone loved Wally and would tell him to open his own business, and then we'd rush back to our ever-so-important casting business with chocolate chips melting on our tongues. Wally would always say that one of these days he might rent a storefront and see what happened. Wally would talk some casting business and move on down the hall while the cookies were still warm. But "one day" came, and Wally begged, borrowed (but didn't steal), and everybody thought he was nuts when he started baking cookies in a retail storefront on Sunset Boulevard that he alone had envisioned. And the nuts he put in his cookies. I personally didn't give the probability of success much of a chance, as it seemed highly risky and speculative, to say the least. Wally Amos did something nobody thought could be done because he believed in his dream and never considered the big companies as any competition whatsoever. He just did what Emerson said: "Do the thing and you will have the power." Only Wally did the thing and he had cookies,

and then money. He was the first independent chocolate chip cookie company. The Famous Amos Cookie
Company was born, proving that you can always build
a better chocolate chip cookie trap. Personally, I'm
trapped every time I see a bag of Famous Amos Cookies,
and not just because they're good, either; it's because I
remember the smile on Wally's face. It was genuine, and
it conjures up memories of very happy times.

Very early one morning I entered the DeMille building to go into my office, and I noticed Millie at her
office entrance motioning for me to come down. Obviously there was a problem, as she never got in early.
Usually, whenever Millie took issue with something I
had done and there was a problem, she would write
"Mike see me" on a document it concerned. This must
be a major problem, I thought, as she's in so early; the
major ass chewing to commence at dawn. I guess I had
always been guilt-ridden for having been so daring and
mischievous at times as a youngster. Therefore, when
Millie would summon me to her office I always felt like
I was going to the principal's office. When I entered her
office, she immediately informed me that Ramsey King
had come down with a terrible case of the flu. What
a relief, I thought. She instructed me to immediately
take on the additional responsibilities of the next *Mannix* episode(s). I had worked on *Mannix* with Bill Kenney when we joined Paramount, and knew producers
Ivan Goff and Ben Roberts well, and liked them. I was
happy and excited to be back, even if for a brief stay, for
the change of it, and to be able to cast some characters
that had more depth and were more complex than

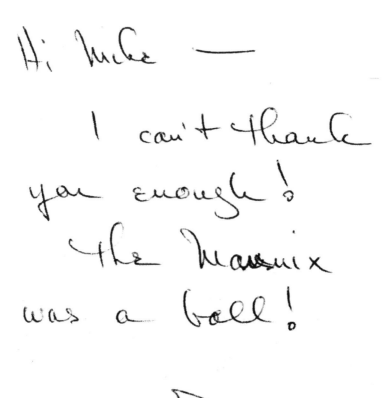

A note from Mike Farrell.

my current casting assignments. Remember that there are actors that won't do television, much less half-hour shows. Some won't do the hour shows, and will try and hold out for big films. So it was a slightly different talent pool. Millie informed me that she was in hopes that Ramsey would be well enough to return in a few days, but that in the meantime I should prepare for the worst, and speak to Ivan and Ben immediately about scheduling the next casting session for the next episode. She further instructed me to read all the scripts scheduled to be next, get some suggestions lists to them as soon as possible, and to start checking out availabilities of whomever I thought were possibilities. A few weeks before on a general interview, I had met a young chap by the name of Michael Farrell. He was a total unknown. I liked his unique quality and immediately saw Mike playing a supporting role in what was scheduled to be the next *Mannix* to go to the stage. I brought him in to read, we hired him, and he worked the following week. Just a very few weeks later, Mike called and told me that Fox's huge hit *M*A*S*H* was recasting the Alan Alda sidekick role that Wayne Rogers was vacating. *M*A*S*H* had requested borrowing that specific episode of *Mannix* to view his work. It was both his biggest role and most recent work at that time. Barely in the can and finished, it took some upper-echelon string-pulling to let the episode off the lot prior to its air date. Mike thanked me and said it was that specific piece that convinced the powers that be at Fox to put him under contract. I was very happy for him. Funny and peculiar how destiny shows itself sometimes, as Mike Farrell was one of only a couple of my original cast submissions I had been able to get the producers to consider. Ivan Goff and Ben Roberts had always been writer/producers that had their own ideas of who they wanted in each role; they wrote with those actors already in mind. Ramsey got well and returned to his duties a few days later. I always thought it was a twist of fate Ramsey King had gotten sick; I know his ideas for that specific role would have been very different.

Mike Rosen's career as a casting director would be short-lived. He became the next to succumb to the chaos of *Love American Style.* After only one year, he said he would be happy to get back to being an agent, to what he knew best. Too much stress, he would say. He returned to the family owned Larry Rosen Agency franchise and then later teamed up with longtime childhood friend and partner Ernie Dade to open the Dade-Rosen Agency. Millie announced the changes at the weekly staff meeting; that I was the best comedy casting director on staff, and that I had been assigned *Love American Style* under producer Ray Allen for the upcoming season. I was pumped up, but extremely apprehensive. After a short hiatus, we would all return for the pilot season and to begin pre-production on our various assignments. I was very happy, to say the least. I was thrilled. I knew it was dangerous territory, but *The Brady Bunch* and *The Odd Couple* were both huge successes and relatively easy to deal with. I thought *Love* would be the real challenge to contend with. Heads were rolling in the front office as well and it was experiencing as many volatile changes, first with Bruce Lansbury (Angela's brother) moving into the VP of production slot recently vacated by ally Doug Cramer. Tom Tannenbaum would then replace Lansbury. I would have cast *Love* for free, just to get the credit. Well, maybe for free, but Paramount gave me a nice increase in salary anyway. In addition to my new casting changes, my wife and I had been blessed with a third bright and beautiful bouncing baby boy, Jonathan Patrick. Life was good.

Ray Allen was a very mellow fellow and his low-key charismatic charm and experience seemed to be calming to all. Of all the producers I had worked with on *Love*, I liked his style the best. He was the consonant gentleman and just wouldn't let himself get too excited about any of the pressures of *Love American Style*. But I would cast *Love* for just one more full season and fall victim as well; the Blackouts and hundreds of exciting "casting coups," for some twenty-four episodes. I had worked very hard to entice the biggest names possible to the show and had been successful some of the time, but somehow I had stepped on the foot of a network jerk at ABC and began getting a lot of bad-mouthing from the powder-sniffing dog. But before my tenure was to end I would cast *Love and the Doorknob*. It was a very short vignette that revolved around a chap who falls and gets a doorknob lodged in his mouth, a segment I could finally suggest my cousin "Laughing Lindy" for. Lindy's character was sick, and when wheeled through the ER on a gurney he observed the man with a doorknob lodged in his mouth and started laughing hysterically. The set was rolling with laughter for well over an hour that morning. Lindy was a very funny guy.

He had worked with Abbott and Costello early on, and had trained and studied in New York, but just never caught much that didn't require his wacky laughter.

At the end of the 1972 season, Millie Gusse summoned me to her office, and it wasn't for morning coffee or drinks. She explained that her department had been pressured by the network to make changes on *Love American Style* and do a revamping of staff assignments. "Unfortunately," she said, "I'm going to have to let you go." Millie then praised me, and said nobody on her staff had worked as hard or seemed to care with as much passion as I did, but that the front office simply wanted change again on *Love*. It was her only option, as all the other casting positions were secure and the *Love* post was the most volatile. She said that I had done extremely well at Paramount and for me not to worry; that she was sure I would find another, better spot very soon. She also said that she had become greatly attached to me, and again that it was her only option, and that if I needed her for anything—a reference, et cetera—to call. We hugged and I left her office in total disbelief, numb. My world of creative work went suddenly upside down. At the end of that week, I said good-bye to all the great people I had worked with; Tony Randall, Howard Leeds, Sherwood and son Lloyd Schwartz, Jerry Belson, Garry Marshall, and Ray Allen. In his best New York delivery, Ray said, "Remember, change is good. Don't worry, kid, you'll find something better. It's a very ungrateful business sometimes. I'll probably be gone in another week, too." I said good-bye to all the friends I had made on the lot, gathered my files and desk stuff, gave Mary Prange and Suzanne Gordon big hugs, but saved the biggest for Sandy Thayer, as I had developed a loving interest in this superb young woman. After more than three seasons of wonderful work, and just as much fun together, we hugged, and with tears and half-baked smiles I left the Paramount lot.

CHAPTER FOUR

Warner Brothers and Garry Marshall

I have always been resourceful; that is, I was only down for a New York minute, and then I went to work looking for work. I went to work looking for something better. My dear mother would always remind me, "God closes one door, he opens another, son." I had investigated all possibilities; it was getting late, past the pre-season period of preparation, and I was having no success in finding a vacant post. I was becoming more than concerned. Then, from out of nowhere I got a call from Garry Marshall, who explained that he would be the executive producer on a new show for Warner Brothers Television entitled *The Little People*, to be shot entirely in Hawaii. He inquired about my availability. I was somewhat reluctant, as this was a location casting assignment, not really where I wanted to be in my career. But it was the only thing being offered, and it was Garry Marshall, and I was sure Garry was going to be around for a very long while. Garry said he liked my work and wanted to put me in touch with producers Duke Vincent and Bruce Johnson at Warner Brothers. The next morning I took a meeting and was immediately offered the position. What attracted me even more was that it would be only a temporary position, to set up the office in Hawaii and to interview, create photo files, and cull through the local talent there, and work until mid-September. A casting person I'd never heard of, and I did some checking, who was the choice of either Brian Keith or co-executive producer Jerry Thorpe, would be coming in at that time to take over. The temporary aspect especially made the job more attractive, as I wouldn't be away from my kids that long and I could continue to scout for other casting openings through Hal Gefsky and other Hollywood agent contacts, with the knowledge that I soon would be available for any sudden staff openings. What they offered and what I was able to get out of Warner Brothers Television for those three months in paradise would be very nice indeed. I would be able to live nicely on the cash per diem expense money paid, send my paychecks home to take care of my family, and sock some of it away. Warner Brothers Television had wanted me to leave immediately for Honolulu, and my son Doyle was scheduled to have some minor surgery the very next morning. I was filled with anxiety about leaving. I knew he was in very good hands, but in retrospect, I wish I had waited. I missed my sons so much it hurt, and I regret to this day not being there for Doyle, but we had to eat, and I needed to pay the bills that been accumulating. I would arrive several weeks in advance of the first production start date in an effort to interview everyone on the islands that wanted to act, organize aforementioned reference files with pictures, and cast the first ten episodes—a piece of cake.

My three-year-old son Christopher would visit me in the weeks to come and do a small part on the show. He had his first experience in front of the camera when he was only fifteen days old, when I was at Fox, on a pilot starring Diane Carroll entitled *Julia*. Chris was a very bright child, and as he got older he was just having fun, play-acting. When he was small I would read him the dialogue, direct him some, and he would memorize and give his natural performance. I had gotten him an agent, Dorothy Day Otis, and he started to get just about every commercial he was sent out on.

Carl Joy's good buddy Richard Lang was the associate producer of *The Little People* and the resident director. He came by immediately and greeted me at my office in the Ilikai Marina Hotel. In our very first meeting, he informed me that the locals had become very upset with the former casting person that had been there when they shot the pilot. They had turned over his car and set it on fire because he had berated one of the local extras in front of other locals—something you just don't do, especially in Hawaii. Richard said the frightened casting director didn't even go back to the hotel to get his things. He went straight to the airport and flew back to the mainland. I'd heard it all before and was wondering to myself, can this be true? I explained to Richard Lang that the hiring of atmosphere/extras wasn't my area of responsibility; someone else there would be doing that. However, Richard advised me that if I had a problem with anyone on the set, to take him or her aside and make my case with patience, kindness, and gentleness. I assured Richard Lang that I was well trained in handling people/problem situations and would never think handling a problem any other way. He directed me to a suite of offices, my desk, and my phones. Immediately,

I called home to check on Doyle and my wife told me that he was fine, and that he was already outside playing with his brother in the backyard. A minor skin operation on a sweet child is never minor to a parent.

Honolulu had rolled out the red carpet for the Hollywood casting director. I would lose count of the luaus and yacht parties I was invited to. Everyone wanted to be my friend: local politicians, presidents of banks, hotel owners. I was wined and dined by all the local power brokers; everyone wanted to be in front of the camera. The local agents—I think there were two or three that had most of the local talent—had quickly spread the word we were setting up offices. Suddenly, people were coming at me from every direction; actors and actresses were dropping by unannounced with pictures and resumes. I shared offices with production so there was some insulation, in that there were a couple of very protective secretaries that had to be approached before getting to my office. I didn't mind the drop-ins, as my general interviewing was ongoing, but a number of local ingénues came at me a very different way.

I had taken an apartment in the Ilikai Marina Hotel, and to get to my apartment and collapse at day's end I found it was a shorter walk home if I used the elevator at the rear of the hotel, the one nearest the pool. As usual, I had been coming in early and organizing until late most days. Often exhausted, I would venture into the bar area, at poolside, and have a cocktail, order food, and watch the swimming for a beat as I thought about tomorrow's duties. Then, almost like clockwork, a beautiful young woman would come up and approach me at a faraway spot I had picked out as my regular away-from-the-action safe place at the bar. Several times they were clad in nothing more than an extremely scanty and very sexy wet bikini. I thought it a coincidence the first couple times it happened; maybe they were meeting someone there, I'd think. But after meeting six or seven aspiring actresses that way, it dawned on me that I perhaps I was being hustled. I would discover that some had other poolside vocations—social farming for business, I called it. I mean, I learned in my first hour there that most working folks on Oahu had three different jobs. These bar beauties would always introduce themselves and then invariably would reveal that they were aspiring actresses, after I gave my job title. It would always be sexy shock/surprise when I would disclose who I was and what I did. Often I had to wait for a picture and resume to be retrieved from God knows where. Yeah, I know, it's tough in paradise. After several such chance meetings, as a lark I gave a young lady a false name and told her she had the wrong guy. I kept insisting that she had me mixed up with someone else, maybe someone that looked like me. She almost got angry, and demanded that I tell her that I was the Warner Brothers' casting director of *The Little People* and that I was Mike Hanks. I put her on for a while longer. Then, she scurried off for the picture and resume. I came to the conclusion that they had done their homework; I was with the new circus in town and they knew where I was hanging after hours. Social farming, and yes, beautiful women were beating down my door.

For *The Little People*, I attended all functions that were necessary for the publicity of the show; the others I pretty much shied away from. On one of the first days I was there I had lunch with Garry Marshall, where we discussed show objectives, writing, and our mutual philosophy of casting. I had discovered this theory on my own, but Garry shed new light and a new affirmation on the psychology of the actor's persona and of casting concepts generally. He asked if I had ever noticed that it wasn't the terribly handsome man or the beautiful woman that were naturals at doing comedy roles. It was always the character, the offbeat weird guy or girl that could best inflate themselves into the comedic portrayal. He theorized that, most times, the handsome and beautiful people didn't have to act bizarre to get attention in life; the world just came to them and lay at their feet. The handsome guy never has to do much to get the girl, he's just there and he gets her, or he gets attention because he's handsome and charismatic. The goofy, offbeat guy has to be inventive and creative to get the same attention. The attractive people never have to develop this aspect of their personalities and therefore don't give to comedic roles what the goofy, off-the-wall person brings. For the most part they've never been there so they don't know what giving an off-the-wall, abstract delivery is, or even that it exists. We both agreed that it's hard to find beautiful people that can be silly and inflate themselves to get zany, silly laughs, but there are always exceptions. A very interesting conversation while eating cool pineapple slices in the warm breeze under the midmorning Honolulu sun.

After about ten days of parties, social meetings, business social meetings, and interviewing more than two thousand people, I was ready to do some exploration of the town on my own, alone, without being hustled. I had been working almost round the clock since my arrival. The only real relaxation I had come to know was my little sons at the end of the day and they were a long way off. One early evening I closed up the office and went out of the hotel for a walk. I had been waiting to be assigned a company car to drive, but it hadn't arrived yet. I walked out on Kalpiolani Boulevard and looked toward Diamond Head, and then back in the opposite direction, trying to decide which way to walk. Then, my eye caught something in the distance, and I thought, No, it can't be, it's impossible; well, certainly highly improbable. I stood there frozen as I watched this chap pedaling his bicycle toward me, in and out of my view, as the many buses and constant traffic that flowed by hid and blocked him. Again I thought, No, it just looks like him. And the mirage became real, as Richard Collier pedaled up and stopped at the curb right in front of me. He didn't even recognize me. I leaned over and calmly said, "Hey, are you following me?" Richard looked at me and nearly fell off his bike and crashed as he broke up with laughter. We both couldn't believe this one. He explained that he was on vacation with his wife. I took his local number and invited him to drop by the offices; that I probably had something he was right for in one of the scripts. He said he was only there for a few more days, and that he had rented the bike and was on his way to return it before they closed.

He said he thought he was late; we laughed again, shook hands and he was off. I shouted as he pedaled off that if I thought of something he was right for I'd call him in the morning, or take a walk looking for him, absolutely unbelievable.

A few steps further down the road I came upon Kobe's Steak House. There were speakers on the exterior of the restaurant and someone was singing, kind of a nice Don Ho quality. Maybe a piano bar, I thought, I should have a look and relax, and maybe sing a couple of songs. It was still early and there wasn't anyone sitting at the bar. I took a seat, ordered the local brew, a Primo beer, and at the end of his set introduced myself to the young singer. His name was Lonnie Kai. I would learn Lonnie was connected to the local Hawaiian community and to a show business family, in that he was the stepson of veteran character actor Woody Strode. I liked Lonnie; he was very talented, a good singer, and had a wonderfully charming personality. Lonnie and I would become good pals during my stay in Honolulu. He had worked on *Hawaii Five-0* and I would be able to use him for something in *The Little People*. When we met that evening, and I casually told him who I was and what I did for a living, he said he had an idea for me to consider. When he took a break, he asked me to join him outside. Lonnie revealed to me that he knew of the other casting director's mistake in dealing with some of the local Hawaiians. He said that he could tell immediately that I was different; he felt I wasn't a snob with a big, condescending ego; that I was honest and a caring fellow that wouldn't step on anyone as the other unfortunate chap had. I assured him that he was right, and that I, too, was a caring, sensitive artist. He explained that the islands are just that, islands, and that if you make enemies there you can't escape because everyone knows everything. It's like a small town. The only way to escape is to get out of Dodge and back to the mainland, and depending on the severity of the mistake, there may not be any escaping the wrath of the locals. He said it was still their island and they were in charge; that if one is to be respected and have power one must pay homage to certain leaders. Lonnie invited me to meet with him on the following Saturday and I did. I picked him up in my brand-new white station wagon, my assigned company car, and we headed to the older part of Honolulu out by Pearl. We passed a bridge on Hotel Street and Lonnie asked me to slow and stop. He pointed to an area on the bridge and said that his real father had been shot and killed at that very spot. He said there's an underworld there, too, and if you make them mad and you're easy to find they'll come after you—it's their turf. We resumed our drive and drove further into the waterfront, the industrial area of Honolulu, no tourist attractions or high-end shoppers here. Lonnie pointed to a small bar and said for me to park. We got out and walked a short distance to the bar.

It was about twelve thirty p.m. on that hot and humid Saturday when we finally entered the place Lonnie had been telling me about all week. Upon entering, Lonnie engaged everyone at the bar and introduced me as being a *haole* (a white man), but a white man with a Hawaiian soul. These guys were huge Hawaiian-Samoan men; the smallest of the eight or so men at the bar was probably 275 pounds. In contrast, I weighed about 165. Lonnie explained to them who I was and what I did on *The Little People*, the new show in town. They asked some questions and seemed unimpressed. I could feel they were looking deep into my eyes and into what Lonnie had referred to as my Hawaiian soul. I liked them, from my perspective; they were just a group of brothers having some beers on a hot day. When we first entered the bar there had been a woman that Lonnie had introduced me to. When she stepped away to play pool, Lonnie confided to me that she was the queen of Samoa and also a very keen pool player. I never really took the time to verify that she was actually royalty, but accepted her persistent challenge to play pool. The humidity was doing a number on me, so I took off my shirt and exposed my pearly white complexion. I was the only *haole* in the place. It was the "when in Hawaii do as the Hawaiians do" philosophy and it worked. Suddenly they embraced me, patted me on the shoulder, ordered me a "special drink" from the bartender, and generally opened up to me with a warmer Hawaiian welcome. It was like they suddenly approved and accepted me, and gave me their blessing. I think it was when they saw me take off my shirt; then, walking around in mere shorts, I could feel they had accepted me. After I had racked the pool balls, I returned to my seat at the bar to retrieve my special drink. As I passed them, they all started making gestures by either covering their eyes or putting on their dark glasses that my being so white was blinding them. Then they would laugh, and then we would all laugh. It was so hot I finished my special drink in a couple of gulps. I liked it; smooth and fruity, I thought. I then ordered more special drinks all around. I was unexpectedly having a terrific time; I was making them laugh and I felt comfortable. I was one of them. I went back to the bar between my pool game and finished another special drink, and they ordered me another. Then, they ordered food from a tiny kitchen in the rear, and when it came it was real Hawaiian cuisine, and each of them invited me to try something different. It was truly a wonderful feast, and a great time. Lonnie was right; these people were the warmest, the most giving people on earth, but don't hurt them and don't steal from them, especially their dignity. I've always been a people person, and I truly loved these folks and didn't care about their titles, either; I liked their souls. My father taught me to play pool when I was nine years old, and as both a young person and an adult I took the game very seriously. When I would drink anyone's special drink, I played even better because I was more relaxed and uninhibited about taking a greater risk. The queen was a very strong player; she was quite a surprise. We were playing eight ball, and the first game she broke my rack, made all her balls and the eight ball, and quickly won the game. I could see she was very good and I would have to pay attention. It would be her last and only win in the ten or so games I played with her majesty, and my pool-playing talents would win her over also. It seemed my new Hawaiian brothers at the bar had been cheering us both on, but I learned later that I had been the only man in some time to beat her, in what had become almost regular Saturday tournament play.

I think they were happy to see a man give her some lessons. A couple of times I tried to return to my seat at the bar, but I couldn't get away from her. She loved the game; as soon as I would make the eight ball, she started the challenges and went to racking the balls for the next game. When we left about five hours later, Lonnie told me I had done the right thing. The local chiefs and the queen loved me, and if I had any problems with anything, for me to get word to my new friends. This was a resource I never called upon, but it was nice to know the locals liked me. The admiration was mutual. It was a great adventure that day. The special drink was, I think, their version of a Long Island iced tea, only with a pineapple spear, more rum, and maybe coconut juice. I was never quite sure of its true ass-kicking content, but I was slugged again as the result of another business meeting.

On another of my first evenings out by myself I went toward Diamond Head to Waikiki Beach. It was early evening and plenty was still going on in the restaurants and bars. Hungry, I wandered into a local restaurant on Kapiolani Boulevard for something to eat before continuing my exploration of the nightlife on Waikiki Beach. I was directed to seating, and as I sat for a moment I saw a young and attractive waitress coming toward me. I thought to myself as she approached that I had lucked out. She, too, was a *haole*. I asked her, as we exchanged alohas, "What's a *haole* like you is doing in a place like this?" She laughed and explained it was her summer job, waiting tables; that she was finishing up at the University of Wisconsin and that journalism was her major. I ordered a beer and a sandwich that my young waitress had suggested. Leta Parks was her name. She was twenty-one years old, tanned, fit, and had one of the very best figures this observer of commercial beauty had ever seen, but that wasn't what drew my attention to Ms. Parks. It was her intellect and her personality. She loved to laugh and would add something even zanier and more intellectually crisp and clever to my observations. I was fascinated; I quickly became addicted to the sandwich, the beer, and to the companionship of Ms. Parks while away from the office atmosphere at the restaurant. Then, we started spending whatever spare time we could find together. Our mutual interest in photography prompted numerous photographic expeditions to isolated and very romantic places on the island of Oahu. I was taken with her, and soon we had fallen into a deep friendship.

When *The Little People* began shooting I had interviewed, photographed, filed, and cross-filed some thirty-five hundred plus people, of which probably less than one hundred were real actors, either living in Honolulu or simply in town working on *Hawaii Five-0.* About another hundred were people that could possibly be directed and rehearsed to handle a couple of simple lines. The remainder I passed on to the folks hiring the background extras. The real problem was that most weren't professionally motivated to be available on specific dates; locals had their own agendas, most working multiple jobs to support their families, and that always came first. They would tell me they were available and then almost always wouldn't be when a specific date came closer; something had changed, usually involving their multiple job work schedules. It was nearly impossible to ever have first choices be available. I had to have as many as five or six alternates for each role, and then there was no guarantee that I'd have anyone in front of the camera on the day of the shoot. I was always chasing down someone's availability, or coaching and rehearsing people for what they would be expected to do, and trying to put them at ease with the unknown acting in front of the camera and the associated pressures to come. It was very different from working in the professional community of Hollywood. I developed a greater sympathy for my predecessor's frustration.

The focus of *The Little People* was Brian Keith, who played a doctor, and his kind of macho persona in contrast to the little cherub-faced beautiful children—the little people of the islands. Kids are always a natural and there were plenty of beautiful kids to choose from. As resident director, which meant he would fill in when necessary, Richard Lang was scheduled to direct several episodes of the shows I would cast. We had started interviewing and reading people, and if we couldn't find the right performance from the talent on the island, we would have the option of having the mainland send us what we needed, but it was far more costly to do so. After several days of meetings and readings, Richard said to me that he liked my reading(s) for something, possibly a role in the next episode. As was my practice when I held readings, I would read all the parts opposite the character I was casting for. I would act out with what my interpretation told me was the correct energy, doing all the different voices and vocal qualities for the different characters that I felt were applicable and necessary. I always did this on every show I ever cast, to give the really good actor something to get his teeth into and bounce off of, and to give the director and the producer more than a mere reading of the material. The actor at least gets an idea of what it might sound like; here, the novice got a taste of the pressures that might lie ahead. When the last of a large group of readings had finished, Richard Lang said to me, "You're still my first choice. I want to use you somewhere." I had to clear it with the front office in Burbank, but because it was more than three hundred miles from the corner of Hollywood and Vine, and what was defined by the Screen Actors Guild as a "location shoot," we had the legal option of hiring anyone we wanted. So I hired myself.

During those first ten episodes I witnessed all the problems of a show in its infancy. In one episode, I had asked that my friend Leta Parks be hired as an extra, and for whatever reason Brian Keith became very upset about her being positioned in the foreground near him. She didn't know Brian, had never met him, but he went into his dressing room and didn't come out until the scene had been blocked and staged as he requested, with no extras. Leta was then placed in the extreme background, a soft blur to camera view. Leta couldn't figure it out, either, and we laughed about it for the rest of the summer. We aired and *The Little People* was an instant hit. The Nielsen ratings were very high. It was Brian Keith's manly, gentle strength and nature in contrast to these beautiful children and the lovely Hawaiian setting that garnered the immediate strong audience. Supported by Shelley Fabares, Nancy Kulp, and the young heart-throb of the moment, Michael Gray, it looked as though it would have a very long run. It was the Art Linkletter *Kids Say the Darndest Things* genre. Brian Keith had controlling interests in the show, and the second season the show was renamed *The Brian Keith Show*, dropping the original *The Little People* title. I can't imagine why. And the stories got away from the children, who were getting the fan mail, with Michael Gray receiving the most. Story content would focus more on the adult characters and story. With the change, immediately the ratings began plummeting, and it would be cancelled at midpoint of its second season. A huge mistake of the "if it ain't broke, why fix it" kind.

In mid-September 1972, I returned home from Hawaii to my own much-adored little people. I had made some really wonderful friends in Hawaii, and for a time fantasized about relocating there. Leta Parks had gone back to Madison, Wisconsin, about a month prior to my departure. We promised each other it wouldn't become just another lost friendship. Today, when I hear Don Ho sing "I'll remember you" like any romantic, with watering eyes and all, I'm drawn back to those beautiful sunsets and have a very warm feeling for some friends that live now in my heart.

Production around town was now in full swing, but with a seemingly tightening economy there were few new openings to explore. I would have to wait for someone to be fired or for the next season. My focus would now lean to the independent casting market and on acting jobs, and I would keep my feelers out for those changes and additions that might occur in the various studio casting departments midseason. In the next few weeks I was sent out on three commercial acting calls and got callbacks for two, and then to my surprise I was hired for one, to play a character in a Ford commercial. Fortunately, the money and residuals to come helped carry us through nicely for a while. I had been continuing my search for work by calling agents and my casting director colleagues, but nothing materialized. Then, in May 1973, I heard of possible openings and changes at Screen Gems Television. I called and made an appointment to meet Renee Valente, vice president of casting.

CHAPTER FIVE

Screen Gems/Columbia Pictures Television

I was offered a staff position under VP of talent, Renee Valente, at Screen Gems, the television wing of Columbia Pictures, located on the old Warner Brothers lot at what was then was called The Burbank Studios. I joined Renee's staff in June 1973, and I was delighted. Renee was another truly a remarkable casting executive, worth her weight in gold, literally. She had an extraordinary eye for talent, every kind of talent, and very creative instincts as an observer/artist. Renee and I immediately liked each other. She respected my achievements and opinions as much as anyone, and as her trust of my instincts grew, she pretty much left me alone to manage my assignments. The staff I would join consisted of Shelly Ellison, Sally Powers, Al "Coronado" Onoroto, and later another agent turned casting director, Paul Rodriques, would join the department. My first assignment as the newest staff member would be a TV sitcom based on the film *Bob & Carol & Ted & Alice*. It starred Robert Urich, Ann Archer, Anita Gillette, and David Spielberg. Jodie Foster had been set to play a sibling role; her little brother was played by Brad Savage, another red-hot child actor. Like the very popular Paramount hit, *The Odd Couple*, that I had cast the previous season, it would also be filmed in a three-camera format in front of a live audience. I thought the show was very funny and had great potential, but the powers that be—the studio executives and those network jerks again—didn't give it enough time to settle into finding an audience or a following. Very short-lived, it aired maybe three of the nine episodes that had been filmed.

Another of my first assignments was a different three-camera financial extravaganza entitled *Needles and Pins*, starring Norman Fell, Sandra Deel, Bernie Kopell, and one of Steve Allen's original "Men On The Street," Louie Nye, one of the true funny men of the world. It had all the elements of a projected huge success. Produced by Mike Frankovich, the story content revolved around the very chaotic and fast-paced garment district in New York. But even with the brilliance of Louie Nye, Bernie Kopell, and Norman Fell, and the touch of Mr. Frankovich, it would be short-lived. I shared my views with Renee, and she agreed that it was a wonderful ensemble cast of characters, but had no real attractive male lead. A young Dick Van Dyke was what was missing.

Renee also had assigned me the daytime drama, *Days of Our Lives*, and a short time later to *The Young and The Restless*. *Days* was rehearsed and videotaped at NBC Burbank and *Y&R* was taped at CBS Television City. I was always in transit. I thought I was being downgraded in casting assignments, as daytime was, in those days, viewed by most of my casting director colleagues as being less than prime time, and it was. But it was also daytime that paid the bills to explore other television program concepts for prime time. I would grow to like doing the soaps; it was fifty-two weeks a year, no layoff hiatus periods, and a regular paid vacation once a year. But I would soon learn that it was a very difficult assignment, because it was often a hard sell to get established talent interested in doing daytime. During the period of time I worked on *Days of Our Lives*, the producer was the elderly Betty Corday. Ms. Corday and Corday Productions also owned a piece of the newer soap, *The Young and The Restless*, but were not involved in the daily production. However, a Corday Productions legal representative signed and approved all contracts for both shows. Betty Corday was a lovely woman that I grew to respect like a fastidious grandmother, as she was extremely opinionated and quite unrealistic about the kind of show she was doing and what actors it might draw. From her perspective, *Days of Our Lives*, which had been created by her late husband, Ted Corday, was second to none, and each one-hour segment might as well have been *Gone with the Wind* or *The Robe* we were casting. I worked for Betty a little more than a year, and for this reason alone it was very difficult to work for her. She would often give me casting suggestions of someone she had seen in a big film or prime-time show to check out as a possibility for the soap. I would always check out any possibility I was given, with a positive presentation of the idea to the responsible agent of the talent in question, mostly to cover my tracks, because you never knew from where or whom the idea might have come. Oh, and I would learn quickly not to say "soap" around her. It was a derogatory term, and she would do a slow burn when someone did, unless it was she who used it. She was often hypercritical, petulant, and extremely moody, and she especially seemed to distrust my concepts of casting because of my youth. Her attitude of suspicion and distrust would escalate drastically when she would learn of something spectacular I had accomplished on *The Young and The Restless.* When Betty would ask me what exactly we were doing on *Y&R*, I would always tell her. Then she would comment that she didn't like the actors we were adding, or that she had thought of them but didn't like them. I would come to learn that she thought I was giving the other show better service, and that I knew too much about *Days Of Our Lives* (DOOL, as we called it) and its forthcoming character development. Ultimately, she confessed to a mutual friend that she thought I was a spy for *Y&R.* For the aforementioned reasons it was extremely tedious and awkward to work for Betty Corday.

On the other hand, I had no problems communicating with the producers of *Y&R.* They were younger and listened to my ideas, and about 95 percent of the time they left me alone to choose the talent for most of the supporting principal/day-player roles being cast. The only time John Conboy or his staff, Pat Weinig and later Ed Scott, would want to explore my thinking was when a character being introduced into the story was slated to be a contractual series regular or potentially could evolve into a series regular role. From my perspective, if any principal role that I would read in an upcoming episode was interesting and had enough substance, I would present it to the agents as potentially being a series regular role. I had my list of names of those who could do the part, but first I would investigate the "name" actors that were between jobs or in the midst of a sluggish career. Then, I had the list of New York stage actors, so I was always covered. Oftentimes, I'd get someone interesting to work a simple principal role, and they would sometimes become more interested in the steady work and ultimately the regular daytime money of the series contract player.

One Friday morning John Conboy called me, half panicked, and said he had forgotten to tell me of just such a new male lead, which would begin evolving into the story in the early part of the following week, and to send him my thoughts and ideas immediately. "There's no time for auditions and readings. Send photographs of whomever you can come up with that would be terrific. We'll try someone you think is right," he said, "and if it doesn't work, we'll keep looking, replace, and get somebody else." About eleven a.m. that Friday, I sent, by rush messenger, the first of three or four packages to John Conboy at CBS TV City. In that first group I had enclosed approximately seven excellent possibilities, all very good-looking and capable actors. On the top of the pile was my first choice, John McCook. I had recently met John McCook and considered him to meet all the prescribed criteria. He was intelligent, charismatic, and charming. I had read him and considered him to be a very capable actor. He had a nice speaking voice and was suave, tall, dark, and killer handsome. I thought he was perfect. John Conboy called and said, "I don't think John McCook is good-looking enough." I knew John Conboy thought he knew what a good-looking man was, and that he considered himself a connoisseur of good-looking men, but I was absolutely floored this time when he gave me his same old "I don't think he's good-looking enough" reaction. I almost fell out of my chair. Perhaps I might be in trouble on this one, I thought; if he doesn't think John McCook is good-looking enough, I may as well get a piece of wood and whittle myself a beak and peck corn with the chickens for a living. "They're ugly," Conboy would say. He requested other possibilities, more ideas, and to get more photographs from John McCook's agent(s). I assembled more, the second package with more pictures of John McCook— everything but his baby album photos—and still I got, "He's not good-looking enough." And then the third package, and then finally I was preparing the fourth package. Sometime back I had found the long-lost photographs of the "ugly guy" Carl Joy and I had used to torment our sidekick Bruce Maidy with at Fox, in an envelope in the trunk of my car. I had these filed away in my "ugly" file in my desk, and for laughs I put one of his two remaining composites in that last package to John Conboy, to show contrast. I thought just maybe that John Conboy had lost focus of ugly reality. I had talked to every agent in town and was out of fresh ideas. I placed John McCook on top, followed by whatever new possibilities I had been able to come up, with the ugly guy under those. Having become even more creatively frustrated, I inserted my own picture and resume in that final batch, in last position. At about four p.m. that afternoon John Conboy called, howling with laughter, saying that I most certainly wasn't good-looking enough, either. He gave me the approval to hire John McCook for the role, and then added, "He'd better be good or it's your ass, Hanks."

I would always be present and attend all such new cast addition trials or screen tests at CBS. The difference here was that I was very confident that John McCook would do extremely well in this role. I met John Conboy in his office, where he usually would watch *Y&R*'s daily rehearsal and then, immediately following, the taping. If he saw something on the screen he didn't like, he'd be on the phone to the control booth of the stage where they were working. When I entered, John was beaming with excitement, almost in a trance-like state, focused on John McCook's performance, and he was very pleased. When the taping had concluded I started to leave. Then, John happily expressed that maybe he had been wrong. Smiling now, he said that maybe John McCook was, in fact, terrific-looking. "You've done it again, nice work." But then his mood stoically changed, as he pointed to his desk and said, "But him; remove him immediately." I noticed all the pictures I had sent him were stacked on his desk, with the ugly guy on top. He again demanded I remove him. I asked, "Are you sure? I mean, you had him out on top, you must have liked him a little." John rolled his eyes, smiled, and laughed, saying, "Ohooo, please remove him." Bill Bell also liked John McCook, and would put him on *The Bold and The Beautiful*, where he's been since its inception.

Jerry Douglas was another example of a very fine actor I had brought in to do a supporting role that they liked so much they created something for him.

Kathy Kelly Lang, another that I had brought in for a small part, later developed into a central character on *The Bold and The Beautiful.* All have survived and been there since I left, the second time, in June 1981. It was night and day working for these two very different productions. *Y &R* seemed more contemporary; younger in story and more intelligently crafted. I thought Bill Bell and his wife, Lee Philip Bell, and his staff (Kay Alden and Elizabeth Harrower) of writer-collaborators were wonderfully entertaining and intelligent, real-world writers. I enjoyed reading what story concepts and fun-to-cast characters would evolve next. John Conboy was a lot of fun to work with; he had a great personality and liked to laugh with me. He was always attentive to my ideas of who might be right for a role, and who we might be able to get for our money and on our dates. We would complement each other extremely well during my two tours of employment, the nearly five and a half years I would make contributions on *Y&R*. However, John would display a white-knuckle, high-strung temperament in the control booth if things weren't going well. I was fortunate not to see that side of him often.

On the other hand, *Days of Our Lives* was very quiet and reserved. I always felt uncomfortable, like I was out of step with their thinking. Jack Herzberg was Betty Corday's right-hand man, the associate producer on *Days of Our Lives,* and understood, as I hadn't been the first to come along that had casting conflicts with her royal highness. Jack was very patient and worked on my behalf to get Betty to come down to earth and be more realistic; he was a good buffer for her cynicism. Jack also had the reputation of being a fellow who burnt the candle at both ends.

One afternoon I had interviews set up for after lunch, for a number of actors to read for some lead principal roles on *Days*. Jack had confessed to me that he was dragging from being out all night. I had purposely positioned a young actress last for this role, as she was my favorite and I felt she would have the best chance to be remembered if she read last. She was accomplished, a fine young New York stage actress. It was a long scene, several pages. At one point while we read and acted the scene, I glanced at Jack Herzberg and noticed his head was nodding slightly and his eyes were shut. He had dozed off. I looked back to my actress; she also had noticed. We kept reading, and she motioned for me to look at Betty Corday, who was slumped deep in a very comfortable office lounge chair, knees almost up to her chin, with her dress mussed just enough to expose her girdle. Betty, too, had succumbed to the warm afternoon. I looked back to my actress friend, shrugged, and kept reading to the end of the scene, and then said loudly, "Okay, very nice," which seemed to awaken the slumbering two with vigor. Jack immediately said, "Oh, yes, that was very good, very nice reading." Betty Corday mumbled something, pushed her dress down into place, got up from her ever-so-comfortable chair, thanked the actress for coming in, and started making phone calls at the end of the long, warm casting session. We then exited Betty's office into the outer office, and when I had shut the door behind us, we burst into very big but suppressed hysterical laughter. Both of us were snickering. I apologized as she gathered her things from the secretary in the outer office. I didn't know what to say. I followed her into the hallway, and we both couldn't restrain ourselves any longer. She kept asking as she laughed, "Was I that bad? I never did that in New York. I never put anyone to sleep before. Please don't tell anyone about this, ever." I kept trying to reassure her that she had been very good, that Jack stayed up late, and that I didn't know what had happened with Betty Corday. We both were giggling almost insanely as I tried to reassure her that she was a wonderful actress and it had nothing whatsoever to do with her reading. I followed her to the exterior of the building, where we were still laughing but speaking normally. She said good-bye and walked away toward the parking area. I laughed and blurted out loudly, "One day I'll write about this in my memoirs." She waved and yelled back, "Never mention my name." She then got in her car and drove off. Actors are very sensitive. I expect she probably still thinks to this day it was her delivery that afternoon that created the impromptu nap-time.

After a little more than a year's time I was becoming very successful on *Y&R*. I had found Jamie Lynn Bauer and numerous other exciting, talented artists that drew in a new audience. The ratings were way up, and I was having a wonderful time, and didn't care much that I'd heard Betty Corday was unhappy and wanted someone new to cast her show. I was unhappy as well. I wanted to work with people that were young enough to at least stay awake during readings. I continued to find other exciting new additions for *Y&R*, and I was very confident and secure in my abilities to assess talent, and very confident of my overall knowledge of the current talent casting pool. Frankly, I thought I was damn good at being a casting director and *Days of Our Lives* was lucky to have me there. The proof was in the pudding; the ratings on *Y&R* told the tale, and it was fast becoming the most watched soap. I always thought I could have done great things on *Days* as well, if only she had been more open and listened to my thinking.

I would then be assigned another half-hour, three-camera sitcom called *That's My Mama,* starring Clifton Davis, Theresa Merritt, Lynn Moody, Ted Wilson, Lile Wilson, Deforest Covan, Jester Hairston, Joan Pringle, Theodore Wilson, and a guy I found and fought for to be tested, Ted Lange. It was a weekend party all the time at someone's house to celebrate life, with drink, song, merriment, and dance, not to mention some of the best soul food I'd ever tasted. *Mama* was one of the first all-black ensemble casts, and under funnyman Alan Rafkin's superb direction it seemed headed for a long run, but would last only a short time. Clifton became ill and the show shut down for a time. It seemed to never regain its momentum and was cancelled.

One very hectic morning, I drove into the lot at just before nine a.m. and the guard informed me that Renee Valente was frantic to find me. Like that kid in me again, I thought, What have I done now? The guard instructed me to get to her office immediately. I raced upstairs to Renee's office and she greeted me with a warm, "Oh, good, you're here." This was a relief, because the tone of her voice told me she wasn't pissed about something. She explained that the billiard player expert hadn't shown up on set of *Banjo Hackett*, a pilot we were currently shooting. She said she had been told that I was a great pool player—superb, she said. I told her I was flattered and humbly said, "I shoot okay. She queried further, asking if I won most of the time. I explained that most of the time, when I was practicing, I could be very competitive and beat most, but I was not a tournament champion. She asked if I had ever entered a tournament. I said no, I hadn't. She then said that today I would be playing the role of the tournament champion, the pool expert. She knew I was a member of the Screen Actors Guild and asked were my dues paid up. I said that indeed they were. She said for me to turn around, immediately head for the set, and go directly to wardrobe, to see if I could fit "Dandy" Don Meredith's shirt size. I shook my head, saying Don Meredith was a bigger man, much taller. Nothing worked. She again said, "To the set," and pointed to the door. "Dandy" Don was playing the lead role of Banjo Hackett. Renee seemed to think it would be a perfect match. Again I tried to interject my concern, that I couldn't just drop everything. I had casting meetings and readings on each show set up, starting that morning, until late into the afternoon. Renee instructed me to have my secretary, Jennifer Jackson Part, call her immediately; that she and the staff would handle my shows while I was away. I pleaded with her, saying, "Renee, I'm not really a pool expert." Renee said, "Well, you're all we've got, so you're the pool expert." She said producer Mel Swope was waiting for me on the set and then ushered me out for my new assignment.

I drove over to the set and met Mel Swope, and he immediately whisked me to the wardrobe person. As she was fitting me with a shirt like the one Don Meredith was wearing in the scene, I told Mel that I was maybe a better-than-average shooter, but I certainly wasn't a pool expert. Mel seemed oblivious to what I had said. He turned to the wardrobe woman and said yes when he saw that the shirt fit perfectly, and then walked off. The set was a western saloon and they were shooting a scene involving horse pool; that is, playing pool while sitting on the backs of horses and riding around a pool table in the middle of a saloon. It was "Dandy" Don and Jeff Cory in the scene. At about ten a.m., it seemed like they were a long way off from shooting any shots of the pool game action. They would fake the pool shots after they delivered their dialogue; the camera angles they were shooting were the master shots and close-ups. They delivered numerous pages of dialogue as they rode around the pool table. Concerned about my assigned shows, I approached Mel Swope again. I suggested to Mel that perhaps we had time to get a real pool expert. Mel said for me not to worry; that they would get to my scene shortly, and he walked off. When the company broke for lunch, I again said to Mel Swope, "Maybe there's time to get somebody really good in here to do this, Mel. It looks like it may be hours away from using me." Mel said he thought we were going to get to it first thing after lunch.

At lunch, I raced over to my office to check on my shows and learned that we had at least two real pool champions on standby, only minutes away. I headed back to the set. At about two thirty p.m., I had checked the shooting schedule again and could see they were still a long way off from using me. I approached Mel Swope again and explained that I had done some checking at lunch, and there were at least two local pool champions standing by who could be there in minutes. Finally, Mel turned to me and said something I've never forgotten. He said, "Mike, you're an actor, aren't you? I know you're a casting director, but you're an actor also, right? I've heard people say you're a pretty good actor, too. I forget who told me, but he said he saw you in a play and you were really quite good." I thanked him for the compliment; I was happy to hear that somebody remembered. He then said, "Mike, everybody here thinks you're the pool expert, a billiard champion. The role you're playing here today is that of the pool expert. Be the pool expert, become the pool expert, the billiard champion. You are the pool champion, get it? It's a role, it's a part, act it." Mel smiled and nodded, with an affirmative look on his face, and trotted off. My fear of inadequacy was suddenly gone. I approached it exactly as Mel Swope's wisdom suggested and how Renee had said earlier. I was the pool expert. It was an acting role. Why hadn't I seen this? I would approach it as an acting role. I would become Paul Newman in *The Hustler*; quiet, methodical. My game would do my talking. It suddenly gave me more confidence. I immediately shed all of my insecurity and went to work creating a character.

What my interpretation had told me was not like the pool expert was left outside at the stage door, including my casting director knowledge and expertise.

For the rest of the day I would be playing a part, that of the pool expert. I was the pool expert, and I couldn't be beaten, wouldn't be beaten. I was anxious now to play, to shoot and show my stuff. I went to a stage phone and called a good pool-shooting friend of mine that had watched me beat all comers one night at the pool hall. He had seen me when I was hot, and I told him where I was and what I was about to do. He started pumping me up; I was feeling even more confident. I kept telling myself I was the best around and it would be my turn to shoot very soon. I thought pool, nothing but pool; I saw shots in my mind and became Fast Eddie Felson, Willie Mosconi, and Minnesota Slim. I examined the pool table when I could get close to it between shots. I held the pool cues and practiced my stroke. I was psyched up. A crew member came over to me and asked if I was the guy he had seen shoot on a show at Paramount a while back. I explained I wasn't that guy but invited him to stick around, "you might see something." He said he would, couldn't wait, and then he smiled and walked away. It was the beginning of my performance. I had a fan, an admirer; now I was even more stoked. Mel Swope walked by and I said, "Rack 'em, Mel, I'm ready." And he said, "Oh, the pool expert has arrived at last. Good." I smiled and replied, "I have, Mr. Swope." Finally, a few minutes after six p.m. that evening, I was asked to mount up on Don Meredith's horse and shoot or run as many balls as possible. Then, I was directed to ride the horse around to several different key positions and make specific shots. After I figured out what they wanted, I made a series of nice runs, some bank shots, and then ran more balls. I made a couple of nice draw-to-position shots, then reared back high on my stallion like the Lone Ranger, galloped around the table some, and ran more balls. I was finished and wrapped by director Andy McLaglen in less than fifteen minutes. Just kidding about the rearing back and galloping stuff, but that was it. I thought, no big game to orchestrate? I was hot to play pool and was wrapped that fast. I would have to stop by my favorite poolroom/horse bar on the way home to shoot a few racks to come down from the excitement high.

My shows had been managed well that day, and I had learned a very valuable lesson about acting: When you get the part, you are the best for the role, the chosen one; do the job and, simply put, become the role; become the expert, and pump up whatever expertise may be required of your character; leave the rest of it at the stage door. I knew this from years of study of the Method. But for me, personally, it was the awareness that I had to let go of my casting instinct; that of always searching for a better choice. When the director says "action," you can only be on one side of the camera or the other. I've learned at every juncture of the acting experience, and for me this experience was nothing less than another metamorphic and very valuable lesson.

The next day I returned to my regular casting duties on *Y&R* and *Days of Our Lives*. There was never a lull in activity on the soaps. I continued with a very hectic

Screen Gems/Columbia Pictures Television

schedule on both shows looking for additional characters. *Y&R* had an ongoing search for a great-looking leading man; always a great-looking leading man, something John Conboy delighted in interviewing for. One late afternoon, I was conducting general interviews for numerous items, and I happened to see out my window a woman I had met previously at Paramount heading toward casting reception. Curious about something, I asked Betty Scott to ask her to drop by and say hello to me when she was finished with her other business. I now refer to this as my James Caan story. I should back up some here. When I was at Paramount and James Caan was shooting *The Godfather*, I had a great many people tell me that I resembled or reminded them of him. Once, an actress friend had come in to meet me on a general interview, and after talking for just a very few minutes she suddenly changed the focus of the conversation away from her, saying that I reminded her of a very good friend that was currently working on *The Godfather*. I played dumb about the coming revelation and she said the name James Caan. "Oh, you think so?" was my reaction. She started talking about physical similarities, but added it was our personalities that were even more similar. She asked if I was from New York or Jersey City. I said, "No, I'm from here, Culver City." I added that perhaps I'd been working around New Yorkers for so long that some of it had rubbed off on me. She said when our meeting was over she was invited to visit him on the set for lunch, and that I should join them. When she left, she insisted that she was going to arrange a meeting with Mr. Caan. I never really thought much about it.

In fact, it made me feel somewhat uneasy resembling a popular actor of the day. In the weeks that followed she called a couple of times, trying to arrange a meeting, but it never happened. He was always busy when I was free, and I always became too busy when she thought he might be available. After I had left Paramount and had been on staff at Columbia Pictures Television for about a year, James Caan had started shooting *Harry and Walter Go To New York*, opposite Elliott Gould, there at The Burbank Studios. I was walking across the lot one day and Mr. Gould pedaled up to me on a bicycle, saying, "Oh, Jim, Jim...oh, you're not Jim. Sorry." I smiled and replied, "Yes, I'm not, I'm Mike, and don't be sorry, Mr. Gould." He smiled, waved, and continued his ride on past me. When that happened, I thought maybe there was something to it, but WHO CARES?

Now, back to this woman who had entered casting reception. She had originally been sent to me through one of Paramount's power brokers, who informed me that she was the wife of another power broker, and it would be to our advantage to keep her husband happy and play some politics; that I should meet her and consider her for acting roles she might be right for. I had taken that first meeting with her at Paramount, and discovered that she had limited professional experience and had trained even less. Her only claim to fame seemed to be that she had been told she resembled Rue McClanahan and Angie Dickinson, and she did. Suddenly, I wasn't seeing her; I was seeing a younger Rue, with Angie's curves and square jaw. At first I didn't say anything, but did encourage her to take more acting classes and gave her numbers of some excellent coaches. I met this woman several times while I was at Paramount; each time, she said she was on the lot for some other reason and would drop in on me, and each time she would tell me exactly the same thing—that she resembled Angie Dickinson and Rue McClanahan. By about our third or fourth drop-in meeting, I got a little short with her and scolded her slightly. I looked her straight in the eyes and said that I remembered her telling me this at each of our previous meetings. I asked if she had forgotten. I then asked, "Why would you want to distract from who you are, distract from your own persona, by painting yourself as someone else?" I suggested further, "You're spinning off on someone else's career and fame." I tried to reach her and not upset her by relating my own look-alike nonsense. I smiled and calmly but firmly presented my feelings. I explained that all of a sudden a lot of folks around town were telling me that I looked like James Caan. I laughed and said, "But who cares?" I said that if I were out trying to get jobs as an actor, I wouldn't want to look like anybody but me; I would want to present and sell me, not somebody else. I'd want the casting person to be thinking of and remembering me, not James Caan or some other artist. I asked again if she had forgotten that she had told me of these resemblances in each of our previous meetings. She seemed somewhat taken aback with my directness. Then, I suddenly thought, I'm going to piss off her power-broker husband. On the contrary; she seemed to take my direction very positively. She said that I was right, and she would discontinue making any mention of having a resemblance to anyone, and thanked me for my "very intuitive observations and advice." In almost the same breath, and with the same excitement she had displayed while telling me of Rue and Angie, she exclaimed, "Yes, I see the James Caan resemblance now!" As I opened my office door for her exit, I asked her not to tell anybody and then said, "WHO CARES!" At which we both smiled and she left.

That was the last time I saw her before looking out my window that afternoon. Now, she was attired in a full-length, very expensive-looking mink coat and matching hat. At about five thirty p.m., Betty called me and asked if I could see her, and I asked Betty to direct her down to my office. When she entered, we greeted each other and talked for a few minutes about her recent triumphs, and then it started all over again. She veered off into what I assumed had become her canned presentation of herself, telling me that she had been told she resembled Angie Dickinson and Rue McClanahan. I guess this was what I was curious about and I couldn't believe my ears. I interrupted her, reminding her that I'd heard it all before. I leaned toward her and asked, "Don't you remember our last conversation we had at Paramount, about this spinning off on somebody else's career thing, and me saying to you that people had told me that I resembled James Caan, and that I wouldn't think of pitching myself as an actor look-alike? Don't you remember our conversation?" She made some lame excuse that she had forgotten. I began to think that perhaps there were forces at work that didn't meet the eye. After a few minutes our meeting concluded, and she asked to use the phone to call a cab, explaining that she didn't drive. I directed her to the guest phone in casting reception and she left.

At about seven thirty that evening, I was finally leaving the office. I had a couple of cars I drove to and from work. My favorite, which I drove only occasionally, was a black 1955 Thunderbird that I had taken great time and expense to restore to its pristine showroom condition. I drove off the lot onto Barham and was thinking about some dinner at the popular Smokehouse restaurant, but didn't like parking in parking lots for fear of door-dings. My wife and sons were visiting her parents out of town and I didn't feel like cooking for myself. I turned south, thinking about food and door-dings, looking for safe street parking, and saw this same woman in her mink coat standing on the corner near the Smokehouse restaurant. I drove to the corner, reached over and rolled down the passenger side window, called her by name and asked if she had missed her cab. She said that she had. I called her by name again and said, "Come on, I can give you a ride home." She said that would be very kind of me, and accepted my invitation. I smelled the scent of bourbon as she scooted in. She shut the door and I drove off. She thanked me and then, to my utter disbelief, asked how I knew her name. "So tell me, how do you know my name? Do you work in the business?" I really couldn't believe my ears. Less than two hours had passed since our most recent meeting. The wonders of good whiskey at work, I thought. The big kidder and the improvisational actor in me needed—craved—to respond. I said, "Why, yes, I do work in the business.

I'm an actor. I'm here shooting a movie called *Harry and Walter go to New York*. I'm James Caan." With bulging eyes and huge excitement, she slowly began telling the tale, as if she alone had discovered this amazing mystery of life. "You're not going to believe this, but I was just with this casting director named Mike Hanks, and he said you look alike, and you guys really do look alike. You could be twins." She scooted a little closer to me, extended a hand for me to shake, and asked, "So, Jim—can I call you Jim?" I said, "Of course you can call me Jim; you can even call me Mike, if you like," at which we both chuckled. She asked again how I knew her name. I said, "I know all the beautiful women." More chuckles as she scooted even closer and placed a hand on the leg of whoever she thought I was—and I don't think it was Mike. A short time later she directed me to a very large estate in Bel Air. She informed me that her husband was out of town and dinner was waiting. She assured me that it would be perfectly okay for her to have me as a dinner guest; that her husband would approve of my being there. I thanked her for the invitation but declined, saying I had another previous commitment that I was already late for. When we arrived, I got out and escorted her up to the front door. The maid had seen us coming and opened the front door, greeting us both. When she opened the door and I got a good whiff of the warm cooking smells, I was so hungry I couldn't resist. She invited me in again and I said I could be late. Anyway, I was really more curious about the palace they lived in, and it was unbelievable—as was the very expensive Scotch, the wine, the salad, and the duck that was served; opulent, sumptuous living, to say the very least. If I hadn't seen her on that corner that night I probably would have had a burger at The Apple Pan on the way home. During the course of the evening and the grand meal, I tried to tell her a couple of times that I really wasn't James Caan. "I'm the other guy, really, I'm Mike Hanks." She was still calling me Jim as I left. "Good night, Jim." "Mike," I said again, and we chuckled as she shut the door.

The next morning, promptly at ten a.m., my secretary buzzed me to say that this woman was on the line. Immediately, she said, "Mike, guess who I had dinner with last night? You'll never guess." I threw the line away as I replied casually, "James Caan." She exclaimed in a kind of whining voice, "How did you know?" I said, "Because that wasn't James Caan, it was me." There was a very long silence; it seemed endless. She wouldn't believe it, she wouldn't have it. It was James Caan she had dined with. I ran into her a couple more times after that at various industry galas and she was still never really convinced that she hadn't dined with James Caan that evening. Later on it occurred to me, WHO CARES? Let her think what makes her happy.

My ongoing, never-ending search for Conboy's good-looking man had continued. Finally, in 1975, I found, through agents Julian and Diane Davis, a young fellow by the name of David Hasselhoff. I was happy because I thought maybe my search for handsome men could slow some. I read David, and was so confident and excited that I had found the object of my searching. I remember jokingly asking him when he became a giant star if he would take me with him to the top, as I instinctively felt he would soon get there. He smiled and said of course. I had a couple more meetings with him to read various materials for the replacement of a regular role that was coming back into the story. I thought he was okay as an actor, but terrific to look at. He had what a twenty-six-year-old John Wayne had had. He was tall, with great curly hair, a great personality, a nice speaking voice, movie-star good looks, and had a nice, honest, real interpretation and delivery of the material we read. He was definitely worth a screen test for the return of the Snapper Foster character. He was hired quickly and went to work. The powers that be at *Y&R* immediately hated him. Columbia Pictures Television and CBS thought he was handsome, but the demands of the story to come needed an artist with more depth. I was told to keep looking for someone better and I did. I let the word get around that we were adding another, similar character and I continued the search. I also advised John Conboy that I thought David Hasselhoff would get better with time. Several more weeks passed and they still hated him. I expressed my feeling again to John Conboy that we just needed to give him more time; that he would grow. Let him get used to being in two scenes, two or three times a week. I suggested we watch David's fan mail. John Conboy said they wanted to replace him; we started serious interviews and met several very strong candidates. And then the fan mail told the tale. It was huge, enough to sway the powers that be at the network and elsewhere to stay with David awhile longer. They might have been wrong, and maybe they did have something special with David. They were

INTER-OFFICE COMMUNICATION
COLUMBIA PICTURES TELEVISION

TO   RENEE VALENTE

FROM   JOHN CONBOY

RE   "THE YOUNG AND THE RESTLESS"

DATE   MAY 30, 1975

Dear Renee:

As per our phone communication on Friday, May 30, just wanted
to again stress how strongly I feel about maintaining Mike Hanks
as our casting director. He has done very good work for me
since he joined your staff, and his taste and knowledge have
most always co-incided with what my needs on this show demand.

I am about to re-negotiate 12 contract players' deals on
"The Young and the Restless", and it would really be unthinkable
to begin these negotiations without Mike.

The show we submitted to the Blue-Ribbon panel for Emmy
consideration, aside from Jeanne Cooper and Beau Kayzer who
appeared (contract players), had a cast of 12 one-shot principle
performers, all cast by Mike.

Enough said. I hope. Again, my thanks for your co-operation
and, as always, it's a joy.

John

cc: John Mitchell
     David Gerber

more convinced that they should give him more time to develop, get more training, and let him settle into his character. David Hasselhoff would do some seven years on *Y&R* as Snapper Foster.

Also that same year, it was rumored that Renee was about to take me away from *Y&R* and place me on another prime-time show, which John Conboy heard. Renee called me into her office one afternoon and asked me to read a note she had just received from John Conboy; that I should be very proud of it, and indeed I was. In the letter, John commended me for my work and knowledge, and gave me credit for the ensemble cast I had put together that earned *Y&R* its first Emmy that spring for outstanding daytime drama. I was enjoying daytime even more by this time; I was almost completely independent and enjoyed a certain autonomy at the CBS facility. Let the others do *Police Story*, *Police Woman*, and other prime-time shows. I wouldn't reveal to them the pleasure of this work on *Y&R*.

Additionally, Renee assigned me a project entitled "Miss Kline, We Love You," christened an *Afternoon Playbreak*; in essence, a two-hour movie drama produced by ABC Television for the afternoon daytime audience. A daytime soap director/producer, who I had worked with on *Days of Our Lives*, was set to direct. Renee's staff, all assigned hit prime-time shows of the day, were less than excited about this melodrama-type project for daytime. An afternoon playbreak? I mean, nobody had ever heard the term before, and it was kind of looked down on by most of the staff. It was daytime; "Let Mikey try it" was the feeling I got.

My staff associates really didn't want to do a daytime show, especially with a slow-paced soap director. It wasn't like it had *Movie of the Week* status, with a big TV director and a big budget to attract thirsty "name" actors and agents. The word of who is doing what spreads quickly within the industry; there's always been a kind of irreverence associated with daytime shows. It's not especially a big-time casting credit for one's resume; no casting status there, it's just work. I think Renee felt it would be easier for me, as I was already set up with daytime connections. Mikey will try anything. And, as an obedient staffer and the perennial new kid on the block, it was a natural.

The thing about doing daytime is you're always trying to entice the names to daytime anyway. You always call the responsible agents to see if so-and-so might be interested in doing daytime that week. Renee had given me the script and all the very tentative production information. A chap I didn't know by the name Al Simon was set as line producer of "Miss Kline." I was directed by Renee to submit casting ideas for all roles to Al Simon and the director. I had been repeatedly told that there wasn't money for any big names in the lead roles. It was just a well-written George Lefferts drama, and I was to think of really good actors. That was all right by me, as I always made exhaustive, very complete, and very creative lists. I always wrote down my first choices when I first read a script, "names" or otherwise. I would use those initial thoughts and qualities of people to vary my thinking to other actors I felt could bring similar qualities to a role.

I had been doing *Days* and *The Young and the Restless* almost from the beginning of my tenure at Columbia, and was still trying to prove myself after leaving Paramount. What do they say? "You're only as good as your last job" or "That's great, but what have you done lately?" I think the artist is always trying to prove himself. Artists are all insecure and need constant reminders of recent triumphs, and that we're still capable of making good choices.

I submitted suggestion lists, with some people I thought would be wonderful, such as Patty Duke Astin in the title role of Miss Kline. I had casually spoken to her agent briefly about the project and had been told it would take much more than we had in the budget, ten times as much, to get her to do daytime. She really didn't want to do daytime, so the agent(s) said. I'd had a brief meeting with Al Simon and mentioned the idea, and was met with, "She'd be great, but we can't afford her. Her agent would never let her do it." I didn't tell him I had just heard the same response from Patty's manager, Grace Lyons. I was advised to keep thinking. Al Simon and I started having some preliminary meetings and discussing recognizable names from daytime that might be possibilities. Then, we began the process of interviewing and taking meetings with some of the "names" suggested by the larger theatrical agencies, and I continued talking to Patty Duke's manager.

The story outlined Miss Kline as a teacher assigned to a group of mostly terminally ill children who, because of their specific condition, lived as permanent residents in a children's ward at the hospital. My vision saw Patty Duke playing the opposite role she played as Helen Keller in the 1962 *Miracle Worker* drama Arthur Penn had directed. Miss Kline would become more than a teacher—a spiritual advisor, a guru to some—who, because of their specific illness, had been raised in the hospital with virtually no home life or any kind of consistent discipline. Miss Kline's assignment and arrival at the hospital would give a stronger meaning to the children's lives.

I had pretty much dismissed the notion of her being realistically considered, as her salary demands had created an almost negative atmosphere. Getting her was totally unrealistic, so I stopped bringing up her name. I was also very busy with the day-to-day casting of *The Young and the Restless.* My enthusiasm for the idea was becoming somewhat deflated and fleeting, to say the least.

Late one morning, I approached Al Simon and it seemed to spill out of me again. This time I pushed hard that I thought Patty Duke would be wonderful; it would be a "casting coup," a publicity sensation for everyone. He sat quietly for a beat; I could feel his wheels turning. I carried on with my thoughts to quiet, no response. I felt I was really pushing and reaching this time, maybe treading on thin ice, almost whining, trying his patience with the stronger pitch. Maybe he was getting mad, I thought, but I plowed on. I said I felt she needed the job as much as we needed her. "If we could get her, that is." He then turned and quietly said, "Let me make some calls." He did, and received favorable response from some. The director thought it a great idea, the studio head remained non-committal, the network brass was lukewarm. Renee Valente loved the idea, but again, based on the money her agent and manager wanted, I was told, "Keep looking, Mike." Patty's agents and manager, Grace Lyons, had said almost the same thing to me earlier that morning, and I was told, "Forget it, Mike." Al Simon gave me more "good work, I like your thinking" praise as I started to leave, then in a rather abrupt and straightforward manner, he said, "Look, we can't get her, we can't get everyone to agree, just continue looking." And then he said something I've never forgotten. He calmly said, "I guarantee you, Mike, somebody terrific will be in front of the camera playing Miss Kline on our dates. We'll find her." It seemed everyone was busy with other, more important items than this *Afternoon Playbreak*, and I was seething with creative frustration. Our start date was still some weeks off before rehearsal would begin.

I had a fairly uncomplicated morning schedule, so Renee's and Al Simon's reaction and the others lukewarm responses motivated me further to play it out and pump more wind into our sails, if possible. I had done some detective work and located Patty Duke Astin's home address. As mentioned previously, I had become a fairly good sleuth at tracking down an actor who had fallen between the cracks. I got great satisfaction out of finding the lost and telling them that their talents were remembered and still valuable in Hollyweird. Patty Duke was certainly not lost, and was fairly easy to find.

I checked out of my office for an early lunch and drove to where she and John Astin lived in Westwood

Hills, near UCLA. After explaining to the housekeeper that I had a script to personally deliver to Patty, she told me she had gone to the market and was expected back at any moment. I returned to my car and waited, and not more than fifteen minutes passed before Patty drove into the drive. I suddenly got very nervous as I saw the real and wonderful Patty Duke exit from her car, gathering bags of groceries like a regular person, I thought. I had no official sanction of the studio or the network to approach her and suggest anything, much less her playing the lead role in ABC's *Afternoon Playbreak*, "Miss Kline, We Love You." Suddenly, I was thinking I could get into a great deal of trouble. As she was pulling a bag from the front seat I walked toward her, presenting my business card and introducing myself. I explained that I was the casting director assigned to "Miss Kline"; that it was a wonderful script and story. I briefly summarized the story, saying it had brought tears to my eyes each time I read it. I nervously went on, saying that I was there as an artist, a frustrated artist, without the sanction of Columbia Pictures Television, the network, or her agent representatives; that all the salary/daytime programming requirements of possibly hiring her had been repeatedly made clear to me, by everyone involved. She stood there listening, and I again mumbled something about being a frustrated artist. I remember saying, "So, if nothing else, you'll have a wonderful afternoon reading this story." She then graciously smiled after she had listened to my passionate plea, and said that she would read it and would call me in the afternoon.

She was really sweet, and I felt great as I waved and drove off. I never really expected anything much to come of it. I thought I'd probably never hear anything from anyone, except a possible scolding for going there in the first place. I went there on a whim; if I had been busier that morning, I probably would have forgotten the whole idea of pursuing her. It seemed like I had just gotten back to the office, but it was a few hours later when my secretary informed me that Patty Duke was on the line. As I jumped on the line, I was sure I was going to get a big "thanks, but no thanks" response. But that isn't what she said. She said she loved the script, that I was right, and that she didn't care what her agents said—if we wanted her, she would do it. She had only one request, and that was that her husband, John Astin, play the role of one of the male leads, that of a doctor in the story. I then told both Renee Valente and Al Simon the outcome of my unauthorized morning meeting with Ms. Duke and her positive response; both were very excited.

Renee and I both knew John Astin could play a dramatic role, but everyone else viewed him only as Gomez from *The Addams Family* of the sixties. Either they didn't remember or they were just too young to remember that John Astin was first a wonderful and experienced dramatic actor, with tons of stage and film experience. I was now confronted with another dilemma. Columbia Television and ABC were stuck on a more handsome, charismatic leading-man type in the role of this doctor; both definitely and finally said no. They loved the idea that Patty wanted to play Miss Kline, but hated—loathed—the idea of John Astin playing along-side her. I was again told to forget it. "It ain't going to work, Mike, keep looking." I couldn't believe it; I mean, they were going to work for one-tenth of their "quoted" established salaries. Renee was calming me down; she knew how hard I had been laboring over this. She put on her boxing gloves that afternoon, danced that cute little figure across her office, and said for me to wait while she spoke with the shoe salesman that ran the studio. During my nervous wait I wandered down a couple of doors and could hear her being, let's say, powerfully assertive. She came back a short time later with hardly a scratch, smiling, and said she had convinced our studio that we should cast them both in the roles, but now we had to get the network's approval. Our studio head had been convinced that we were right, and now he was on the phone with the network, hammering them. Later that afternoon Renee informed me I had won the battle; that the decision was unanimous, and I could immediately make a deal to hire Patty Duke and John Astin. To say that I felt satisfied and complete by convincing them of my vision is an understatement. Additionally, I would get the handsome fine actor Fred Beir as the third lead to satisfy those daytime programmers who always were thinking of that suffering housewife audience draw.

At the Emmys that season, the director of "Miss Kline" won an Emmy for best director of a daytime drama and immediately was considered a very hot director. Following the awards, in a New York minute he was pacted to a term contract to direct nine episodes of *All In The Family* at CBS. Through the Hollywood grapevine, I heard Carroll O'Connor instantly hated his slow style, and he was terminated and paid off almost as fast as he had arrived, after fulfilling only a couple of his contractual obligations. With all due respect to this director and his style, it wasn't the director that made "Miss Kline" great. It was the great tearjerker script, and what I was able to assemble in the way of an ensemble supporting cast around the wonderful Patty Duke Astin that gave it real direction and life. It was the honest delivery of the children that touched one's heart. A senior cinema student could have directed this project, and frankly it was the casting that made it special, but they don't give Emmys for casting, do they?

Casting people are a very curious breed of artists. If they're good at what they do, they're always chasing people they like and remember, be it from a general interview, a reading, a film, a stage play, or the constant recommendations of a hardworking, persistent, trusted agent, like Hal Gefsky, Ron Meyer, or Julian Olenick. Like a good detective, height, weight, vocal or other qualities that cling to one's memory banks help bring them back into focus. Memory banks being jarred awake, it was one lazy morning that I had run into Irene Bunde at ColGems Square, again. She was such a talent that I always seemed to be trying to get her for something. I had met and read Irene at Paramount and had become an instant huge fan of her energy and talent. She was a very beautiful young woman, model beautiful, and also a very good actress. Because of her looks, she was also experiencing the rush excitement of a modeling career, which was a rare combination. I had found that model beauty doesn't necessarily guarantee that someone has a clue what acting is all about. Irene took it very seriously, and was studying and had done some East Coast theater. After that initial first meeting I had been in constant pursuit of Irene Bunde. I had tried to get her in to read for different shows numerous times, and had invariably been told by her agents she was off doing a shoot for whomever, or interviewing in New York or elsewhere, always very busy. Initially, when I first came on staff at Columbia I had tried to get her in for a lead on *Days*, with no success; not in town or available. I loved her talent and she knew it. Several times, I got return calls from her after she would learn of my persistence in inquiring with her agents about her availability. We would talk like kids for long periods of time. I suppose I had a crush on her, and I feel confident that she felt something for me as well; maybe nothing more than a mutual brotherly-sisterly, artistically induced caring for each other. I also felt confident that one day I would get her for the right project, and it would be instant stardom and success for her.

At Columbia, I had the first office on the right after you passed through casting reception. It was after three thirty p.m. on a Friday afternoon and I propped my office door open. It was highly unusual for me to do so, as I had learned early on that I would risk being disturbed with actor/agent drop-ins, which would inevitably happen if I dared leave it open, even on a slow-paced Friday. I went back to quietly reading a script and was distracted by someone walking by. For a half a beat I hesitated to respond. Suddenly, my mind's eye told me Irene Bunde was the person passing I had seen out of my peripheral vision. "Naaah," I thought, I just want to see her. It couldn't be her, but I had to check it out. I sprang from my desk and tried to get a glimpse of the person before she made the turn in the hallway that would take her out of sight, about twenty-five feet from my door. I looked out and got a glimpse of her just as she turned the corner, and it still looked like Irene. "Naaah," I thought again, as I quietly called out her name. I got to the turn in the hallway and said it again, only louder this time, "Irene?" The person was now ascending the stairway to the second level. I could see only her feet and legs as I looked up. I then heard, "Yes? Is someone calling me?" She looked downward and I could see her beautiful face, and I said, "Irene, it's me, Mike Hanks." Her face lit up, and with a big smile she rushed back down and gave me a warm kiss and an affectionate hug. Hurriedly, she explained that she had been trying to find me; that her agent had told her I was on the lot at Columbia Pictures Television somewhere. She went on to say she didn't exactly know where I was and didn't think she was going to have time to look me up on this outing. She said that she had been really busy; that she had rushed into Los Angeles to take a meeting for something at Columbia Pictures and she late for that meeting, and then had to race to the airport as soon as the meeting was over to meet her boyfriend, to leave for location on a project he was directing for Wolper productions. I understood that she was in a big hurry, so we hugged and kissed again, and made plans to meet and talk first thing Monday morning, ten a.m., my office, for coffee and to catch up. It was a date. As she again ascended the stairs, I shouted, "I have you on my calendar, ten a.m.!" She shouted back, "I'll be there with donuts!" I was energized to see her; it must have been fate, I thought, leaving my office door open. We were destined to know each other better.

Then, that evening I learned of the horrid events on the late-night news. The aircraft carrying the entire Wolper production crew had hit the side of a mountain near the location site where they were shooting. All aboard, including Irene Bunde, were lost. God does only know the reason I left my door open that Friday afternoon.

The Lindbergh Kidnapping Case was a major project that came to Columbia Pictures Television as a movie of the week. It was a collaborative casting work under Renee Valente's supervision. Everyone on staff contributed casting ideas, but it was Renee's project, and it was her niece, Shelly Ellison, and I that assisted mostly on *Lindbergh*. It had a huge cast, and director Buzz Kulik requested authenticity. Renee Valente had acquired a film of the actual Lindbergh trial, and casting suggestions should look like the real persons involved in this tragic story. I watched the film of the courtroom action, getting a glimpse of all the principal characters, including Bruno Hauptman, where he avowed his innocence, probably five or six times. Renee had suggested unknown Anthony Hopkins for convicted killer Bruno Hauptman. Upon meeting Mr. Hopkins, I mentioned to him that there was a film of the trial, and that I had watched it numerous times.

He, too, thought it would be very good to view. Renee asked for me to arrange for Anthony Hopkins to see it. I think he watched it a hundred times.

Renee's instincts were right on target, as usual. We all thought there was a slight resemblance to Hauptman, but Anthony Hopkins studied each nuance and mannerism. He would become Bruno Hauptman. If you could watch the original trial footage and the trial sequence with the master Hopkins playing Hauptman, you would think they were one and the same. At the time of its airing, there were probably a great many still living that remembered seeing Hauptman in the Movietone News Reels during the time the trial was actually in progress. I remembered seeing this footage at the movies when I was a kid an infinite number of times. I think it's very effective when an artist can accurately duplicate and/ or emulate a well-known character from history when there's a well-known film sequence available for study. Anthony Hopkins was brilliant in the role, and the brilliant casting idea of him as Hauptman was that of Renee Valente, master casting director extraordinaire.

At Columbia, in corporate finance under another a junior executive, there was a guy I had seen at several different company meetings, including a pre-production meeting for *The Lindbergh Kidnapping Case.* It was at one of those meetings he whispered to me that he was a reserve deputy sheriff and carried a gun. I immediately thought "wienie." The meeting still in progress, he opened his briefcase and showed me. I looked at him while the leader of the meeting was speaking and whispered, "Wow, can you do a fast draw?" He smiled back, and I thought he might take it out and start twirling it, and shoot up the meeting to prove his manhood. The meeting concluded and he continued trying to impress me with being able to legally carry it with him or on his person. If I had to describe this poor fellow so that the reader might have an image, it would be the George Costanza character on *Seinfeld*— bald, short, and a total wienie; the kind of guy who is determined to try to impress somebody, anybody, with his power. He never told me he was an architect or a marine biologist, like *Seinfeld*'s Costanza, but he had tried to impress me with other dull bull crap, like his gun power. His role in this unfolding story will become obvious.

Renee Valente had offered to send me to location on *Lindbergh,* to see if I could make actors out of some of the locals for approximately twenty-five speaking, scripted roles. If this can be accomplished it saves the company money, as they're able to buy cheaper actors and save on transportation and lodging expense. Renee asked me to cast the extras also; reluctantly, I accepted. I found this possible work-holiday assignment hard to refuse, since I was experiencing more marital disharmony and thought it might be a good time to again be apart for awhile. I took a pre-production meeting on the project, and was told I would have this snappy little vehicle to drive to location and for use the days I would be there prior to the company's arrival. I was also informed that, because of union rules, on the day the company arrived I should cease to drive myself and have a driver pick me up and drive me where I had to go.

I met with director Buzz Kulik, and he explained that the extras amounted to approximately 160 people, and asked that about thirty look very sinister and unfriendly, or just plain ugly. The latter was for a special scene/moment to be shot through a fish-eye lens, to evoke a threatening, menacing, and distorted feeling toward the innocent Lindberghs as they were leaving the courthouse and being approached by hordes of people trying to get close to the popular aviator hero. Everyone hired would be paid in cash, a guaranteed daily rate, and be provided lunch and/or dinner if it was a night shoot.

In my absence from my regular duties on *Y&R*, my colleagues on staff were to fill in for me and I would get this little work-vacation. That next week I drove straight to the town of Colusa, in northern California, arrived late, and checked in at the downtown Colusa Motel. It had been arranged that I would live and work from this location during my stay there. I wasn't really ready for business at nine a.m. the next morning, but I opened my motel room door and was surprised to see several hundred people waiting for me in the parking lot. Tired already, as I hadn't slept very well, I went promptly to work interviewing and photographing people in groups of three, gathering names, phone numbers, and vital statistics. All the local newspapers and radio stations were running ads for the talent we needed. Mostly it was locals from Colusa and the neighboring towns of Williams, Marysville, and Arbuckle, but people were coming from all over, San Francisco and elsewhere, in hopes of finding work or being discovered. The stream of possibilities never stopped and it didn't slow for days. Someone would always be knocking on my door. I would work late into the evening every night, reading, directing, and coaching people, trying to teach acting in three easy lessons. I wanted at least three possibilities for each of the approximately twenty-five one- or two-line speaking roles, so that Buzz Kulik had some choices.

About two days into culling through people I heard a knock at my door. I opened to find this man of about seventy-five standing there. He immediately said, "Name's Joe James. I hear you're looking for ugly people." I said, "Well, we sure are, and we ain't got nobody as ugly as you, so come on in." We both laughed as we shook hands. Actually, Joe James was too handsome for that one special sequence, but I used him elsewhere. He was a great fellow, country wise, with a happy and humor-searching personality, exactly like my dear old dad, Vernon.

Another person, a young woman, that got my attention was Janice Duminie. Janice was a hemophiliac, a bleeder. She had a terrible dental problem, with every tooth in her mouth being in some degree of decay, if not rotten to the gum line. She told me that a dentist had an extremely difficult time effectively treating her condition, since she would start bleeding and it would be very difficult to stop. Even a simple cleaning was next to impossible. A close-up of her approaching open mouth would be ugly and she knew it. When I first met her, she would talk with her hand in front of her mouth; she didn't want anyone to see her teeth. I asked her to take her hand down and explain. I then suggested to her the possibility of making the negative positive; let her make whatever money she could from the problem to help solve the problem. She accepted the notion and then offered her services to help me. She had secretarial skills, and could see I had a lot of organizing to do. She would become of invaluable assistance to me. I really don't know how I could have done that job there without her help. A few days had passed, and in conversation she commented on a ring I was wearing. I had recently received it as a gift from Renee Valente for my birthday. It was a beautiful ring, inlaid turquoise on silver. I had never gotten used to wearing either watches or rings, but this ring from Renee had a special feel and meaning, and I attempted to get used to it. On a second occasion, we were working and she noticed it again, and said how beautiful it was. Immediately, I removed it and told Janice it was hers. She was shocked, saying she couldn't take it. I told her it was no longer mine; it was hers as a remembrance and as payment for what I would owe her for all her help. With some prodding she finally accepted. It was a Christmas-morning-like moment as I saw the glow in Janice's eyes when I handed her that ring. It was now where it was meant to be.

The company began arriving and started setting up for the exterior courthouse shots and a number of other shots around the streets of Colusa. I immediately got a call from a Columbia Pictures transportation captain requesting the location of the company car I had been driving. I told him it was in the parking lot of the motel, and he said that's fine, and that I could continue to drive it while I was there. I was relieved, as I still had some business to do about town and it seemed inconvenient to have to call a driver every time I wanted to go someplace.

Then it happened; I got a call from the Wienie with the gun. He had been sent to location to handle the disbursing and payment of the extras cash payroll. Any person hired to do a speaking part would sign a Screen Actors Guild contract that I would prepare, and then receive a check in the mail from our offices in Burbank. I would be responsible for giving first calls for anyone used, and beyond that it would be the responsibility of the assistant directors to give additional work calls.

I had met a number of really wonderful, down-to-earth people that I truly liked, besides Janice Duminie and Joe James. These included Cheryl Turnbull, Dan Gouty, Adrian and Beulah Tanner, Agnes Morton, Kelly and Evelyn Kilgore, Paul Kilgore, Josephine and Joe Turano, Joan Cousineau, Mary Myers, Wilma Smith, Allen Priner, Jackie Newsom, Claudia Lucken, Mary Elide, John Garrett, Gary Weathers, Dennis Schnall, Larry David, Gloria Foos, Jean Paccioretti, Jim Souza, Tom Reeves, Paula Neise, John Hardt, Odius Eagle, Betty Stevens, Melva McBride, Allen Stromer, Rita Stayton, Rebecca Landis, Jacqueline Moorehead, Rose Buria, Hope and Ron Beatty, C.F. Trailer, Warren Purcell, Emma Deuel, Lillian Boss, Vickie Kimbler, Delores, Richard, and Jon Lawson, John Chastain, Lisa Green, Karen Soito, Martha Gonzalez, Margo Beal, Julie Brown, Barbara Brown, Dan Hart Shorn, Rose and Volet Shipp, Kent Shirley, Laurie Stone, Pam Whittaker, John Brown,

Margaret Verezik, Ron, Gay, and Dana Caudill, Al Porterfield, Marlene Charlton, Gladys Dodd, Howard Gerber, Darlene Garrison, Neal O'Brian, Richard Williamson, Mike Stone, Robert Lee, Kathy Reppo, Jenae Medford, Virginia Schneck, Conrad Arbaugh, Letha McGowan, Scott Loddesol, Jeff Burleson, James Bruno, Steve Bower, Jack Smith, Wallace Williams, Robert Streit, Vicky Cezario, Bill Vogle, Ester Lim, Wayne Harrison, Marcia Sylvester, Jan Walter, Linda Thompson, Gloria Briley, Helen Davis, Mary Ross, Philip Huerta, Judy Coon, William Froines, Kim Tomney, Judy Otto, Tracy Dixon, Eulie McDougall, Ann Dixon, Mabel James, Sylvia Provence, Margarita McGratin, Katrina Bodenhamer, Sean Rymer, Larane Rymer, Donald Kahler, Hannak Thiara, Daisey Proctor, Kathryn Mark, Gloria Trygstad, James Garcia, Paul Walton, Tom Heenan, Conrad and Doris Kersch, Gloria Boyer, Rodney Jones, Joe Ramus, Steve Harris, David Smith, Nancy Wilman, Ethel Gillis, Sam Hodges, Frank, LaDonna and Lorna Munar, William Denson, Linda Stevens, Marilyn Turner, Dorothy Duncan, Shirley Clarke, Jerry Willis, Dorothy McKinley, Elaine Bowden, Shandra Davis, Linda Cornell, Janice Vaughn, David Anderson, Linda Norris, Vannie Lundquist, Agnes Morton, Sondra, Linda and Rox Kahler, Mary Seagraven, Helena Ernst, Kim Cox, Claire Cox, Julie Steffes, Minnie Walton, Mary Lee Scholl, B. Hunter, John Teague, Richard Goddson, Stephanie Schenk, Philip Jackman, Imogene Pasley, Hans Hanson, Earl Fitzsimmons, Glen Lepine, Sharon Garner, Virginia Greiner, Harriet Potoski, Joane Admire, Flora Twilley, Susan Gibbs, Edith Protine, Peggy Cooper, Geneva

McFadden, Clement Miller, Marine Sanders, Kim Sherfield, Michail Buse, Donna Gore, Janeice Crawford, Richard and Christine Ercolino, R. Allen Morrow, Linda Chima, Bill Gentry, Bill Lower, Alice and Lonnell Debnam, Mike McNatt, Scott Patten, Toby Stubbs, Earl Laux, Joyce Raue, Cherry Sawyer, John Eggett, Deborah Serger, Gladys and Clay Hemphill, Sherie Collingwood, Linda Boyer, James Dunn, Ada Larabee, Edith Burright, Shirley Ragen, David Retner, Carol Tyer, Bonnie and Randy Tomlinson, Vickie Sanders, Marcell and Andrew Bink, Lucille and Warren Strohlein, Roby SkinnerNorma Ward, Lucille and Juanita Myers, Danny Iles, C.W. Potoski, Noel Helphenstine, Rodney Mercer, Mark and Susan Juntunen, and Donna Hickson. All of them made me feel very welcome in their small town. (Forgive my spelling; a great many names on the old Polaroid photos/records I took back then were smudged.)

Joe James came to me and informed me that there was a group of ugly, old, retired rice farmers that gathered every morning like clockwork at nine a.m., at the town square. Joe said they would always sit for a while in the sun, talk current events and business, and when the mood struck they would wander over and have breakfast together at the local cafe. Joe said they had great craggy, sun-baked, weathered faces, but were also very rich and he didn't think they'd work for our money. Curious, I had to meet these old boys. Joe gave me directions of how to get there, so I jumped in my hot rod and drove over the next morning, to see what a group of ugly, old, rich rice farmers really looked like. Joe had exaggerated slightly; they were about as weathered as Joe was, but weren't what I considered ugly. I introduced myself, and explained who I was and what I was doing in town, and that I could use them all in *Lindbergh*. Then, when I told them how much we were paying, one of them said it wasn't enough for him. He then pointed to his pal sitting across from him and said, "Maybe he'll work for ya, he probably needs the money, he's only got about ten million." They all broke into laughter. I tried selling the possibility of having fun working in a Hollywood movie and being discovered, and we all laughed again. One of them offered that they'd probably break the camera, they were so ugly. They started pointing to each other, saying that the other was uglier, and laughing. It got very serious, though, when I told them I was looking for ugly; that ugly was a good thing here.

Then the older gentleman of the group thanked me and offered to teach me the rice farming business when I got tired of the movie business. He said he could make me ugly, too, and rich. We laughed again and I said I might take him up on it one day—that is, the rich part of it. He added, "Yeah, you're already ugly enough." It was a good time to exit, on the laughter. He offered that he and the others were half dead, so I shouldn't wait for a terribly long time to try rice farming. Still snickering, pointing, and muttering "ugly" to each other, I shook each of their hands, wished them well, and headed back to where I had parked.

I had been invited to a number of events and gatherings, Saturday/Sunday afternoon barbecues. Just prior to that first day's shoot, I decided to attend one of them and had a great time. We began shooting the next day and encountered the usual location problems. One merchant was already unhappy that his small business entrance had been blocked and he hadn't been compensated for the use of his store. He was very upset and fit to be tied. It was out of my area of responsibility, so I passed on his grievances to the production manager and mentioned it to the Wienie.

Another problem began to evolve at the end of the first day, when the Wienie began calculating wages based on hours worked instead of the modest guaranteed day rate I had told everyone they would receive if they simply showed up. We had taken over a storefront office to handle payroll, and the Wienie entered with his briefcase handcuffed to his wrist like he was James Bond. He opened it, uncuffed, and started to pay out—in cash—a fraction of what these folks expected to receive. Some of these people were the special group that Buzz Kulik had hand-selected for the special moment at the courthouse.

The Wienie left his briefcase open, with thousands of dollars piled in plain sight, and his gun next to it, also in plain sight. I asked him several times to put the gun away before someone was accidentally shot; that is, if he wanted me to continue helping him with payroll. As a former U.S. Marine, I was very confident around firearms, but was very nervous about the Wienie having one that close to me. He was arguing with almost everyone, especially the people that came in for a few hours; people that had changed their schedules to work for the day rate and then were handed a few dollars for their time. They were told, "You misunderstood.

If you didn't work eight hours, you get paid a prorated hourly rate." This was not my understanding of what was to be paid as compensation, and it wasn't what I had presented to everyone. It was late in the evening, people were tired, and there was a near-riot. From the outset I had argued their case with the Wienie, with no success. I announced to the crowd and told everyone to trust me; that I would get it all straightened out, and for them to keep copies of their work voucher receipts for what cash amounts they had received. I then went to the unit production manager and called Renee Valente. It took a few days, but Renee got it corrected and the Wienie straightened out. But he had made a lot of local people really unhappy, and we were still doing the late-night payroll with the gun. I assured everyone that there would be no further misunderstandings, and asked them to please come in to work if requested. I personally called all the people back that had been paid incorrectly and made sure they received the appropriate payroll corrections.

Toward the end of that first week, we had moved from the courthouse to a number of other areas within the small city of Colusa for other exterior shots. There was a large crowd of people walking from one end of town to another location, all dressed in very heavy, layered winter attire, and we were shooting on a very hot day. It was very hard on some of the older people, but everyone was helping each other. I was walking with Cheryl Turnbull and a group of my new friends, one of whom for the sake of this writing I'll call Wilbur. Wilbur was kind of a Gomer Pyle-type country bumpkin, a character-looking chap we had selected and used in our special scene. Wilber became my tagalong friend; wherever I'd go, if he wasn't in the middle of shooting a scene, he'd be within arm's length, trying to help me do something. "Hey, let me pull the flush for you." It was almost that bad. If I said his name, he'd come a-running. I had to be careful which way I turned, as I was likely to bump into him. He'd go for this, he'd go for that. And I liked Wilber; he was such an amusing real-life country yokel. He worked every day of the shoot because he helped everybody, but Wilbur had a terrible body odor problem. It was like it gagged you, and when he was around you, occasionally you had to step away to get fresh air. I tried to keep him further away than arm's length because of it. A couple of times he got on my nerves with the constant but harmless offers to help, and his body bouquet in the heat made him especially hard to be around for any length of time. I would send him off in the direction of the assistant directors and remind him to stay close to them.

We were all walking along to this new location when suddenly, from between two buildings, out darted the Wienie, his briefcase handcuffed to his wrist. Seeing me, he shouted, "Mike! Don't let them catch meeee." For a nanosecond I thought somebody might be trying to rob him, and I stepped forward and pondered how I might defend him. Then, I saw that it was two uniformed Colusa police officers that were doing the chasing. The Wienie was now out of sight. The police had turned the corner in pursuit and had to be gaining on the slow-waddling Wienie. As quickly as it had begun, it all disappeared. Then, a deep voice said loudly, "Get a rope." Over two hundred people broke into a well-deserved, knee-slapping laugh as we continued moving up the street slowly. We moved some further and noticed that, at the end of the street, the Wienie was now talking casually to the police. I asked him later if he expected me to throw a body-block to the police officers chasing him. He explained that the proprietor of the business, whose entrance we had blocked, had filed suit and they were serving him with papers. I casually asked him if he had been taught, as a reserve policeman, to run from other policemen, and added, "Don't you know they always get the crooks?" He didn't think I was very funny.

I had been invited to another cookout that evening and thought I needed a break, if I could get there before it was too late. There was nothing to do in my room but sleep and watch what I could get on the fuzzy motel TV. I had already called my boys, as I did every night, early in the evening before they went to bed. I was really stressed out and thought I wanted to try hard to make this party; Cheryl Turnbull would be there, and she was very intelligent and offered a different conversation since she had little interest in show business. I called and they said everyone was waiting for me; to just come, it was a party and would be going for a while.

I headed out of Colusa about seven thirty that evening. The sun was setting behind me, but it was still light. As I got further away from town, I saw a young man walking along the desolate country road ahead of me. I got closer and he turned, and I could see he was hitchhiking. I recognized him as one of the young men that had been working as an extra that day. I pulled over, he got in, and we shook hands. I drove him to where he had to go—home, I presumed—a few miles further out of town. We talked during the drive, and he seemed to want to open up to me, and was hungry for my opinions. He spoke of his plans of going to college; he wanted to turn his life around, and I encouraged him to do so. I gave him my favorite Emerson quote: "Do the thing and you will have the power." He smiled and said, "Absolutely, right on." He also confessed to me that he was a felon and had just recently been released from the penitentiary for armed robbery. He pointed out that the direction I was headed was what some people referred to as the badlands; that there were a lot of social misfits and criminal types living in hard-to-find places around the area. We drove further and he pointed to a distant area, and said that was where Juan Corona had murdered numerous farm workers he had hired because he wasn't able to pay them. He said that he and his brother killed them and buried their bodies in the fields. He also said that the Wienie had pissed off a lot of folks, and his having all that cash might be very tempting to some. As he got out of the car, he thanked me for the ride and the words of encouragement, and said that everyone thought I was all right, but he warned me to be careful.

The conversation left me with an unsettling, haunting feeling. I drove on to the gathering, but was feeling a little paranoid and out of place. I tried to put it out of my mind and relax for a while, but it was difficult. I arrived to a grand welcome, had some really wonderful barbecue, a couple of beers, and a lot of laughs. Two plus hours later, I started to make my exit back to the motel.

Early the next morning, I casually mentioned my conversation with the young hitchhiker to another production staff member. At lunch, I ran into the Wienie and he asked if I had heard the news. I asked what news? He then informed me that there were people out to get him; there were badlands and bad people close by, and rumor had it that they were coming in to rob the cash payroll. The Wienie was now becoming Barney Fife. Suddenly, it felt like the game we played in second grade, where all the kids in class told a story and by the time it got to the other side of the room it was completely different and distorted. I then asked Wienie-Barney the obvious; whom had he received the information from? He said he had heard it from our aforementioned mutual staff member associate. I then explained the distorted exaggeration, and that I had started this erroneous rumor. I had been the one that had relayed the story of what I heard about the so-called badlands. I reminded Wienie that there were numerous police around during the times we were doing payroll, and there wasn't anything to worry about; that he should relax before he prematurely ejaculated and shot himself in the foot; even worse, me in the foot. That night, every time a new face came to the pay window he would reposition his gun. He was very nervous, which made me very nervous.

I was very relieved and happy when the filming finally ended and I was told I could drive the sporty little car back to Burbank. The night I left everybody turned out to see me off. The women all brought me something nice out of their private stock of canned goods. Evelyn Kilgore brought me jams. Josephine Turano brought me a huge jar of pickled olives. Janice Duminie brought me flowers from her garden. It didn't end. I took home-canned goods home from about every pantry in town, including those of Minnie Walton, Adrian and Beulah Tanner, Violet and Rose Shipp, and Cheryl Turnbull. Kids drew me pictures and sent little notes that they had had fun and liked me. Wilma Smith brought me home-made cheese biscuits, still warm from the oven, for me to eat on my journey back to Los Angeles. Finally, when I had just about finished packing and was almost ready to check out of my motel room, there was a knock at the door. I opened it to again find Joe James standing there. I'll never forget what he said, because I knew it came from his kind, generous heart. He pointed at the hills to the north, behind him, and without even looking he said, "If you look up there, Mike, back in the buttes, I know where the trout are; and if you get up here again, Mike, I'll show you where the trout are." I told him I was coming back, and he could show my sons and me how to fish up there. I shook his hand and could see in his eyes the essence of the good things that should be in us all.

I would eat biscuits and think about those buttes Joe James had pointed to on my drive back, and for many years to come, and about the kindness all the people of Colusa and Marysville had showed with all that they had brought me as gifts. It all had touched me deeply.

On my return to Los Angeles I took it very slow driving home. I was tired. I stopped and rested, called my kids, and focused on getting back to them, relaxing, and showing them how much I had missed them. I stopped several times to get them more surprises. I always brought them presents when I was away. Then, I was driving into the driveway of our home. There's absolutely nothing on this planet quite like hearing three adoring little sons saying excitedly, "Daddy's home! Daddy's home!" and racing to you, arms wide open, for hugs and kisses. Absolutely nothing compares. A couple of years later, I called Joe James to take him up on his offer to take me fishing in the buttes of Colusa and learned from his wife that he had passed.

I returned to my regular duties the next Monday morning and learned that the transportation captain had reported me for driving the car on location. This cat denied ever having told me I could continue driving the car, and had requested that a heavy fine be levied against the production company for the union violation. I'd been had.

A couple of weeks passed and I drove onto the lot, through the guard station, just like I did every morning. On this morning, inside the guard station was a man moving almost in tandem behind the guard, shadowing his every move. The guard stepped out to greet me and gestured that the man behind him was there to see me; that he said he knew me and was my friend. I looked at him again and vaguely recognized him. His hair was slicked back; he wore wraparound dark glasses, a bright yellow flowered shirt, shiny white patent-leather shoes, and a matching white patent-leather belt on some maroon-colored slacks. While the guard leaned into my car to tell me this, the man had been peering over the guard's shoulder, bouncing from side to side and trying to get a better look at who the guard was talking to (me). And then it hit me—the aroma, the bouquet, the stench. It was Wilbur. At the same instant, he said, "Mike, it's me, Wilbur. I've come to Hollywood to be discovered." He went on to say that he thought he had been paid incorrectly. I pointed him in the direction of casting reception and my office, and told him to wait for me there. I drove off and he proceeded to trot behind my car to my parking space, like he hadn't heard a word I said.

We entered casting reception and Betty Scott was at her post. I had gotten to know and love Betty Scott, and in time had discovered that Betty was a no-nonsense, shoot-from-the-hip old-timer. As a young girl, Betty Scott had denied President Harry Cohn access to the entrance at Columbia Pictures Hollywood, because she didn't know what he looked like and Mr. Cohn didn't have any identification with him. She denied Harry Cohn entrance to the company he had built. Later he commended her actions, and said they should have more people like her at Columbia Pictures. Betty Scott and I always laughed our brains out most of the time; she had a wonderful, fun personality and a great cackling laugh. I knew it was coming when we entered reception and she got a whiff of Wilbur, whose bouquet had immediately permeated the air. She exclaimed, "Phew!" and asked if I had forgotten to shower. Then, she whispered to me, "They're going to remodel out here next week and remove the wallpaper; this will help," and then started cackling.

I ushered Wilbur into my office, turned back to Betty, and asked her to call and check that all air-conditioning systems were up, on, and working properly. She cackled and said, "It won't help." She made a face and put her fingers over her nose.

I was happy to see Wilbur and probably wouldn't have rushed him so if it hadn't been for the scent of dying goat he brought with him. He said that the town of Colusa missed me and that I should come back and visit. In his high-pitched, excited voice, he said again that he thought he had been paid wrong; that he had received a check in the mail for well over six hundred dollars. I pushed the pencil around for a minute, and based on time worked, my calculations indicated he was right, and the balance still due him was a little over one hundred and twenty-five dollars. He said that he had forgotten the six-hundred-dollar check, and had left it lying on the dresser in his room at the Arbuckle Hotel, in the exciting town of Arbuckle. I asked Wilbur to go down to reception for a few minutes and talk to Betty Scott, to see if he could help her remove the wallpaper. I had other concerns that morning, and I honestly needed some fresh air because I was starting to gag. As soon as Wilbur trotted off in Betty Scott's direction, I propped my door open, turned my air to high, and got on the phone to accounting, and they verified my calculations were correct. I suggested they place a stop payment on the check Wilbur had back at the Arbuckle Hotel, pay him in cash, and dismiss him from the premises with Godspeed, as he had horrible body odor.

I called Betty to send him back, and told her to ask him not to trot to my office, so that it might lessen his excitement and thus calm his capacity to perspire. Betty cackled and said, "It's too late, it won't help." She cackled more and hung up. And there came Wilbur, trotting to my office. I cut him off in the hallway and immediately directed him upstairs, where he would collect his money in cash. The forewarning that the stench was coming prompted accounting to make haste in the matter. A few minutes later, he came back down to say a final good-bye, and said for me to keep him in mind; that he'd come back, since he wanted to act and be discovered and become a big star. We waved as he left casting reception, and Betty turned to me, cackling, and once again exclaimed, "Phew!" She said she would be smelling his bouquet for days to come, and would now begin the freshening process by calling her husband, Scottie, who worked with Hazmat at the Burbank Fire Department. She then cackled more as I disappeared into my office.

Later, Betty Scott told me she had tried to engage Wilbur in conversations about her preferences in men's colognes and basic bathing hygiene, at which point I offered that I was surprised she hadn't tried to get him in the nearby bathroom and give him a quick scrub. She cackled again and said that she would have done exactly that, but she couldn't give baths and answer the damn phones at the same time. Then she cackled again.

But Wilber would get the last cackle. Several days passed, and accounting called to inform me that Wilbur had returned to the Arbuckle Hotel and retrieved the six-hundred-dollar check, only to cash it at a local bank. The bank had missed the stop payment on the check and had cashed it for smelly Wilbur. They, too, were probably in a rush to get him out of the bank, and had overlooked the stop payment made days before on the check. We were covered; the bank had to eat the loss, as it was their mistake.

I called the Arbuckle Hotel several times and was told that Wilbur had checked out. Off to see the world with all that money, I thought. I left word that if he returned or if anyone saw him, to have him to call me immediately; that he'd been discovered, I had a big part for him, all was forgiven, and to come back to Hollywood. He never returned my call; I never really thought he would. That was the last time we saw, or smelled, loveable Wilbur.

The following morning I got a call from Renee Valente, inquiring about my schedule for that afternoon. She explained that Al Onoroto, who was the assigned casting director of *Police Story*, had his hands full with a pilot project and they needed someone to cover for him on the interviews and readings set up for late that afternoon. After some canceling and changing around of my schedule, I called Renee back and explained I would be able to cover the readings for Al. I stopped by his secretary's office and retrieved a copy of the script the actors would be reading from, and a copy of the interview schedule, which indicated who was coming in and for what role. *Police Story* always had a fairly large cast and the interviews usually consisted of seeing a lot of actors, sometimes three or four for each role, and readings lasted for several hours into the early evening. Old-timer Virgil Vogel was directing this episode. I had known Virgil prior to my being called to help out that afternoon, but had never worked with him. Originally, we'd just run into each other around the Columbia Television offices and had hit it off. When I'd see him, we'd talk and kibitz, tell each other jokes and make each other laugh. For a time, I really didn't know who he was or exactly what he did. But when we'd get around each other, I could sense that we were both searching for something humorous to enlighten the other with. I would learn that Virgil Vogel was a very experienced old-school director. He had directed dozens and dozens of television episodes, western movies, Ma and Pa Kettle films—a little of every genre. He'd do several *Police Story* episodes each season, and was always busy with something.

That afternoon, when I showed up and informed him I'd be running the interviews for Al, he said he thought it was splendid. I then commenced by seeing who had arrived and was ready to read, and started by bringing in the first actor on the interview sheet to meet Virgil and line producer Hugh Benson. The talent being seen were all people that Al Onoroto, the producers, and Virgil had talked about meeting and reading for the various supporting roles. There were the arresting police officers and the bad guys and bad girls. I had read the script and, as always, had familiarized myself with the characters being cast and the scenes being read. In this episode there were some very whimsical characters. One was a goofy country bumpkin, a Wilbur type, that had attempted a bank robbery with his very nervous buddy, who was waiting in their getaway truck around the corner. In the sequence, he charged the front door of the bank with his unloaded frontier Colt .45 in hand, and because the bank wasn't open for business at the time and the doors were still locked, he hit the heavy glass door with his head, rendering himself unconscious. It was reading for the supporting role of the policeman that found him lying in front of the bank doors where I started having some real fun with this bumpkin bank robber character. I had read the part of this old country boy with three or four actors reading for the role of the policeman when Virgil started laughing and suddenly said, "I think we've got our bank robber." I had felt my country-boy performance growing better with each reading; I was having fun.

At the end of the casting session, I double-checked the choices they had made for the roles being cast, so I could inform Al and he could hire or "set" them the following morning. As I started to leave, Virgil turned to me and said that he had enjoyed my character interpretation; that he thought I was a very good actor and he wanted me for the part of the hayseed bank robber. I was flattered by his comments, and felt like he had come backstage at the end of the play. He then asked if my SAG dues were paid up. I said they were, and he said he'd talk to Al. As I turned to leave, he smiled and said, "Know your words and be on time," like he'd say to any other actor. I shook his hand, and we both laughed and I left.

My good friend Al Onoroto informed me the next morning that Virgil Vogel had taken the fight for me to play that little part all the way up to executive producer David Gerber. He had asked Virgil if I was a casting director or an actor, and said that I couldn't be both. The day of the shoot, I went over to the set and thanked Virgil Vogel for his artistic tenacity extended on my behalf. He leaned toward me and quietly said that he liked me better. I had sensed frustration before, but not quite to this extent. I had seen a great many roles I hungered to play while casting shows, but none that a director had fought for me to play. Later I saw the final cut of that specific episode; the actor they used in that role was excellent, but I know I would have been very good, too.

When first assigned *Days Of Our Lives*, I had met a talented young woman by the name of Sharon Thomas. Sharon was an excellent actress, and expressed to me that she had no qualms whatsoever about doing what AFTRA had designated as roles under five lines, which we paid at a scale rate, plus 10 percent agents' commission. Of course, she desired the principal roles, those greater than five lines, which had more depth and paid considerably more on a daily or weekly rate. But Sharon just liked to stay busy and work. If I had something, anything, we needed to see her for, she was there; a true professional. I used her on *Days*, but now was considering her for a recurring role on *Y&R*. I liked Sharon; she was down to earth and became a regular pal. She had popped in on me one afternoon and we were chatting, and I kind of went into one of my hayseed voices. She knew I was a frustrated actor, too, and my character change suddenly prompted her to reveal to me that her husband, Chris Cain, was a film director, and that he was going to be doing the first of a couple of low-budget films soon, one entitled *Elmer*. She had disclosed this to me before, but I never paid much attention, as it seemed everybody in Hollyweird had a feature script in his or her back pocket that he or she was developing. Sharon insisted that she thought I might be right for one of the country bumpkin-type leads. This encouraged me to give her more hayseed, and then we spent as much time talking about my experiences as an actor as we did her recent work. I explained that it was likely I would be on an extended vacation soon, as I might be laid off for an additional period beyond the designated vacation time.

When we finished our meeting, she said she'd call me. Frankly, I thought I was being hustled; the kind of hustle where someone tells you they're going to do something grand for you, and then you really do something grand for them and nothing happens in return but the hot air of the conversation. Although it got my attention, I was used to this kind of happy Hollyweird hype and didn't give it much credence. I used to get all sorts of offers all the time; anything I wanted was there for the taking. Unless it was show-business related—tickets to a play, for example— I just didn't pay any attention to the "hustle," no matter what was offered. I had learned that payback day comes, and you don't want to owe anyone special favors or have any allegiances except to the company you're working for.

A week or so later, Sharon Thomas called and asked that I come and meet her husband; the more elaborate hustle, I thought. I drove out to their Malibu home, and met and talked with Chris Cain. I found him to be a very genuine, low-key, mellow gem of a guy; an actor's director. Like any actor, I was hoping it was on the up-and-up and that I'd get the job and be able to work it into my schedule. He said he thought I'd be good in the role; it was a likeable character, a family film. After reading some lines as my best country-boy character, he thanked me for taking the meeting and said he'd be in touch. Was I ever excited—a lead, playing a character I'd been rehearsing all my life. I'd play it like my dear father, Vernon; young country-boy Mississippian, somewhat like the role Virgil Vogel had fought for me to play, but country-boy smart, intelligent—and a lead, no less. That is, if I get it, I thought.

Columbia Pictures Television was definitely experiencing a production slowdown, with the loss of shows and a pilot season that hadn't been as fruitful as anticipated. Renee's newer staff member Paul Rodriques had been let go after only a little over a year as a casting director on *Days of Our Lives.* Paul, a former agent, he had little success in changing Betty Corday's views and had been pink-slipped. With the overall economy slowdown and production coming to an end, I was becoming less secure in my position, too, as with Paul's departure I now had less tenure than anyone on staff. It was going to be a long hiatus.

It was about this time buddy Carl Joy called and informed me of a project called *Close Encounters of the Third*

Kind that Steven Spielberg was directing at Columbia Pictures, and asked if I was available to go to a nearby dubbing stage and audition for a voice-over job. I explained to Carl that what I was doing on *Y&R* wouldn't safeguard my security that season; that it was likely one of the other even less active senior casting directors would take over on *Y&R*, and that I probably would be laid off due to an overall production slowdown. I told him it was feasible I'd soon be available for anything "ugly." He laughed and I thanked him for thinking of me. Carl called back the next afternoon and confirmed my audition time and date. A couple of days later, I showed up and read some lines into a microphone—that was it. I was told it was a highly secretive project, with only a very few having seen an entire script, and other than what the title indicated of the story's content nobody knew anything.

About three weeks passed and I had completely forgotten about it when I got a call requesting that I report to the dubbing stage for work the next week. I then went to Renee and explained that I had auditioned and gotten the work call, and asked permission to work for two or three hours for a few days. Renee thought it was splendid that I had been chosen, and gave me her blessing and approval to go ahead. This was one of the reasons Renee was so loved; she was not a corporate wienie, she was an artist. She was a great casting director/executive/deal maker, but mostly a visionary artist. She understood this best because her husband, Burr Smidt, was a wonderfully talented art director, but I think what he enjoyed most was working with watercolors.

Beautiful stuff. He was also a very good actor and a delightful, intelligent author. Renee clearly understood the concept that perhaps art is related to other arts, and thus creative people occasionally desire to don different creative hats.

I worked longer hours than anticipated on *Close Encounters*, and for three days. They wanted me for the whole week, but I declined after the third day. It proved to be another great, wonderful, and enlightening experience, but I was afraid I really wouldn't have a job if I stayed any longer. There were about twenty of us; Howard Hesseman being the biggest name among us. I recognized him as an actor of "guest star" status. I don't really think he knew who I was; I was just another actor working a job. A short time later he would be cast in the role of Johnny Fever in a new sitcom called *WKRP in Cincinnati*. I was honored to be working with him. I had always liked his work and considered him to be an intelligent, inventive, off-the-wall talent.

In the dubbing room, there was a large projection screen and a control booth where the projectionist and Steven Spielberg would remain during takes. Most times while dubbing, a director will give direction to the artist(s) via a two-way intercom system activated from the control booth. At first, Steven came down and explained that we would be shown sequences that had been shot without sound, and we should view the sequences, pick out people in the crowd scenes, and improvise and ad-lib subtle, applicable dialogue to whatever character we chose. Steven spent about half the time going back and forth; he would come down and explain something and then return to the booth. We would see the scene projected on the screen maybe three or four times, rehearse, and then do an audio take about as many times. Steven Spielberg was shooting home movies most of the time we were recording. Once, he scribbled down some words on a piece of paper and said to me, "Mike, go over and say this." I stepped to the microphones and he gave me a signal from the booth that it was a take. We did it a couple of times and then it was off to another sequence.

There was one sequence when Richard Dreyfuss and cast were in the back of an Army truck and were all wearing gas masks. Everyone stepped up to the microphones and donned a real gas mask. Steven wanted real muffled breathing sounds. In the film, it was an intense, very dramatic moment, with no dialogue. We tried it several times and Steven didn't like the way the real gas masks stifled our natural breathing. The audio wasn't picking up much of anything. One of the actors was drinking coffee from a Styrofoam cup, and it suddenly came to Steven that it might sound different if we all simply breathed into a cup. He went to the coffee service, took one from a stack of Styrofoam cups, and then played with it a moment, breathing into it. He commented, "I think that might work." He then asked everyone to lose the gas masks, take a Styrofoam cup, and breathe into it at the microphones to see how it sounded. He returned to the booth. "That was the one," he said, "it works." The rest of what I was involved with for those three days was recording the background technical dialogues when the alien spacecraft landed at Devils Tower.

Individually, we were given pages to read, but we didn't understand much of what we were saying. We just read the technical jargon and tried to make it sound authentic. Later, those recorded dialogues and speeches were inserted where needed. Another very different and creative experience working with a brilliant director, and I got paid for it, too. What was it Picasso said about being at one's leisure when one is at work? And, I wonder what became of those home movies Mr. Spielberg shot?

I would return to my regular duties on *Y&R*, soon to be laid off for the anticipated extended period, beyond my usual two-week vacation. Sharon Thomas called and said it looked like it would be a green light on her husband's project soon and asked if I could think of an actor that could play my sidekick and was within their budget. Almost at once, I thought of a funny actor/writer chap I knew named Jamie Reidy. I had never used him, but instinctively thought he and I would work well off each other, as our chemistry together was very energetic, inventive, and always humor seeking. I set up a meeting for them to meet and talk about the project. Sharon immediately called me upon its conclusion and said that they loved him, and told me if they got everything in place they wanted us both. So it all might work out very nicely, I thought; my hiatus/vacation would begin with making a little movie. Some days later we got the call, and we were hired (set, booked) to begin filming on the anticipated start date.

The first day of the shoot I drove to the location early to meet Jamie. I was sitting in my car with Jamie, going over our lines and waiting for the crew to arrive, when Chris Cain approached my car. We greeted each other and he asked if he could see my script. I said of course, and he reached in, took it, and said, "You won't be needing this." He literally threw my script out in the field next to my car. I had only heard of directors doing this; that is, "throwing the script away." He said, in his very gentle and convincing manner, that I knew my character, the action, and the story, and basically knew the dialogue, and that we would improvise the rest. I would later retrieve my script from the field at a time when Mr. Cain was not around, since I wanted to keep it as a souvenir.

How truly exciting, I thought. I had studied at several improvisational theater groups, read the books, and considered myself quick and good at the art; now would come the real test. *Elmer* was a family film about a lost boy and my character's quest to find the boy and be a hero, be famous, and above all, make the hometown newspapers. We shot *Elmer* in about three weeks. Jamie and I worked well off each other. We'd improvise what wasn't scripted and polish it with three to five rehearsals, then Chris would say, "That's it," and we'd shoot it. It got big laughs at the premiere, which was held at a little theater in North Hollywood. I was especially proud when Mickey Rooney, who was in attendance, approached me and in front of my elderly father said, "You're really a good actor." We passed him later and Mr. Rooney said it again, with my proud father now beaming. My dad turned to me with a big smile and said that Mr. Rooney was a great artist, as good as they come, and that I should respect his opinion. Then my dad snickered and whispered to me that when he was at MGM and Mickey Rooney was still a boy, everyone called him Macaroni. I was very proud that Macaroni had noticed and encouraged me in front of my dear father that night; I did indeed respect his comments greatly.

I would return to my assignments at Columbia Pictures Television for only a short while longer, and then Renee Valente would deliver to me a message similar to what my colleague Paul Rodriques had received. It was economics; with the loss of shows, the department would have to downsize even further and cut back on staff, her only option. Renee was optimistic, however, and she tried to connect me with other production projects around town. Her gracious efforts met with little success, as all the "majors" were experiencing a similar slowdown.

CHAPTER SIX

Low-Budget Films and Independents

Sharon Thomas had called again, checking my avail-ability, and informing me that Chris Cain was near getting the go-ahead for his next project, *Charlie and The Old Buzzard*. She said it was a similar offbeat, amusing character and story, but I didn't care—I needed the continued cash flow. Chris Cain wanted me for one of the two adult leads, and then asked if I had any ideas for a boy of about eight to ten years old to play Charlie. Without hesitation, I explained that in all my experience of casting *The Brady Bunch*, "Miss Kline," and generally working with young people, I knew of one of the best child actors around, and that boy happened to be my eldest son, Chris. The next afternoon, I drove him out to Malibu for a meeting where he read some lines, but basically Chris Cain just talked to him about different situations and then asked my son to show him how he might respond. Sharon called me shortly after we got home and said they wanted him and thought he was perfect, and when the film funded and it was a real go, they'd be calling with exact start dates. They got the green light and I began another casting hiatus, working in a film opposite my eldest son, Christopher. What a gift, I thought; it's a great life. *Buzzard* would also include Chris Cain's sons, Dean and Roger Cain, and Chris Penn in the roles of the older and antagonistic neighborhood kids. Character actor Bruce Kimball also played a lead role as the owner of the buzzard. The shoot lasted another three-week period.

I had moved away from my wife in more than a trial separation this time, as unfortunately the marriage seemed ill-fated. I was temporarily staying in one of guest rooms at Hal Gefsky's home off Sunset Plaza Drive in Hollywood. Hal had always been very generous with people; his home was like a hotel, with close friends coming and going. A young lady that also lived there was Ava Redy. I had become friends with Ava long before I moved into a room (Simon Oakland's) at Hal's. She was a discovery of casting director Hoyt Bowers, who also lived at Hal's after a divorce. Hoyt had been trying to help her become more established in town. I liked Ava; I thought she had talent and possessed a unique quality beyond mere physical appeal. Originally, I had met her at Columbia Television at Hal's suggestion. I read her, thought she was very good, useable, and perhaps that she even possessed star quality. I firmly believe she'd be working today and would be a recognizable name if she had just stuck it out and not gone back to Podunk. We lived together, in rooms a few yards apart, but our relationship never evolved beyond being very good and close confidantes. During the months I hung at Hal's, whenever I could, I would bring my sons by to swim in the pool, and Ava would come out and swim and play with them like an older sister, very caring and protective.

When production on *Charlie And The Old Buzzard* began, Chris was about nine. I asked Ava to help me with managing my son on the days he worked, or when I was working and he wasn't. On one occasion during the shoot, we decided to go up the road to get some real lunch at a local eatery, which we were soon to rank as a "greasy spoon." We ordered food and I excused myself to the restroom. When I had returned and sat down at our table, Chris said, "Watch this, Dad." I looked in his direction and saw him hurl a missile of some sort out of a napkin he had in his lap. I looked to the ceiling as Ava responded, "Good one." There were about four or five yellow pats of butter sticking to the greasy spoon's dark, noticeably dusty knotty pine ceiling. As a nervous, soon-to-be-apprehended father, I immediately looked around for the butter police or the waiter police, or the real police ordering donuts and coffee in the next booth, but no one even noticed. Everyone was too busy putting greasy food in his or her bellies. Chris would make a deep pocket with his napkin, place a soft pat of butter in its center, and then by snapping it taught, outwardly from the sides, would send the projectile up to dangle with the others. This was Ava's way of keeping the creamy dairy products far from her slender thighs.

Chris's work in the film was even more inventive and entertaining after even less direction. He had some really amusing moments, but the film as a whole wasn't very good, although it was another very good experience for both of us.

My casting director contacts and then Hal Gefsky directed me to Andy Kuehn of Kaleidoscope Productions in Hollywood. It was my understanding that

Kaleidoscope was a well-known post-production company usually hired for editing, sound effects, or simply saving a film by editing it somewhat differently. This would be its first venture into production on its own. Immediately, I called Andy's office and confirmed that Kaleidoscope was interviewing casting directors. I was again late in submitting myself; he had already interviewed a number of people, and I felt that perhaps it was all a waste of time. And a few snooty agents from the big theatrical agencies offices weren't helping me find the more desired staff positions because I hadn't played their politics very well, as I noted earlier. I would learn that one had already paid a visit to Kaleidoscope and was stepping on me, pushing for his company's choice for the job. I also learned that a couple of other staff jobs had surfaced, and I would hear later, through friends, that an agent had badmouthed me to the casting department head. By the time I had gotten the lead and followed up with calls, I'd been told the jobs were filled. So, I would focus on what was available and would take what was offered in the independent job market. Ross Brown had always done well there, so would I.

Andy Kuehn was readying several low-budget projects under his own banner, as well as several others in co-production with other production companies. One such company he had teamed up with was Bill Osco's. Among other slated projects, Bill Osco was spending a great deal of money writing a script and building sets for a spoof R-rated version of a classic; his version was entitled *Oz*. In 1976, Bill had released his X-rated version of *Alice in Wonderland* starring Kristine DeBell, and even earlier he had done quite well with *Flesh Gordon*, which starred Jason Williams. It wasn't my intention to be involved with these kinds of productions, but I needed to keep the dollars flowing. I met with Andy Keuhn at Kaleidoscope and he almost hired me on the spot, saying he had disliked all the people he had met previously, and especially mistrusted the aforementioned agent's suggestion. That afternoon, I drafted a simple agreement that we signed for casting services rendered and he showed me my office, where I went to work. I liked Andy, and thought perhaps I might have consummated the first of many such nonexclusive pacts as an independent casting service, there and elsewhere.

The first of the scripts that went to the stage was *Flush*, an R-rated farce, which Andy Keuhn would also direct. I suggested a favorite of mine in the lead role, funnyman Bill Callaway. I had met Bill Callaway while casting *Love American Style* and had cast him in numerous Blackouts at Paramount. Bill was a gifted, inventive, keen, quick, and very funny improvisational actor. I brought in six or seven other strong possibilities for *Flush*, but the powers that be chose Bill Callaway. An amusing concept, *Flush* revolved around a young chap that cleaned out septic tanks for a living, and in so doing found the fortune of a Howard Hughes or William Randolph Hearst eccentric-type billionaire in a septic tank. I assembled some really funny people to this film and most sequences proved to be hysterical, but the film didn't have the advertisement and distribution it should have or I'm sure it would have done better.

The next project was *Bus 17 Is Missing* or *Cheer-leaders' Wild Weekend*, whichever you prefer, directed by Jeff Werner. Not much story content; the title says it all—T&A (tits and ass)—and evidence that it's very difficult to get even an adequate performance out of the beautiful and the untrained. They had retained me for a while longer to do some preliminary casting on Osco's *Oz*, but it never got off the ground. Bill Osco once summoned me to his office, scribbled a phone number down on a page from his desk calendar, and said, "Call this guy for the role of the Wizard; tell him that I'll pay him a million dollars for one day." The name he had jotted down on the torn calendar was Richard Nixon, and it was his San Clemente phone number. I was never able to reach him; I learned that people of that stature have rotating blocks of numbers that change frequently. However, I was able to contact a representative agent through SAG and was told that Mr. Nixon wouldn't be interested in doing such a project for any amount.

Then there was *Racquet* for *Westside Story* dancer-turned-producer/director David Winters. Again I was retained to cast the movie as an independent casting company, with the complete autonomy to cast other in-dependent projects simultaneously, and for a specific period of time and a specified fee. Harlequin Produc-tions, David's company, would supply office space and staff, the beautiful Victoria Pearman to fall in love with and assist me when needed. And Bud Botham—well, Bud wasn't so beautiful physically, but what a gem of a fellow. He could do anything; hired as a cinematographer, he gently helped at every task. He even acted in a scene. Bud's management skills proved to be the glue that held the production from coming apart a couple of times; give credit where credit is due.

David was a mover and shaker, first cabin all the way, with big, impressive offices on Sunset Boulevard, and he wanted the same big-name A-list cast. He felt if we could get a bankable name interested, he would have the script rewritten to a star's satisfaction. I would explain that, in my experience, this was sometimes done when the big names came aboard, but more often than not projects for the really giant names were set years in advance. We might get lucky if I could find an A-list actor whose slated project had fallen apart and he became available on our projected dates. I advised that I thought this was unlikely to happen, and we might be looking at months before we got final approvals on script, director, et cetera. But if an agent or manager liked a project and was interested, and liked the director and the other supporting cast being assembled, and the talent and money was available, anything was possible. Most often, possible script changes would generate first through that interested agent or manager. I've seen few bankable names that didn't have ideas for changes that they would bring to the foundation of a working project, and that's just what a script is; a foundation to build upon. David Winters would have let someone else direct if he could have gotten a major name interested. Just too many ifs; too big a gamble for the top A-list male artist.

It's very exciting to find a barn and want to entertain and put on a show, like Mickey Rooney and Judy Garland did, but this was real show business, a big money business, and a casting coup was not to happen on this project. Putting the cart in front of the horse never works. As usual, I always explored what seemed impossible, but continued to remind David that most of the big names we were talking about were booked for years in advance, and if we could get someone interested we'd have to wait until he became available. After David realized we couldn't get a Harrison Ford or some other bankable name for our money, script, or assigned director, he settled for the good actors that were available and interested for the bucks we had to spend.

Racquet was another slightly farcical story. This one revolved around the life of a tennis pro who was getting older and starting to realize the associated personal changes. We met with the young Robert Urich, who was interested, but even he, who had come to meet at my personal request, wanted a great deal more money than we could offer. *Racquet* went to the stage with Bert Convy in the lead role. I tried to cast the stars of tomorrow; I made deals for newcomers Tanya Roberts and Kitty Ruth in supporting roles. Phil Silvers and Edie Adams were hysterical and added to the comedic frenzy. David and I met personally with Mr. Silvers to entice him into doing the project. He walked out of sight into the kitchen of his Century City condo and said he wanted a bag of cash as payment—cash. I think David ended up paying him as much (cash) as anyone in the movie. He was really funny that day as well. What a crack-up; he was his own money-hungry agent, preceding the formal deal making with his agent/managers. I suspect this was the way it was done in his day. It would also feature tennis greats Bjorn Borg and Ilie Nastase, and numerous cameos of people that just ate up the budget and brought no real value to any potential box office. David Winters or one of his entourage were constantly coming up with other name ideas after reading *Billboard*, *Rolling Stone*, *Variety*, or *Hollywood Reporter* on any given morning. Once we began shooting, we tried to get anyone who seemed hot at the moment for something—anything.

Racquet always seemed in constant rewrites and changes to adjust for some added name's schedule. My duties and contractual obligations having concluded, I would often drop by and watch the daily shooting if it didn't interfere with my schedule, and would continue to handle issues that always seemed to surface when I was about the set, gratis. I liked David Winters, everybody did; flamboyant, yes, but also very bright and inventive; a charming adult/kid with a salesman's personality and wonderful sense of humor. We, too, laughed a great deal.

On one occasion, David Winters took me aside and told me of a character they were writing into the story that he wanted me to play. I was delighted. After weeks of casting, he had become quite familiar with this chameleon actor that lives within me. In a nutshell, it was a farcical sequence where Bert Convy's character is being chased by the police, and to escape he jumps into the front seat of a car at a huge Greek-type wedding. The car he jumps into is the one tagged at the rear "Just

Married" and the customary tin cans are affixed to the bumper. The character I played was the best man at the wedding. As the police cruise by searching, Convy is slumped down in the front seat, hiding. He begins hearing amorous utterances from the rear seat, and discovers it is my character and a woman, passionately kissing and trying to undress out of their formal attire, with her saying ego-inflating things like, "Oh, oh, you really are the best man". To evade the police, Convy's character starts the car and races away. The couple remains deliriously lip-locked and oblivious to any of the chase until the car finally comes to a crashing rest in the middle of the wedding reception feast, with tons of cake, food, and bizarre-looking extras being tossed about. My character finally breaks away from this very steamy moment when he's told by the young lady that her husband, the groom, and her father are approaching the car. The young lady was nothing less than *Penthouse* Pet and centerfold beauty Darwin Hastings. It was a very difficult scene for me to play—a stretch, a real stretch. I won't bore the reader with the rest of the sequence, but I will tell you this: I have never been prouder of a moment I was involved in as an actor than that silly one. I did my best befuddled delivery to the father and the husband as they yanked, jerked, and finally pulled me from the car.

Veteran stuntman George Fisher, who I hired to oversee the stunts and step in for me if necessary (yeah, right), came over and congratulated me. I had stayed in the car as it careened through the air, crashed, and came to rest. He said I should be a stuntman and gave me a Stuntman's Association patch. When I went to dailies the next day, the screening room was packed—standing room only. The investors, Darwin Hastings, Bert Convy, and everyone that had anything at all to do with the filming of *Racquet* was there. Just prior to the start of the running of dailies, the projectionist buzzed David Winters. Seemingly annoyed, David then announced that one of the reels had come in from the lab without the sound track. I immediately thought the worst; it's probably the stuff I was in, and it was. The pleasant surprise was, we started watching the silent action of my antics and everyone roared with deep, nonstop, rolling, hysterical laughter. And folks were still laughing for a long time after the lights came up. Everyone was patting me on the back and saying really wonderful things about my comedic talents and the visuals, and what I personally added to the scene. David Winters was still on the floor, laughing, and said he hoped the rest of the movie was that funny. I could see a strong Stan Laurel influence in this work; I was very proud. The following day, I was told that everyone had checked and double-checked, and they would have the audio to run with the film that evening. I thought nothing could top last night's audience response, a tough act to follow. Again the projection room was packed, and when it got to the sequence I was in the room went bananas with laughter, only bigger and longer this time. The audience loved this sequence, and the dialogue gave the scene more life. They were rolling on the floor. I couldn't believe it was happening again. I thought, I just want to have this kind of audience the rest of my life; I'll work for free.

To this day, I don't think I've ever had moments quite like those two evenings in the projection room; three minutes of beautiful performing fame and laughter. Unfortunately, most all of the sequence ended up you know where—on the editing room floor—and was not used.

The good news that week was that Hal Gefsky called me with a lead about three young guys from the University of Wisconsin film school who were readying a film project. Hal had said good things to them about me while I again had been tenaciously banging on doors all over town trying to find my next assignment. I called and arranged to meet with Jerry and David Zucker and Jim Abrahams, at the very popular local theater of the absurd they had created, Kentucky Fried Theater. The theater was located on Pico just west of 20th Century Fox studios. They explained that they had little money for casting. The movie project was entitled *Kentucky Fried Movie*. It was composed of numerous comedic vignettes, the longest being about fifteen minutes, with a projected cast of some 150 plus speaking, solid, character-acting roles. They would be the writers and executive producers of *Kentucky Fried Movie*. Their director of choice was John Landis, who was just as off-the-wall funny and energetic. John had a number of acting credits and earlier had produced, directed, and starred in another farce, *Schlock*, his only directing credit at the time, which has a kind of cult following today. Other than that, I really didn't know much about him. I would learn that besides being very bright, quick, and funny, he was also creatively very demanding, bordering on temperamental if he didn't get exactly what he wanted. I also would quickly learn to love these guys. It was constant silly, continuous comedy, a wonderful exchange in an arena of highly creative comedic energy. I was a wee bit older than they were, but we all liked each other immediately. Samuel Bronkowitz Productions, the spoof name of their production company, had already shot two short, very funny sequences in 16 mm, funded with their own personal money, about ten thousand dollars. Based on the response from those first sequences shot, they were able to raise additional funding and go into production.

I wanted to work with these guys, no matter what they offered; it would be four weeks of work and a very good independent casting credit. I did my best to sell my comedy experience(s), having done similar for Paramount on *Love American Style* and the other independent credits I had accumulated recently. Jerry and David Zucker, Jim Abrahams, and John Landis (the boys) gave me a lot to think about. I took plenty of notes on the back page of a first draft of the *Kentucky Fried Movie* script they had given me. In the next few days, I made a deal with them for my independent casting services and went to work making lists of possibilities for the many segments. They then hired a crew and set the start date. I was excited. I felt as though they were the Marx Brothers redux. It would be a search for funny, and when the polish for something funnier was found we would all laugh again, harder. A new twist could come from anyone involved, mostly from the Zucker brothers, Jim Abrahams, or John Landis. A few times, it was something I did or a way

I interpreted a character's words during auditions that inspired a change or rewrite. Sometimes, the actors being considered for a role would bring another new twist to the material that nobody had thought about until it had been read several times by different people. It had been my experience that this would always occur when writer/producers were present during casting sessions.

We began shooting several weeks later and shot the rest of the constantly changing script over the slated four-week period. Overnight, I started getting calls from people all over town, companies I'd never heard of, inquiring as to my availability for their various projects, and asking if I could take a meeting as a possibility of casting for them. It would be safe to say I was suddenly a hot and sought-after casting service and it was exciting, but I chose to stay focused exclusively on *Kentucky Fried Movie*.

For the next few weeks, I would bring all my casting experience and resources to *Kentucky Fried Movie*, but it would be no different from any other project I would cast. I would work very hard to assemble the very best talent for what we could offer. I took it very seriously and endeavored to make it another signature example of my work, my expertise, perhaps to take to the Academy. Oh, that's right; casting directors don't get Oscars or Emmys. Not to minimize anyone's contribution, especially that of the director, producer, and the writer, but is it makeup, wardrobe, lighting, editing, music, and other craft departments that assemble the first creative visions of the writer? When is somebody going to realize and recognize that, more often than not, without the fundamental creative ingenuity of the casting process—the casting director, specifically—no one would get any awards for anything? Often, it's some casting director who brought something to the table that gave a story life; a new life, and perhaps a new direction that gave the project viability or the legs to walk into financing and get the money for further development.

Kentucky Fried Movie had several vignettes that required nudity of both men and women. My casting experience in television gave me little knowledge of which agents specifically had actors that would do nudity. However, during the preliminary casting on Bill Osco's R-rated project, *Oz*, and on *Racquet* and *Flush*, I had met a number of agents who seemed to feed on this kind of T&A casting call. On *Flush*, but especially *Racquet*, I had used numerous young, sexy women who would do nudity, and I had current lists of many more possibilities to call on. Once I put the word out, by way of my own script breakdown, I was flooded with submissions for all the roles, even some from the top agencies. Suddenly, everyone knew someone, or had an idea of someone not necessarily on a client list—the girlfriend list, perhaps. It was just a matter of culling through what I thought were the very best and setting up interviews for each constantly changing sequence. With the exception of cameos played by Donald Sutherland, Bill Bixby, George Lazenby, Tony Dow, Henry Gibson, and Dick Yarmy, the remainder of the huge cast consisted of supporting character actors, mostly total unknowns. We weren't paying much and that factor alone eliminated a great many possibilities. For the Exit the Dragon sequence, originally entitled Fist Full of Yen, I met and read every martial-arts-trained, Bruce Lee look-alike actor I could find. It would prove to be not nearly as much fun as interviewing and reading naked women. A spoof of martial arts genre films, we cast Master Bong Soo Han as the antagonist, the evil Dr. Klan, and Evan Kim in the Bruce Lee look-alike role; both were wonderful. We had seen some amazing exhibitions of martial arts skill on the little stage at the theater during interviews. Prior to bringing him in to meet the boys, I had asked veteran character James Hong if he had ever studied martial arts or had any self-defense training whatsoever. He confided to me that he was in his sixties, but still trained daily to stay fit. I thought he might have been exaggerating some, so at the end of his reading we asked him to do something. He bowed graciously, then punched, spun, and kicked very high, and then flew through the air, at shoulder height, completely across the width of the stage. We were amazed, almost as much as we were with the constant flow of naked women we had been interviewing.

It was very hard work and we had to do it. We sat in the audience seats and it was like a private strip show. Lenka Novak, Betsy Genson, and Nancy Mann were finally selected after the usual numerous, tiring callbacks. From day one, Jerry, David, Jim, and John teased me about Betsy, saying, "She likes you, Mike, go for it." I never liked to mix business with pleasure in my career; it was not a good practice to follow. But I was recently divorced, and was feeling a strong honest human attraction for lovely Betsy, and she for me.

There was another sequence in the script entitled Catholic High School Girls in Trouble, in addition to the scenes lovely Lenka, Betsy, and Nancy were involved in. This scene not only involved nudity, but also a simulated lovemaking scene in a shower. I had met the beautiful and sensual Ushi Digard when I was at Paramount. I was told she had done adult films, which to this day I have never seen. Ushi was now attempting to make the very difficult transition to legitimate work. I loved Ushi, I fell in love/like/lust with her the first time I met her. She exuded honesty and sensuality in a very real, low-key, earthy way. It wasn't a performance; she was sincerely a warm, sensitive, affectionate, and naturally very sexy and beautiful young woman, very similar in quality to Liv Von Lindenland. We became friends, and I really liked her heart. Sure, I would have jumped at the chance to be something more than friends with her, but she was married and having a happy life with her husband.

I mentioned to the boys that I knew Ushi Digard and they started to howl, literally. I was asked during howls to get her in, find her, and see if she would do the shower scene. I had several ideas for the male chap in the scene, but few for the female role. With this other dimension it became more difficult for me to make a list of possibilities. I called Ushi, explained about *Kentucky Fried Movie* and the many humorous sequences involved in it, and exactly what her part would entail. She said again that she had absolutely no qualms about nudity, but was trying to get away from it. She reiterated her views that she had expounded to me previously; that she would be interested in the right project, with the right director, a meaningful story and scene, and hopefully opposite a star. I didn't blame her for her caution, but continued selling the project, saying that it was really a funny farcical script and bound to get a lot of attention at the box office. She asked me to send her the script, to let her look at the scene, and asked about who she would be working with. I told her there were a number of possibilities, to which she replied, "Maybe you could do it with me, Mike?" I immediately felt my libido heart rate increase. My mind's visualization of being in the shower with Ushi Digard was suddenly waking up my entire being, definitely breaking up my hurried day. She then laughed and said, "Yes, I think that's it. If I like it and want to do the part, I want you to be the man in the shower with me." I was nervously laughing with her, said that I was flattered, but started blathering other excuses. "I just couldn't do it, my mom might see it." I explained that I had kids; that one of my sons was being considered for a part in the film and might be working the same day this sequence was being shot, and John Landis wanted me for something else to be shot later, something with more substance and lines. I came up with every excuse I could think of. Her repartee was, "Aren't I more substance?" And then, "Don't your kids see you naked? Certainly your mom has." I nervously laughed again and confessed to her that I'd really like to be in a shower with her, but not this shower. Then, in a very sexy voice she said, "Do it with me, Mike, do it;

we'll get all soapy and wet together." I gave her the nervous laugh again and told her the script was on its way, and for her to let me know and that I'd fix her up with somebody she'd like. We made some kissing sounds, laughed, and she said, "See you in the shower, Mike," and hung up.

The next morning, I relayed my conversation with the boys and they were howling again, with a sense of comedic-orgasmic voyeurism. It now was almost a demand that I play the part opposite Ushi; that is, if she wanted to do it. "And we won't tell Betsy," Jerry snickered. That afternoon, Ushi called to say that she thought the whole film was very funny and she would do the part, but only if I worked in the shower with her. The boys had requested seeing what she looked like in person and asked for me to set an appointment for her to come in and meet. Unlike the other roles that required nudity, no one asked Ushi to disrobe. We chatted a while, where she again stated that she would love to do the role, if I worked with her in the shower. The interview then concluded, she thanked us and said to me, "I'll bring the shower soap, Mike." I gave her another nervous laugh, the boys' eyes bulged, and she left. John Landis, Jerry and David Zucker, and Jim Abrahams were really howling at me to do it, selling me on the idea. "Maybe you'll have to rehearse the shower scene in private with her. Yeah, that's a good idea," John said. They all agreed I should have lots of rehearsal time with her for the shower scene. I emphatically explained that I couldn't do it. "I have kids, and my mother is deeply religious and would fry me in a skillet of lard if I did it."

Jerry Zucker responded, "Ohhhh, it's the old skillet of lard excuse again."

For the next few days the boys actually wore me down. I was prepared to soap up and jump in the shower with Ushi under the guise of the "it's a tough job but somebody's got to do it" maxim. And Ushi was calling me and telling me what it was going to be like. It was early phone-shower-simulated-sex chat. John Landis began assuring me that the camera would be focused more on Ushi's ample loveliness than on me. There was part of me that definitely wanted to work with Ushi, in the shower, naked, soapy, and wet. The bottom line: the actor in me wanted words and lines, not grunts and moans. Once and for all, this puts to rest the age-old question of primary human drives—is it food or sex? Neither; it's lines. Those indescribably delicious, well-thought-out words we say to an audience. The actor can live without food and without sex, but not words and lines, in any project. It doesn't even have to be a meaningful project; just give me words! At the last minute, I told the boys I couldn't do it for all the aforementioned reasons; I wanted lines. I frantically suggested Michael Kearns to replace me in the shower scene. He was tall, handsome, and didn't mind getting wet with Ushi. I had used Michael in a supporting role in *Flush* and he was very good, and he had no compunctions whatsoever about working in the buff. I went to work on Ushi and convinced her of the change, but I would hear from her for a long time after the film's completion that I should have showered with her when I had the chance. John Landis then decided that he wanted me to play a news reporter in a segment to be shot later in the schedule entitled A.M. Today. More lines, yes; more camera time, yes; but the thought of not getting soapy with Ushi will always haunt me, especially when I go to the shower.

My fondest memory of casting *Kentucky Fried Movie* involved my son, Chris. I had suggested him for a role in a sequence entitled United Appeal For The Dead. The boys thought he was perfect and we hired him. This vignette was morbid, dark humor. It revolved around a family that had found a way to have their prematurely dead and decaying child's cadaver still be involved in their family activities. There was a montage of shots: the family at Thanksgiving dinner, football games (sons Doyle and Jon worked in this scene), children at poolside gatherings. In the opening, Henry Gibson narrates and presents this new program for keeping a loved one still fully involved and intact at these family functions—black comedy, to say the least. Chris was in the makeup chair for hours at a time for the days he worked, for the application and removal of the decay makeup material. He would sit there calmly and let them affix the stuff or remove it from his face, and would talk incessantly with the makeup artists about anything under the sun.

On this specific day's shoot, the company was on location at a very beautiful and stately mansion in Pasadena. Chris's makeup call was six a.m., and the first shot of the day was the swimming pool sequence at approximately seven a.m. The water was like ice. I dropped Chris off at makeup, and had gone to the pool and dipped my hand in the frigid water after overhearing some conversation about somebody trying to get the pool heater on and working. I had heard them say it would take more than an hour for the heater to warm the pool; that is, if they could get it to work. Needless to say, I was concerned, but hopefully when Chris was out of makeup it would be at least a little warm. In the script, the dearly departed family member is floating the dead man's float in the water very near where other children are frolicking, splashing, and tossing a ball around at the pool's edge. Chris's makeup time that day would be a few minutes shorter because the camera would see only a portion of the side of his face and some of his forehead, but it was still well over an hour.

Jerry and David Zucker and Jim Abrahams had joined John Landis and the crowd of crew and technicians gathered at poolside to watch the filming of this segment. Everybody was feeling the early morning chill and anxiously awaiting Chris's entrance from makeup. A nervous John Landis had placed the camera and had assembled the shivering extra children, still in bathrobes, to the edge of the pool in anticipation of Chris's entrance. He directed the children to disrobe and get in the water, and was met with whining resistance from them all. The oldest of the three, his niece, yelled, "It's freezing, John, it's like ice!" He asked them again to get in and move around, and said that they would get warm when they did. All three were complaining even louder and still no one entered the water. John was moving about nervously in the face of a full-on mutiny, directing the kids to get in the water. Technicians from the crew were also moving about, still trying to find remedies for the faulty pool heater. John continued reassuring the kids that it would be okay if they just got in the water and moved around. Everybody was dipping a hand in now, me included, and it was still very, very cold since the heater had never come on. It was a unanimous opinion that at an earlier time that morning there might have been ice on the pool. Now, more like a concerned parent, I was getting very worried about my own child's well-being and less concerned about the picture's shooting schedule. John Landis had finally convinced his shivering niece and the other children to at least dangle their feet in the water at the edge of the pool; again assuring them it wouldn't take long to shoot if they would cooperate. Giving them a large beach ball to play with helped them get in the mood. Then, a few minutes after seven a.m., Chris entered the pool area at the far end, the deep end, bundled up in a bathrobe and wearing sandals. An immediate hush came over everyone at poolside, as if the volume had been turned down. I think everyone sensed a bigger mutiny about to commence, with Chris entering the equation, and my obvious nervous concern. John then loudly gave Chris the direction that he wanted him floating, facedown, at a point at the end of the pool farthest from where he was standing. He pointed and said near where the kids were at pool's edge. Standing at about midpoint of poolside, John directed Chris to walk along the path on the opposite side down to where the kids were and then get in the water. Chris listened to the instructions, and before I could say a word he immediately dropped his robe, kicked away his sandals, and without hesitation made a perfect dive into the pool's deep end, swam leisurely to the bottom and then beautifully the distance of this very long pool. The gathered crowd was even more silent and still, with all completely mesmerized by his swim underwater. He came up for air exactly where the other kids were positioned, to rousing, enthusiastic, spontaneous applause; a true hero's welcome. Suddenly, it was a new day; everyone was in awe of what he had done, with no complaints whatsoever about the water's temperature. It was an inspirational and motivational moment given to us all by a ten-year-old boy. I was beaming with pride. Chris went into a dead man's float and John Landis got what he wanted, as I recall, in two takes. Naturally, the kids got warm and wanted to play in the water more, but we were moving on. Everyone congratulated Chris for being a real trooper with a pat on the head or a "Way to go, Chris." He was everyone's little hero from then on.

Later, I explained what had happened prior to his arrival and the impact of what his dive had done for everyone that morning. It was the kind of unique, brave moment in life you almost have to witness to fully understand. For the rest of the days he worked, someone would always remind him of his inspirational dive into a pool of very cold water on that chilly morning. I would hear "I wish I'd done that" many times.

CHAPTER SEVEN

Metro Goldwyn Mayer

I had found a small but very unique apartment a step or two south of and overlooking popular court eight at the Paddle Courts in Venice, California. I thanked Hal Gefsky for his generosity, gathered some things from my house in Culver City, and moved. I would soon learn that my new alarm clock would be the pop of the first ball hit at about seven a.m. Paddle tennis sounds would increase to a very steady, constant popping at about seven thirty a.m., when I would finally roll out to embark upon the beautiful day. Court eight became an extension of my apartment, and with my boys digging the game, too, we discovered all the courts. I would sleep just steps further east of where anybody really good would play. I could watch the best, I thought, with a view of the ocean, no less. The world would travel by like a large screen on one side of the room; passing people, often looking up at me, on Ocean Front Walk. It was like a fishbowl, unless I pulled the drapes closed at the front windows. Two immediate left turns out of bed, and I could throw my stuff on and be in a game with the best, perhaps nudging enough to fill in for someone late. I often became a warm-up game for the best, the players that would gather at court eight. At the time, York was the best player I ever saw play the game; extremely fast, with a deadly cross-court approach shot.

He let me beat him a few times, or maybe I was getting better, but I beat him; he was teaching me.

Depending on the weather the sounds of play usually would last until the sun went down. Fortunately, I could close the doors and windows, and the old building would muffle the sounds. But when you love something, the sounds of what you love become a part of you; they don't disturb you. It's like sleeping in the theater where actors are rehearsing, working, training, and/or filming; it all becomes inspiring, and then relaxing at the same time. Like in the arts, in paddle tennis would be die-hards, myself included, that didn't want to go home. They want more play, and would be out hitting balls with the aid of only streetlights until late, sometimes in pouring rain. I was learning the game fast and loved it.

I had gotten the *Kentucky Fried Movie* assignment at just the right time, a period that had become extremely slow for the entire independent market. All those when-you're-hot-you're-hot calls became when-you're-not. The previous job possibilities had been filled and quickly faded. I had taken most of the meetings for *Kentucky Fried Movie* at the Kentucky Fried Theater or the Samuel Bronkowitz Production offices on Pico. There were a few additional roles that I conducted interviews for at my beach apartment and the word quickly spread to the local Venice actor community. I started getting a few knocks on my door and some wacko inquiries. But for the most part, the casting on *Kentucky Fried* was a wrap.

My routine would start early, with either a run or it was straight to courts. One morning I was out for an early brisk walk/run on one of life's great stages, Ocean Front Walk. I had discovered this great local eatery at Windward and Pacific Streets. I was never quite sure of its name; my boys and I called it Dupar's. After my run that morning, I sat down at the counter for coffee, the German pancakes, and the eggs and home fries special. I noticed that immediately next to me was a chap I had met and had hired previously for several projects at Columbia Pictures Television, Ed Griffith. Coincidentally, I had recently hired Ed to play a role in *Kentucky Fried.* He had done a marvelous segment in the film called Thrill Seekers. He explained that he lived not far, just a couple blocks north at Windward and Ocean Front Walk. Ed was a consummate actor, a very genuine chap, and was also divorced with a child. We had a lot in common and became good pals. Ed didn't play paddle tennis, but he roller-skated, and we began spending a lot of time that first summer racing each other on roller skates—that is, if we weren't seriously busy—from the Venice Pier to the Santa Monica Pier. He was a good athlete and a very good skater. He beat me most times we raced, but I was rapidly improving. Like kids in our mid-thirties, we'd play tag and race back and forth from the uncompleted bike path through the heavy pedestrian traffic on Ocean Front Walk at midday, from pier to pier. We nearly bought the farm more than once pushing the old speed envelope, trying to beat each other and ultimately break Mach 1 on roller skates. We finally scared ourselves; with too many crashes and very bad pedestrian near-crashes, we gave it up, thanks be to God.

Ed and I also found ourselves deep in conversation about acting techniques, as he had done several years on *As The World Turns* in New York. Among other interests was a very competitive backgammon tourney, and we shared information on the local single-lady scene— the Venice Debutantes, we called them. Once, he came by my place with a beautiful and very intelligent young woman by the name of Theresa Hunt. Theresa lived nearby, and she and I hit it off immediately. I saw her a few days later and she confirmed what Ed had told me; that they were just friends. Trendy Robert's Restaurant was directly next door to my place, and there was always a party there. If I couldn't sleep due to the noise of it, I would invite Ed or Theresa, or both, over and we'd join the celebrity crowd gathering late.

My sons and I were inseparable, and they had become addicted to paddle tennis and began staying more than half of the week with me, Thursdays to Monday mornings most weeks. They loved the game as much as I did. Addicted, I would often open a window and set the phone out on the windowsill, steps away from court eight. I'd play for a while and return to rest, make some calls, or check my machine for messages. Theresa and I had started to see each other more. She was a remarkable young woman, driven to further herself with education, and was finishing up at Cal-State Los Angeles. We had an enormously good time together and shared a great many of the same interests, but she ultimately would become another beautiful woman I let slip through my fingers. One thing I remember vividly about Theresa was the tiny bedroom of the tiny house that she rented in Venice. How tiny was it? Her bedroom was so tiny that her mattress, which I think was a double, rolled up against each of the three walls and met you at the doorway as you entered. When you went to her room, there wasn't anything to do but jump in and lie down. We had a lot of laughs there, as well as many loving times together while I lived in Venice.

With my work on *Kentucky Fried Movie* finished and the shoot near completion, I was listening hard for word of other projects. Christopher and I would watch the Super Bowl with Jerry Zucker in his apartment above the theater on Pico Boulevard the following January. The release of *Kentucky Fried Movie* would bring the Zucker brothers, Jim Abrahams, and John Landis enormous recognition; a low-budget sleeper, it did much better at the box office than even they imagined. For the boys, it opened more doors within the industry, as they were suddenly acclaimed as the young filmmakers of tomorrow. John Landis went on almost immediately to *Animal House* and *The Blues Brothers.* Jerry and David Zucker and Jim Abrahams collectively produced *Airplane, Police Squad,* and the *Naked Gun* series. Jerry Zucker would direct the huge hit *Ghost* and later *A Walk in the Clouds,* co-produced by brother David. They would all collaborate on *Ruthless People,* directed by David Zucker, and Jim Abrahams directed *Hot Shots!* Jerry Zucker commended me on my work. He said what I brought to *Kentucky Fried Movie* "was genius, a hundred and fifty-six speaking roles, a brilliant contribution." I appreciated his comments, and was extremely elated and flattered by them, but I never heard from him, or David, or Jim Abrahams, or John Landis ever again. The Zuckers, Abrahams, and Landis were being rushed, wined, and dined by the big studio operation and casting services. I don't know what happened with Betsy, but she didn't return my calls, either.

I was banging on doors again, talking to everyone in town about possible openings and casting job changes, and seeking a staff job when I got wind of an opening at Lorimar Productions in Culver City. Close by, Lorimar was located in a new complex of offices on the MGM lot. I called and learned that they were in the midst of interviewing candidates to head up their casting department. I was able to arrange a meeting with production head Phil Capice. I thought our meeting went very well; in fact, I heard through the grapevine that I was being seriously considered, but then one learns not to believe everything one hears there, too. Several days later I would hear that my much-respected colleague Barbara Miller had been selected. I was happy for her and felt that, of the people around that were available at that moment, besides yours truly, she was an excellent choice.

I continued with my search diligently; I had put my ear firmly to the ground listening for work, and was more than persistent in calling and bothering everyone I knew. Finally, it paid off. In late May 1978, Hal Gefsky called and informed me of production and casting changes that he'd learned of that were occurring at that very moment at MGM. Gary Shafer had left his position just the afternoon before. He had cast the first nine episodes of a new police show entitled *CHiPs*. Hal advised me that I should call the new producer of *CHiPs* immediately. I put down my paddle tennis paddle and did so. This new producer was Cy Chermak; he returned my call moments later. They must be seriously looking, I thought. We would meet the next morning. That afternoon, I made more calls and inquiries about what had happened. I heard all sorts of things. That Gary Shafer had a horrible time of it with the police officer/producer/creator of the show. Then I heard this police officer/producer/creator had battled the studio, and then had been barred from further access to the studio lot. Production had shut down after the first nine episodes that had been shot in that first season, and the show was placed on hold. I also heard that it was a breath away from being cancelled. I called Hal back and learned that among the many shows Mr. Chermak had written and produced were *The Virginian*, *The Bold Ones*, and *Ironsides*; probably his most successful achievements at that time, all quality programs. I talked to several more agents that afternoon and learned that Cy Chermak also had a reputation for being extremely demanding, difficult, and moody, all spawned mostly by an enormous ego. I also heard that there were few casting people who really wanted to work with him. But I needed to work and hadn't known the luxury of turning work down as I had been advised to do. The stories I heard all led me to believe that some of it was probably true; the "where there's smoke, there's fire" truism.

Cy Chermak was a forty-seven-year-old, better-looking Hugh Hefner type. If I had had to cast Hugh Hefner and Cy had been an actor, I would have had Cy at the top of my "to meet and read" list. Cy and I hit it off immediately. He seemed impressed with my background and qualifications, and I sensed that perhaps mine might be the kind of personality that would complement his well. He admitted that he had a reputation for being all of what I'd heard, or would hear, and maybe more. Simply put, he wanted things done his way. We laughed and talked, and other than the few minutes we talked about my salary requirements, we chatted about everything other than casting and production. His response to my salary requests appeared to be favorable; I couldn't really tell. I would learn that this was Cy; he played his cards very close to his chest. I told myself I could work with this guy regardless of what I'd heard, and I liked him. He was a charming, intelligent man, and I reminded myself that sometimes there's a bigger price to pay working with creative-genius types. I left MGM feeling fairly confident and excited about the possibilities.

The next morning, I got a call from Cy saying that I should come in and take a meeting with the president of MGM Television, Ed Montanus. I came in that afternoon for what seemed like the callback and was squeezed in to meet with Mr. Montanus after lunch, on what his secretary told me had already been a very hectic day. This guy I really liked; he was all personality, a dynamic, bigger-than-life salesman, the presenter type, a four-star general. He opened by saying that I was the young fellow that had been recommended to him for the position of director of casting, to head the MGM Casting Department, that he had done some checking around town and that he liked what he had heard about me. He then said that he knew I could handle the post. He added with a chuckle that the money I was asking for was outrageous, but thought perhaps I was worth it and would surely earn it in the days to come. He further explained that in the capacity as director of casting I would answer to only him; that I worked for only him. Moderately stunned by his revelation of the title of the post I was being considered for, I rambled nervously for a beat, detailing a brief story of an injustice I had once observed directed upon a casting director by an ego-driven, maniacal producer. Suddenly, Mr. Montanus interrupted, leaned toward me, and said, in a very commanding, powerful, General Patton-like voice, "If you want the job, it's yours, Mike. And if anybody ever does that to you, you tell me and I'll throw them right out that fucking window. I mean it, right out that damn window." He pointed to a large window just to his right. Below was the entrance to the Irving Thalberg Building. My mind's eye suddenly saw him throwing people out the window to land on the tiered steps below. I thought, seems just, that's what studio presidents do, throw people out windows. I'll never forget his words, and he was big enough; he looked like he could throw somebody out a window. I wanted to be on his squad. He was charismatic, to say the least. I felt like when the battle began I would survive and maybe even earn more stripes. He said MGM was going to be very busy and successful in the months ahead, with both *CHiPs* and *Lucan* (that was the one about the boy with animal powers who had been raised by wolves) set to start and a number of pilots slated. I told him I'd be happy to work for him. He then took a call, shook my hand, and said, "Welcome, and remember what I said, right out the friggin' window, on their friggin' head. You work for me, you answer only to me, and that door is open to you any time. Don't forget it." He then said, "Oh, almost forgot, meet Ann down in casting. If you want somebody else, it's your call. It's your department, you're the director, bring in anybody you want. Oh, and Mike, NBC has their hand on the flush with respect to *CHiPs*. We got to pull it out of the crapper, Mike; the former producer is history here. He's barred from the lot, so don't worry about that. And Mike, Lew Gallo, a great guy, he's the producer of *Lucan*, the wolf-boy show. My girl will give you his number. Take a meeting with him as soon as possible." He then whispered, "I got to take this call, I'll talk to you later."

Needless to say, I was dancing on air as I left the Irving Thalberg Building. Hal Gefsky was right. It's psychological; always ask for more than you think you'll get. If you sell yourself at a bargain price they think you're ordinary and just average. If you seem expensive, they want you because you appear to be the high-end quality, top of the line, the more expensive choice, the best money can buy—and I was. I had no idea the position I had put my paddle tennis paddle down for was the director of the MGM Television Casting Department. I thought it was a casting assignment on a single show. I was ecstatic, to say the least. A department head title, no less; next I would earn a VP stripe.

I returned to Cy's office and informed him that I was official. I had accepted MGM's offer and the appointment of director of television casting. He congratulated me and then asked me to never look at any of the nine episodes that had been produced the previous season; it would serve no real purpose to do so, and could possibly taint my perception of the show. He then asked his secretary to take me downstairs to the casting department suite, where I was introduced to Ann Jarboe.

Ann Jarboe had worked for Gary Shafer during that very chaotic first season. Ann was some years my senior, a beautiful woman with an even greater inner beauty who postured strong organizational abilities. She had originally hailed from Kansas, and as a young woman had joined the Navy and worked her way up through the ranks to chief. She had been at MGM since the end of World War ll. Instinctively, I concluded an immediate evaluation and appraisal of the offices and decided that Ann Jarboe was extremely efficient, a team player, and probably would mother me some—maybe more than I wanted to be mothered, or was used to—but would give her all to any assignment. Mr. Montanus had said I could bring in any secretary I wanted, but after meeting and talking to Ann those few minutes, I loved her, trusted her, and felt her allegiance could be won, especially in that I had been in the Marines, and the Marine Corps was a part of her Navy. Ann reminded me of my mother and a dear aunt; it all felt very comfortable, like family. I took the position of "if it ain't broke, why fix it." Ann did warm to me; she always took care of me, and never let the slightest detail get by without reminding me. She was always checking and double-checking everything. "It's cold out, take your coat, Mike." I would learn later that Ann had never had children of her own, so I didn't mind.

For the remainder of that first day, I made calls and put the word out to the industry that I was back, and tried to forgive and forget any past misunderstandings that might have occurred through a clash of young, aggressive personalities. Theatrical agents often change offices and territories as well, and people grow up and mature, myself included. I turned the other cheek as I had been taught. I viewed it to be a new day and thought that perhaps those conflicting and clashing personalities were covering other studios and/or other shows. And if not, maybe like the other kid in the sandbox, they had grown up some, too.

Cy's office had delivered several scripts for me to read and start thinking about, and informed Ann and I that they were all in some stage of rewrite. Production on *CHiPs* was to begin about two weeks hence, with *Lucan* to follow, but the exact start dates were unconfirmed. When I left at day's end, Ann walked me out of our offices and gave me a short tour. She pointed to the direction of the studio commissary, where she said the food was a little pricey but good. She indicated that the offices just across the way were the Chartoff-Winkler suite, where Sylvester Stallone had done *Rocky* and was presently working on the sequel. Alan Carr was upstairs from us, producing the multimillion dollar television extravaganza *Super Train* (twenty-five to thirty million spent on just the set alone) for NBC. Considered a project under NBC's banner, they had their own casting director assigned out of Burbank. She indicated that the building just to the west of our offices was going to be demolished in the next weeks to make room for the new multimillion dollar MGM Film Laboratory. It would be a state-of-the-art facility, second to none, and we would have to deal with all the noise and dust of the project for the months to come.

The casting offices were mere steps from a guard's station on the east side of the lot I remembered coming through with my dear dad when I was not much bigger than a toddler. Ann went on to say that the talent for interviews would be checked in at the guard's station (Stan Sarniske and Danny Stein), and that an interview list was given to the guard sometime prior to the interviews, usually in the morning. Talent would then be directed to the casting office in the Gable building. Initially, when I had arrived for the interview with Cy Chermak I had passed through this guard's station, but he hadn't said the name of the building. The guard had just pointed for me to go upstairs. This was another surprise that day; the name of the building where my office was located was the Clark Gable Building. Ironic, I thought.

In the next few days, I met Bill Young, the unit production manager and associate producer for *CHiPs*, and California Highway Patrol technical advisor Bob Hayden (later Dave McDannel). I had meetings with Lew Gallo on *Lucan*, which was also readying scripts and hiring directors. Old friend Vic Morrow was set to direct at least one episode. I had worked with Vic at Columbia and was excited about working this genius talent again.

I had known Lew Gallo as a capable actor, a member of an ensemble cast of a television show I had assisted on while at Fox, spun off from the movie with the same title, *12 O'Clock High*. Lew had done a ton of work as an actor in supporting roles in huge films, opposite a great many very big stars of his era. He was certainly on the A-list for supporting roles, but never quite made the star list. I liked Lew a lot; he was very creative and had ambitious plans for the show's ultimate direction. The show's star, Kevin Brophy, was a complete unknown to me. I was totally unfamiliar with his work when I joined MGM.

The following week production start dates would be set, and I went to work making suggestion lists and checking availabilities for what would be the first possible episodes to go to the stage. I was also getting the rush from every agent in town, and had a constant flow of them and their tagalong clients coming through my office to talk talent and/or to set up meetings for other possibilities before I got bogged down with the slated production schedule. Another agent mentor of mine was Lew Sherrell. Mr. Sherrell had been with all the big offices in his early days, but had been on his own for many years at this point of time, and was old school. He was a regular at casting offices, after the Friars Club. He knew talent and had a very strong working client list. To him, I was the punk kid casting person that he liked. We would always kibitz and make each other laugh. I never forgot what he said to me once: "If you want to make the sale you have to look the buyer in the eye; the buyer you don't see face-to-face is the sale you won't make." I was still unpacking boxes when Ann buzzed and informed me that Lew was outside. I really liked and respected this guy a lot, but we played with each other's ego. I shouted "Whooooo?" loud enough for Lew and Ann to both hear me through the walls. At that, Lew entered doing Rodney Dangerfield's "I get no respect." I could hear Ann laughing in the outer offices. He congratulated me on my assignment and said immediately he had a great new kid in his stable that was going to be a big star. I interrupted him and said, "Lew, you're not going to believe this, but the guy you passed on your way in said exactly the same thing." Lew just smiled and took it in stride, and then said, "Forget what he said. I got a kid that can go the distance, he's very funny." He said it was a talented young chap named Jay Leno, who had already been a guest on *The Tonight Show* as a stand-up comedian, and he assured me that he was also a very good actor. Lew said that for the time being he's available, but that we'd better get him quick before somebody wrote a sitcom for him. Lew knew I liked funny, and I invited him to schedule an appointment with Ann for me to meet with him as soon as possible.

A few days later, I met with Jay Leno and immediately saw what Lew had seen in him. He was open and honest, charming, and a very witty young guy, but also quite offbeat-character-looking. At our meeting we talked mostly of old cars and shared information about some local collectors and car shows. I told him about my dad and Clark Gable, and of a 1941 Ford I had recently purchased with only sixty thousand original miles that had belonged to *Oklahoma!*'s Charlotte Greenwood and was still in marvelous shape. We even talked about getting together sometime socially; we liked each other. Lew called me later in the afternoon doing some follow-up and I told him that he was right; Jay Leno was funny and had a witty, very likeable personality. I had read a scene with him and thought he was a very good actor. I also told Lew that it would have to be some sort of character role; that he's not the run-of-the-mill, nondescript type; he had a very unique quality and look, with a jaw and chin that seemed to reach forever, maybe to Pasadena. Lew snickered and then said firmly, "Well, find something for him, he's going to be big." I said I'd try; that I liked him and would keep him in mind. I had jotted his name down a few times and talked to Lew about him, but as it turned out I was just never able to bring him in for anything; he was always busy. The next thing I knew, I heard he was guest hosting for Johnny Carson in his absence on *The Tonight Show,* and the rest is history. Guest hosting for Carson was tantamount to superstardom. I would have to have a bigger role and more money. Lew Sherrell would come around and rub it in, saying, "See, you had your chance; you had your chance, Hanks."

To the right of my desk at MGM were windows that extended the complete length of my office. Almost immediately the demolition of the building next door began. Between it and the Gable Building was no more than twenty feet, with the buildings being separated by this narrow street that ran south to the perimeter of the lot to Culver Boulevard. MGM's Music Department was located at the very end of the street. After several days of demolition, Ann and I smelled the repugnant scent almost at the same moment. I walked hurriedly into her office, and before I said a word she asked me, "Do you smell that?" It was very strong. A skunk had made a move out of the building being torn down and into the Gable Building. It was a horrible stench and permeated everything. At first, we thought of the country; skunk stories were coming from everybody in the building. Then, it wasn't funny anymore. They would send in animal control and pest extermination teams, never to find the little critter. At a meeting with Ed Montanus, he commented on the foul smell and threatened again to be rid of the problem by throwing the skunk out his window. "That is," he exclaimed as he chuckled, "if I could get my hands on it." Now my mind's eye saw a skunk come flying out his window, landing on the top of a heap of bodies. The foul skunk smell would linger; the ghastly odor seemed to worsen as our tolerance weakened. It would almost make us nauseous some days—disgusting. I would find any reason whatsoever to get out of the office. For about the first ten days after the great skunk invasion, I spent many hours viewing film or videos of suggested talent in screening rooms. I would take the Academy Players Directories with me, make calls, and prepare suggestion lists for both *CHiPs* and *Lucan* away from the office. It was refreshing to work without the nauseating skunk smell up my nostrils, poor Ann.

It was midmorning and I was still at my office desk, trying to get away and off the phone to leave to the fresher air of the viewing rooms. The morning had begun with a flurry of activity; the phone hadn't stopped ringing, and a number of agents had stopped by to see me. I needed to get some fresh air, away from the lingering smell, when my attention was drawn to the window to the right of my desk. A young woman was passing by, walking toward the music department. I had seen her pass once before, but this time I saw something that propelled me up and out of my office, and it wasn't the skunk smell. I had to meet her; there was something about her that I found enormously attractive.

My people instincts had been honed and fine-tuned to such a degree that I could sense honesty and integrity by watching a person for only a moment, especially if I could look into his or her eyes. Call it instinct, body language, or what have you, most times, even before the artist had said his or her name to me, I knew whose performance I was going to like best. I think it was Lee Strassberg who first pointed out this observation, this awareness, and I shared his conclusion. I excused myself to Ann, told her I'd be right back, and walked briskly around the corner of the Gable building and up the street. I caught this young woman just as she reached Ann's window, where I introduced myself. I explained that I did casting for MGM TV, and in an effort to make conversation I asked if she was an actress. I didn't really think she was, but thought that perhaps there was an outside chance and she had a meeting with someone, somewhere. She smiled and said that she wasn't an actress, and had no aspirations to be one, either. She said that she had recently relocated from Arizona to go to school, and that for the time being she had secured a position in the music department. I was so taken with her that I immediately asked if she might be interested in getting some dinner with me after work. She declined, saying she had plans, and then added quickly that the plans were with her aunt and uncle, whom she was living with temporarily. I think she felt my disappointment; I sensed she was explaining further because she wanted me to know she was single and available. I also sensed a very strong, immediate, mutual attraction, a natural liking for each other; the mystic energy. She gave me her extension number and I told her I would call.

I came back into the office bursting with another kind of excitement. It was that magic something happening that I had forgotten really existed. Since my separation I'd dated a few high-maintenance, beautiful women, but none that I had been truly attracted to spiritually, not for a very long time. I was thinking she might like me for who I am as a person and not my power-brokering job. Ann said she could see it all over our faces as she watched us through her window. She added, "She likes you, Mike, I could tell." I smiled and said, "I didn't even smell the skunk when I was out there, Annie." Ann quipped, "It must be love." I smiled big and returned to my desk, to continue making casting suggestion lists and setting up audition interviews, but my mind was filled with the scent of this beautiful person. She had filled my being.

The next day, I called and invited her to the viewing room during her lunch to watch some film with me. We talked and began to really open up to each other. It was all very nice; I really liked this young woman. An inner honesty and a beauty much larger than mere surface appeal was what I saw through my window that morning. She was very intelligent and there were no facades. She came from a large family, with five older brothers and two older sisters, and I would discover she had learned to fend for herself; she was very real and fearless. Several lunch dates, and just as many meetings viewing film and actor's tapes had passed, and I was again enjoying her humor and fresh, unaffected views and input as we watched more film in the screening room on her lunch break. She knew who and what she liked in film and what she didn't. She knew current films, the old ones, and the ones that weren't big at the box office, but she thought they were good and knew why. She had strong intelligent opinions and I liked that. Then it happened; I very innocently leaned in her direction when hanging up the phone after speaking with Ann and our eyes, lips, and hearts suddenly seemed to be drawn together like magnets, symbiotically all interwoven. Eternities later we came up for air, and I thought I knew what a passionate kiss was. I was soon to forget every beautiful kiss I had ever known. It was a wonderful first kiss, a bewitching moment. She whispered in my ear, "What took you so long? I thought you'd never kiss me. I wanted you to kiss me when we first met on the street." And we kissed again, and I whispered that I had felt the same attraction for her. Instinctively, I felt those first kisses had begun a romance where we wouldn't be able to keep our hands off each other and the passion didn't care about where we were, either.

That first evening together was so very special; we fell in love. We were entranced with each other, and it was so much more that mere physical attraction. The world had taken on a whole new appearance and had an exciting new energy and meaning that had begun to reveal itself, as if it all happened before. My apartment at the beach was a one-room flat with a very small bath, and was drafty and cold at night. When the lights were on you could see almost everything, even some of the bathroom. I turned toward my postage-stamp-size corner kitchen and started hustling to gather some wine and snacks. "It's nice bumping into to you again," she would say, as she had followed to assist me. The kitchen floor space was only big enough for one person. It was hard not bumping if there was another person there, but human-attraction magnets were at work, too. I had learned to prepare a nice meal for myself, my sons, and occasional guests, fast, if nobody was in my way. Suddenly, she was crossing and we were bumping in the mutual search for stuff. It was very cramped, and those magnets were bumping and attracting, and we were liking it. We hadn't been out dancing yet; this would be our first, stand-up slow dance, I really liked being close to her. She was me and I her, we both could feel it.

Then came another sweet, wonderful, life-giving kiss, after which she turned and disappeared into the bathroom. A moment after the flush I heard the tub filling with water. Perhaps she wanted to take a bath, I thought. I placed the wine and snacks close by and went to work trying to get the heater on for some room warmth. I was about to give up on it when I noticed steam filling the room. As she entered, she gently suggested that I suspend my attempts with the broken heater, to warm with a hot bath before going to dinner. I hadn't taken a tub bath with anyone since my brother Irv and I flooded the house when I was about seven; this is what I saw, the great house flood again. I hadn't even taken a bath with my wife before for this reason; a shower, yes, but not a bath, in a tiny tub. As she continued her sweet persuasion, this time after the kiss she whispered that she'd learned the two warmest places on earth were in a hot bath or under the covers. Those images and sudden thoughts of tender kisses began to warm, mesmerize, and arouse all my senses. I was truly enchanted now and thinking of other warm things. This would be a first of many firsts with this angel and no flooded house. For another heartbeat we continued sharing bites of apple, sipping wine from first our glasses, then our lips. Maybe it was the wine, maybe it was her beautiful kisses, or maybe it was the wine-kisses, but my shyness of the possibility of being childlike naked with her in a tiny bathtub was quickly diminishing. Then, back into the steam she would disappear, and then reappear, angel-like, through the surrealistic cloud, stepping from the brightly lit bathroom with more enticing, affectionate, distracting, wine-flavored kisses. I suddenly felt embryonic, like something inside me needed to swim in her water. Her warm touch was finally getting more of my attention than the defective heater. "Get warm with me, we don't need the heater," she would say. As we kissed again, I smiled and whispered that I could get warm without the bath too, that I had a built-in heater.

She laughed, then kissed me again and asked that I warm her with it.

She had taken control without hesitation. Like a couple of very natural, healthy and happy young people, she would lead me, and I would follow, and I loved it and I loved her. I'll never forget the laughs as we rolled and sudsy-splashed and frolicked around, trying to stay warm in that very small bathtub on that cold night, creating indelible moments. I adored this young woman and I knew I had blossomed in her heart as well. It was real, very real. We were suddenly one, and we would become inseparable.

Production had begun and it was becoming very busy and hectic on both shows. Both Tim Carey and my laughing cousin Lindy Heidt visited me at my new post. Tim would look out my window and point in the direction of Veteran's Memorial Park, remember where we had met, and say something like, "Look at you now, the head of casting—at MGM, no less." Lindy would laugh his hysterical laugh, get Ann laughing, close my office door, and say that I should give it all up and become a full-time actor; that I had too much talent to do casting. I replied with something like, "Yeah, right, you'll be my agent and pay my bills too."

The workload those first few months prompted me to get to the job early, and I often worked late into the evening reading scripts and making suggestion or interview lists for the shows that were slated ahead. My beautiful friend had become even closer to my heart and was always waiting for me at home; often calling and telling me of waiting gourmet meals and sudsy baths, among other naughty visual and very pleasant thoughts she would conjure up for my distraction. On about her second or third call, I would decide to be finished and go home to the food of life.

The revitalized, reenergized *CHiPs* would become a huge hit, too. Those first ratings were extremely good and the audience continued to grow. Production changes had brought a new creative energy to all involved. I had honestly thought the show's concept and the production values to be little better than *The Brady Bunch*; at best, a kids' cop show. The demographics said I was slightly wrong; that a great many adults were watching as well, a possible captured audience of the huge teenage girl following of Erik Estrada and his blond partner, Larry Wilcox. People were watching; what did I care if it was mindless television? For the moment I was gainfully employed. When it was canceled I would be assigned a more favorable and realistic MGM project, I thought. Cy had firmly stated to me that there was only one casting director on *CHiPs* and it was he who held that position. I had learned not to make waves and to go with the flow. Although Mr. Montanus had made statements about throwing people out windows, I knew that this possibility was especially unlikely to occur when confronted with the huge and enormous egos of the so-called "hit-show producer."

At various times at the beginning of the season, I had received a number of calls checking my availability and my contentment at MGM, as I had once again reemerged as a "name" casting director. John Conboy had even called and made a very pleasant inquiry about the possibility of my returning to *The Young and The Restless.* He would say *Y&R* wasn't the same without me; that I had brought an energy to the show that was very much missed; that it had been a huge mistake allowing me to leave. I thanked him for his complimentary words, but explained that for the time being I thought I would stay at MGM. It was home to me, and that's what I chose to do.

I would continue in diligent pursuit, to bring to *CHiPs,* and the other MGM projects slated, those very strong and interesting actors that could draw an audience to even the smallest of character supporting roles. I had always felt almost any knucklehead could draft the A-list names onto a suggestion list for a role; it was knowledge of the supporting actor list where the real casting talent lay. I always first approached those that I thought were the very best and the most appealing, no matter how offbeat or unknown. I went for the talent I thought was right for a role, and always tried hard to sell the idea, with little regard to the always-present theatrical agency politics or to a production manager's budget. My creative first choices were always at the top of my lists, even though I knew I wouldn't be able to get some because of money or the "he doesn't do episodic television" factor. "Names" and choices at the top of my suggestion lists would always spawn ideas of other actors that were similar in some way. Actors that I could get for my money and weren't above doing television, and I always had numerous unknowns as backups, the talented untried and untested always close by.

MGM had always considered itself a motion picture film production company first, with television being an evolutionary by-product. During my tenure, MGM enjoyed one of its most successful television periods in its history. Ann Jarboe said to me one day that I left no stone unturned looking for talent; that previous department heads had never brought so much attention, vigor, excitement, and publicity to the MGM Casting Department before. I was proud of her comments and thought perhaps my tenacious methods and actor/sales abilities were again paying off some.

In that second season, my first on *CHiPs*, Paul Linke would reoccur on a freelance if available basis for a number of episodes. I had known Paul's talents mostly as an improvisational comedic actor, but he was also being pitched as a fairly good dramatic actor. We finally put him under contract as a series regular for fear of losing him. I was also informed that we would add a few more characters to the regular cast, one of which would be a possible foil to all the cast members, but probably to Paul Linke's Officer Grossman character most. This character was going to be the intellectual mechanic who was neat and orderly in the greasy garage setting. He was a scientist who was efficient, meticulous, and a very natty dresser who never seemed to get dirty. His character name was Harlan. Grossman and Harlan were to be the fun, the comic relief in most scenes that Cy and the writers would create. Viewers began to look more and more for their comedic interaction and exchanges. I had several ideas for the Harlan role, but Lou Wagner was one I thought of right away. His agent, Pat Amaral, had been selling him to me every week. I brought in Lou during the first group of Harlan interviews. Cy seemed to approve of Lou almost immediately, but we backed ourselves up with several other good choices to cover our buttocks with those jerks at the network. Lou Wagner would get network approval and be "set" in the role of Harlan on our first go-round.

Cy, MGM, and NBC then decided *CHiPs* should add a female to the ensemble cast, that of a cute, perky, intelligent, and personable young woman. At first it was Brianne Leary, but for whatever reason we replaced Brianne with Randy Oakes. Jerks is jerks. They were both fine for what this show was, but somebody at the network wanted something different. There was also the addition of a black policeman to the *CHiPs* squad. The handsome Lew Saunders was first set for the role, and worked on a freelance basis in a number of episodes. But word came down to me that, for similar reasons, somebody at the network didn't like what he was doing. I was even more ready for this change, as Ed Montanus again informed me that MGM was nearly ready with a pilot script based on the distinguished black Army regiment of the late 1800s known as *The Buffalo Soldiers*, to be directed by Vincent McEveety. Having done *That's My Mama* in the early '70s, I had fairly extensive lists of the more established black artists, but was less confident of the younger talent pools.

New talent is always evolving and emerging from the New York theater and off-off-off-Broadway. Every free moment I had was devoted specifically to interviewing, reading, and culling through every new black actor/actress I wasn't familiar with. I would meet anyone who was recommended and, as always, those that had no representation. After several months of these general interviews, I had strong ideas in all categories. I was very confident my newcomer first-choice replacement for the Lew Saunders role was going to around for a while, and that I could sell him to Cy Chermak and NBC. His name was Michael Dorn. I had advised him several times to be patient; that I would eventually find a role in something for him. He did his homework by staying in touch; he stayed in front of the people doing the buying, at MGM and elsewhere. He would call or drop by to first visit Ann and then me. Above all, he was a good actor who was personable and likable. I'd always found it easier to think about someone if you knew he or she was well adjusted and pleasant to be around. Sometimes, the artist is a nutcase personally, or boasts an inflated perception of himself or herself, but what he or she brings to the camera is magic. So, in spite of his or her abilities to make dazzling contributions, most folks don't want to be around this kind of artist on a personal level for very long. But Michael Dorn was a very pleasant young man. And when I called him in for the possible series regular role, I think he fell out of his chair, he was so shocked. I think I was just as happy as he was when I called him and told him he had been approved by the powers that be, and that we were going to try him.

Earlier that week I had read a script, and for the second time had tried to find Regis Philbin and get an availability from his agents/managers for a lead character on *CHiPs*. Was he in town and could he be available? Would he work for our money? The usual inquiry. Remember, this was at a time when Regis was between gigs, too, not really doing a whole lot. No daytime morning show yet, and not much else. But when you talk to the agent, he's hotter than a baker's apron, up for this, up for that. Well, he was certainly up for us, so it was likely that likeable Regis Philbin was wanted by other programs as well. I always thought Regis was a huge talent. As a young man I watched as much of *The Joey Bishop Show* as my young, busy, hormones would allow. I grew up on Regis and on that show. He was definitely a positive role model, a positive image, and a glib reactor for Joey. I would have been happy to have used him on anything I was involved with at MGM; I liked him, and my instincts were that he was a good guy. Remember what I said about leaning toward hiring nice folks; it just makes it easier. When I walked in the next morning, Ann informed me that Regis's agent had just called and that I should call them as soon as possible regarding his schedule. I asked Ann to place the call and I got on the line. I heard her announce my name and that I was returning the call, and then I heard Regis say loudly, "Mike Hanks, he's the only one that ever thinks of me." We both laughed as he came on the line. He was very gracious, thanking me again for trying to get him on an MGM show, but said he thought our dates were going to conflict again with another, less meaningful previous engagement. We chatted for a few beats and I could sense this man was a true, gentle, sincere person with a keen comedic edge. I liked him in spite of his allegiance to Notre Dame; nobody's perfect, I thought. Anyway, due to the way he recognized me as he came to the phone, I became instant-fan-forever man.

My new love had almost moved in with me at the beach and my sons loved her; we were absolute bliss together. We seemed to have so much in common; we were so alike in so many incredible ways. In those first months we had vigorously discussed nearly every topic that was of interest to us. Often, our in-depth conversations would prompt one of us to report back to the other with additional information, from some published scholarly sources, for our mutual edification. We seemed to enjoy the same kinds of books and films, and word games, and if time permitted she would attempt to beat me at my favorite table game, backgammon. We always seemed to know what the other was thinking, and always, always would be searching for what might make the other grin and laugh, from dawn to lights out and beyond. She seemed to be a natural extension of me and I of her. Once, she would say that it was her belief that our chemistry, our attraction to and adoration for each other was like an energy that's always existed, as if we had known and loved each other before, in some other time and place; that we were made for each other and predestined to connect again. A penetrating notion, wisdom perhaps, spawned from intuition way beyond her years. I, too, had felt from that first moment when our eyes had engaged and had become filled with each other, that I had known her before in some other orbit of time; perhaps only in my dreams.

Then I received a call from my former wife, who explained that she wanted to relocate to Hawaii with her new fellow. I was happy for her, but diametrically opposed to either my sons moving out of state or of liquidating and selling the family home to possibly further disrupt and unsettle their world. Finally, after long, hard discussions we reached an agreement whereby I would return to our home as the guardian of our older sons, and would foster their care until they finished high school without further disruption before we would sell and split the assets. Our youngest son, Jonathan, would accompany his mother. It was very difficult to concede on this point, but because of his age maybe he needed her most. Ultimately, I felt that he would want to return and rejoin his brothers and me when he began missing us more. At first they all went to Hawaii, but Chris and Doyle would return for school in September. I had given up the Venice apartment and moved back to my home in Culver City, where my best friend and I set up housekeeping and proceeded to fall deeper in love.

The new film laboratory next door had been completed and the skunk fragrance was almost completely gone. Occasionally, we'd get a whiff of something that would bring back the awful nauseous times of that first season. Well into the second season I got a call from Tim Carey one morning. Tim was of Italian heritage; his real surname was Agoglia. He apologized for the short notice, but explained that he had been able to arrange an impromptu screening of some of his film work for his Italian brother and his huge fan, Sylvester Stallone. A very nice fan to have, I agreed. He wanted me to come to the screening, and asked me to drop what I was doing and join them in a projection room of the Irving Thalberg Building. Fortunately, I wasn't knee deep in readings and had a lull in my morning schedule. I could break

"Rocky's" lunchtime opponent now guards my backyard.

away for *Rocky*, and it was close. The truth was, I would tear away no matter what I had scheduled.

I met Mr. Stallone when I entered while Tim waved and proceeded to give the projectionist instructions of what he wanted on the screen first. This was a performance in itself. Tim had acted, directed, and produced, with the aid of family and friends, a couple scenes from original screenplays he had written (Tweets, ladies of Pasadena). The lights faded and for about ten minutes Sylvester Stallone and I howled and belly laughed like we were old-time buddies. We had the rare distinction of seeing Tim Carey doing comedy, a genre where he had always been overlooked. When the lights came back up, we exchanged comments on his work and were still chuckling as I hurriedly shook their hands again and excused myself.

As I rushed back to the casting office, I noticed something out of my peripheral that caught my attention. In front of the of the Chartoff-Winkler suite where Sylvester Stallone's office was located, I saw a life-size cutout photographic poster of George C. Scott in a policeman's uniform, from a film he had starred in for Chartoff-Winkler entitled *The New Centurions.* It was the kind of life-size cutout display utilized at the theaters to advertise upcoming films. At the bottom it had the Chartoff-Winkler production credits. The heavy cardboard and black-and-white photographic material was broken across the middle, across Mr. Scott's stomach. It was also broken at the neck, with Mr. Scott's head bending forward slightly. I actually had to push the broken head up to see who it was. There he stood, holding a police baton at the ready,

George C. Scott, LAPD. I stepped into the Chartoff-Winkler office, inquired about it and was told it was trash, headed for the dumpster. The receptionist went on to explain that it had previously adorned Mr. Stallone's office while in production on *Rocky*; that Mr. Stallone had at times gotten the best of Mr. Scott during the filming and had beaten him up with flurries of unprovoked and uncontested punches on his lunch breaks. I replied that I'd always heard Mr. Scott was bit of a tough guy, too, and that he hadn't fought back was hard to believe. I was invited to take it if I wanted it, and I did. I thought my boys might like to have it hanging around in their bedroom. I was still amused at Tim Carey's antics when I returned and explained to Ann what I'd seen and had been told of how Mr. Scott had sustained his injuries. I introduced her to George C. and then propped him up in his new temporary position, at the far corner of my office entrance, just in time for my preliminary casting meeting with the next week's *CHiPs* director, John Florea.

A few days later, I was again working late when the regular lady that cleaned my office stuck her head in and said, "Oh, Mike, you're still here." She then started laughing, shaking her head and snickering. She said, "The other night I was dusting and cleaning and singing and talking to myself. I hadn't seen big ole George standing there in the corner before, and I turned and George there seemed to jump out at me. I jumped back so hard I fell over backwards onto into your sofa here, and then I started laughing so hard I had to go to the restroom." She swore to me that George had moved at her. "Trying to get me on that couch." She laughed and went on, "Everything I've heard about those casting couches must be true." She said she would come back to do my office later if I would see to it that George would just stay still. We were both laughing as I assured her I'd have a talk with Mr. Scott about his behavior.

In early part of 1979, I heard through the grapevine that John Wayne was very sick. I felt I wanted to contact him, and send our good wishes and heartfelt prayers for a complete and speedy recovery. I didn't think he would remember our meeting at Paramount. I composed a short note and asked Ann Jarboe to get it off to him as soon as possible. In the note I asked some off-the-wall questions concerning stories I'd heard about him, Ward Bond, and Victor Jory. I didn't really expect to get a response; I just wanted to tell him that we were thinking of him. Almost immediately I received a note in return, answering my questions. It made Ann and me feel really good that we had somehow touched him in his last days.

My love had been much missed on her most recent visit to her parents' home. Her previous visits back home had been for shorter periods. I had missed her terribly, and my sons, who had bonded with her big-sister presence, were showing signs that they, too, missed her fun and energy. It had been our longest separation, four days, and I couldn't wait to hold her in my arms. When she came in the door, we didn't let go of each other until I had to get up and start getting ready for work the next morning, and even then we kept falling back into surrender. We both would be late for work that Monday morning.

Items that came up that morning included a conversation about us getting married and having at least one little blessed child that would be hers and mine together. The concept of marriage didn't bother me; what was becoming a problem for me was the idea of having more children. She wanted to have children with me. She loved me deeply and I, her. The thought of having a child with her was an absolutely beautiful idea, but my concern of starting a second family was due to my youngest son being so far away that he might begin to generate and harbor resentments and jealousies of a new sibling. My older boys were here and could be part of it, and not be threatened by their dad giving love to a new baby. I was really concerned about my youngest son, Jonathan, and how he might feel. I expressed my feelings to her, and she would say in the most enticing way something like, "Don't you want to make a baby with me?" I loved this woman so much I wanted anything she wanted. I even wanted this with her, but I was having a very hard time committing to it. Long periods would go by and it would not come up, but then we would see a lovely baby somewhere and we'd be talking about it. This would become the only issue where we had a real difference of opinion, where, in the final analysis, our individual needs and desires were very different; our only source of conflict.

The work load seemed to increase, I working longer days, spending more and more time at the office. I started considering the idea of getting an assistant. I had thought about it a couple of times before, but had

March 16, 1979

Mr. John Wayne
Newport Beach,
California

Dear Mr. Wayne:

We here in the MGM T. V. Casting Department (which
consists of my secretary, Anne Jarboe, and myself)
would like to relate to you the countless good
wishes and thoughts of love we see and hear, on
a daily basis, from your friends in the Industry.

Get well, and let's do a picture.

                    Sincerely,

                    MICHAEL O. HANKS
                    Director of T. V. Casting

MOH aj

PS: Is it true that Victory Jory took you and
Ward Bond in a scuffle one night somewhere in
No. Hollywood? It's Industry scuttlebut.

A note to an American legend.

JOHN WAYNE

9570 Wilshire Blvd., Suite 400
Beverly Hills, California
March 27, 1979

Mr. Michael O. Hanks
MGM
10202 West Washington Boulevard
Culver City, California 90230

Dear Mike:

I appreciate very much your thoughtful note.

To answer your question concerning Victor
Jory, we have always been good friends
with respect for each other. Victor Jory
out-manuvered, let's say, Big Boy Williams
one night in a pretty heated scuffle; and I
guess both of them have taken Bond, but I
never had trouble with either of them--not
even a nice friendly fight. I'll tell you
something; that Victor Jory was a helluva
man. Pound for pound, I guess he was as
good as any man in his era.

Again, many thanks for the kind thoughts
from you and Miss Jarboe.

Sincerely,

John Wayne

JW/mm

A pillar of strength to the end.

kept telling myself I could handle it until such time as more pilots were slated. I had thought that maybe it would be a good idea to get someone to help Ann with the phones and setting up interviews. Once, when it had gotten really crazy, we enlisted assistance from the secretarial pool, of what was referred as a "roving secretary," to come in and help Ann for a few days. In Ann's office, there was another workstation all set up with phones and a desk. We were at a steady, very busy pace, and I was seriously thinking about some real assistance. I had casually and very discreetly made inquiries around town of some possibilities and availabilities. I hadn't started the interview process, but had made some notes of whom I thought I might like to meet.

A few days later, I got a call from Sidney Lassick of *One Flew Over the Cuckoo's Nest* fame. Sidney played the cigarette-obsessed role of Cheswick. Sid and I had become friends long before *Cuckoo's Nest*. He had always reminded me of Abbott and Costello regular Joe Mell. I loved Joe Mell and Sid had a similar sissy-funny quality. If I had something Sid was right for, he was there, on the interview, but he seldom worked for me. Sidney informed me that he had heard that I was looking for an assistant, and that he had always wanted to learn casting. He said he thought casting was very creative work. I explained that it was my belief that the colors/qualities of the film canvas are shaped by the qualities of the actors used, and to have those keen insights and do it well was great art. He enthusiastically and wholeheartedly agreed. He convinced me that he could help out, would do so without interfering, and without pay for a while

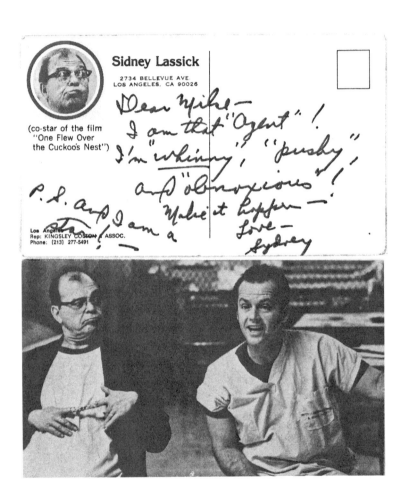

Sidney Lassick

2734 BELLEVUE AVE.
LOS ANGELES, CA 90026

(co-star of the film
"One Flew Over
the Cuckoo's Nest")

Los Angeles
Rep: KINGSLEY COSTON & ASSOC.
Phone: (213) 277-5491

Dear Mike —
I am that "Agent"!
I'm "whiny", "pushy",
and "obnoxious"!
P.S. and I am a   Make it happen —
                    Love —
                    Sydney

until we could make a decision about hiring someone. I talked it over with Ann, and called Sidney and asked him to be at the office the next morning, at about nine thirty a.m. He was delirious with excitement.

The next morning he showed up promptly as instructed, but by noon we both knew it would never work out. Ann was so used to handling every detail by herself, and to have Sidney's very inquisitive, nervous personality invading her each and every move was too much for her. At about five that afternoon, Ann came into my office, shut the door behind her, and expressed in a very kind and gentle tone that she had become very fond of Sidney; she liked him, and said she thought he was wonderful in *Cuckoo's Nest* with Jack Nicholson. But then her tone changed. The former Navy chief blurted out, "But he's driving me crazy, too. This is the real world, it's not a *Cuckoo's Nest.* It's either him or me, Mike, either he goes or I go." What followed was a kind of nervous laugh from us both as I calmed her. He was driving both of slightly stir-crazy in less than eight hours. I fully understood. The bottom line: Sidney Lassick was not right for this role. A superb talent in the right role, but sitting next to the former Navy chief was not it. I called Sidney into my office and explained it all to my friend. We laughed about it, and with a teary-eyed look he said he fully understood, and I explained that I felt Ann just simply worked better alone.

We were now well into my second season of *CHiPs* and I was feeling fairly secure with the show's continued and growing success. *Lucan* was not so fortunate, it had been cancelled. I had cast MGM's *Buffalo Soldiers* pilot, and had assembled another distinguished cast that included John Beck, Stan Shaw, Don Knight, Angel Tomkins, Charles Robinson, Hilly Hicks, and Richard Lawson, to name a few. Production was completed, but not even a minimum order would come in from the network. Astounding. It was now down to just *CHiPs*, and I was starting to sense some clashing and uneasiness between Mr. Chermak and myself. I had finally been successful in selling the idea of using Tim Carey for an episode entitled "Kidnap," opposite another favorite actor, Warren Berlinger. Chermak had finally relinquished and consented, as the possibilities for the role we were considering him for were limited and our choices meager at that point in time. At least Tim Carey was a well-known, recognizable face. Most of what we had listed as acceptable first choices for this role didn't want to do television, or especially *CHiPs*, which wasn't considered a real drama or a show that an actor needed on his resume. Some agents had called it "junk," trendy TV, and didn't want or need their name clients to work it. But they always had someone down on their lists that would work it, who needed a recent credit, but these choices weren't the ones we sought.

Tim Carey had always been a hard sell to anyone due to the fact that he had a reputation of being a very unconventional, off-the-wall Method actor that would sometimes bring his own improvisational dialogue twist to the action and story. If you were unaccustomed to working with this kind of artist it might throw you, because you might not know what would come next or how to handle it. And it might disrupt your timing, delivery, and performance, and just plain piss you off. A lot of great actors have been quoted as saying they detest this style of performance. But, too, many of our best and most memorable film moments have been improvised acting. "Are you talking to me?" DeNiro improvised those moments in *Taxi Driver*. Tim had done a lot of work for Cassavetes in *The Killing Of A Chinese Bookie*, for Stanley Kubrick in *Paths of Glory*, and for Marlon Brando in *One-Eyed Jacks*, but these were big films, with lots of time and money, and we were doing television. In television, every word on the printed page has been weighed very carefully for story substance and timing, so that it can be edited together precisely without having to re-shoot someone's close-up to fit an unexpected improvised change. With all the above concerns, Cy Chermak reluctantly had given me the thumbs-up to hire Tim Carey.

In this episode, the great Warren Berlinger and Tim played two dimwitted escaped convicts. Warren Berlinger had no problems working off Tim's unpredictable style. Unfortunately for me, from Mr. Chermak's view, it was a casting calamity. I would be reminded and scolded almost on a daily basis, in front of anyone who was close, that using Tim Carey was my idea, that he wasn't sticking to the written dialogue, and that it was quickly becoming a disaster. Cy Chermak was most unhappy. After the browbeating dust had settled, I closely observed the outcome of this specific episode. The director, film editor, and other technicians of film were able to put it together with little more difficulty than any other problem episode, and most episodes had some sort of problem. Problems happen when a show is not on the stage every day and is constantly on the move like *CHiPs* was.

When the "Kidnap" episode aired, the Nielsen ratings during the second half hour were actually higher than in the first half hour of the show. This might suggest the possibility that a viewer who doesn't necessarily recognize an actor's name from *TV Guide* or the newspaper listings has channel-hopped and seen a recognizable face; this was Tim Carey. The viewer doesn't necessarily know his name, but recognizes him, stops, and watches another interesting performance. "Kidnap" was a very amusing episode of *CHiPs*, if not the funniest and most memorable one, especially for me. Warren Berlinger laughed as he told me later, "It's not *King Lear*, Mike. I don't know what the fuss was about, it was a fun shoot."

Then there was the chap who claimed he was an expert on a motorcycle. He had read and met with me, Cy, the director, and the associate producer, and we liked his acting and hired him. He was a competent actor for what it was, but when it came time for him to ride a motorcycle, he nearly fell over. His riding skills were a total fiasco. No one ever thought to test his claim of being a skilled motorcyclist; the producer, associate producer, and director never thought to make it clear that this specific role required good riding skills. After the actor got to the set and when he kept falling over, I knew more browbeating would come, since casting got all the blame. Again the director found solutions, but I wouldn't hear the end of it for some time. The lows of the casting process.

One morning, it was about ten thirty a.m. when Erik Estrada dropped by to see me. He would frequently stop by my office and introduce me to one of his tagalong friends he was trying to help out; he was very generous this way. On this occasion he had no tagalong friends, he just popped in to see me, punched George C. Scott a couple of times, and laughed his infectious laugh. We were chatting and laughing, as I had followed him out of my office to the exterior of the Gable Building offices. We were just talking about anything, but mostly the show's progress, when into the guard's station drove the giant talent, Steve McQueen, in a very bright and shiny Rolls-Royce. Like a little kid, Eric suddenly whispered to me, "That's Steve McQueen! That's Steve McQueen!" We were both star-struck. Erik caught Steve's eye and approached him, saying, "I've always been a fan of your work," and extending his hand. Steve McQueen returned the compliment by saying that he had watched him on *CHiPs* and liked what he was doing. Erik then said, "Do you know Mike Hanks? He does our casting." Steve McQueen and I shook hands and he said, "You're doing very good work, Mike." I responded with, "It would be an honor to work with you one day, sir." He said, "Well, maybe we'll do that. Maybe we'll all do that." He waved to Erik and me as he drove onto the lot. I was beside myself with excitement, but I think Erik was even more excited. We walked around for a couple beats, just like a couple kids, uttering, "Steve McQueen. That was really Steve McQueen."

I had always thought Steve McQueen was one of the most unrecognized artists around. Several months later, it was disclosed that Steve McQueen was ill. We would lose him before the year's end.

Then the poop hit the fan again. I had talked Troy Donohue into doing an episode of *CHiPs*. Previously, Troy Donohue had received as much notoriety and worldwide publicity as anyone on the planet, and to get him for *CHiPs* was huge, even then. I had suggested my son Christopher for the role of Troy's son in the episode, because he looked like he could be Troy's son, and without being biased he was the best child actor of his type and age around town. Chris came in and read for Cy Chermak and the director, and I was given approval to hire him for the seven-day shoot. Everything was fine until Cy Chermak discovered that Chris was actually my son. He said, "You slipped one past me." I could tell he was pissed. My position was that I presented, for consideration, all talent suited for the role and that he had selected my son. He had seen all possibilities and had selected the best there was, which happened to be Chris. I had brought him in under another name because I didn't want anyone to be influenced knowing that he was my son. I felt it should not be a factor; that it should be an unbiased selection. No explanation worked. He found a reason to give me more hell, and he was seething. I honestly had thought it the only fair way for Chris to be considered, but Cy viewed it as deception and chose to make it into a disaster. I felt that if Cy could have fired me right then and there, he would have. After I had given my best explanation on the matter, he then leered at me and I stepped out of his office. For several days I would feel his wrath. Chris knew nothing of this.

Then, about the fourth day of the shoot, Chris barged into my office and closed the door loudly behind him. I was sitting at my desk sorting through other problems when he shouted, "Dad, I hate this fucking business! I just sit around and wait! I want to go and play baseball!" I remember that the hair on the back of my neck actually bristled. I reminded him to watch his language. I was immediately thinking that if I had to replace my own son, in light of what already had happened, and they were forced to re-shoot what they already had in the can, I would be history at MGM, for sure. I asked him to calm down and tell me what the problem was. He calmed down and repeated to me that he wasn't having any fun anymore; that he could care less about working on the stupid *CHiPs* show. He repeated his desire to go to the park with his friends and play baseball. I confided with him that I shared his conclusion and felt the same way about the stupid show, but reminded him it was the stupid show that was paying the bills. I explained that I never really cared that he work or that he should pursue acting as a vocation, but that it was simply an opportunity that had presented itself to our family, like the artist's son that becomes an artist or the doctor's son that becomes a doctor. I further explained that because he was around it, he might learn and gain something from the experience. I expressed my feeling that I always wanted him to follow his heart and do what made him the happiest; that his mother and I had thought it a good way to sock some money away for his college education, as long as he was having fun and it wasn't affecting him in a harmful or negative way. I also pointed out the reality to him; that is, if I had to replace him, it would probably be the last thing I would do at MGM. I then asked Chris if he would agree to finish the shoot for me, and in turn I would call his agents at once and tell them emphatically, in his presence, that until further notice Chris Hanks had gone into retirement. He agreed, we shook hands, and as promised, in his presence I made the calls, to his satisfaction. We then hugged each other, talked of his pitching, and I walked him back to the *CHiPs* salt mines, where for the next several days he finished his job. For the rest of that summer he played baseball, and hasn't worked as an actor since finishing that episode.

I was having problems at home as well, experiencing a great deal of personal conflict within myself. I had been destroying and pushing the love of my life away for what I viewed as very noble reasons; her maternal instincts were her right and her need was intense. I wanted her to leave me for only this reason, to have that experience. I was tormented; it hurt me deeply to suggest that she leave. She had packed her car with all her belongings three different times over this very same issue. Two of those times, I had watched her cross back and forth at the intersections at both ends of the street. Then, I would hear her car coming around the corner with a burst of speed and brake to an abrupt stop in my driveway. We would smile and laugh, and then race to each other with open arms and watering-eyed kisses. That third time, her plea to have a family with me was met with coldness and seemingly uncaring rudeness. I loved her so much, but wanted her to find her happiness. I felt compelled to let her go.

She returned to my arms that last and final time, but when I woke in the morning she had gone. I didn't want to accept it. I raced through the house feeling like an abandoned child, searching to discover her hiding, to finally teach me, but she was gone. I was beside myself with grief; she had finally left while I slept. We had several lighthearted conversations after her return to her parents' home during the days that followed. I missed her; maybe I would change my position on this one item, she would say. We spoke of her coming back; we also spoke of her finding work and other options.

I ventured along in my work, more time passed, and I was completely miserable and lost without her. Then, she came to visit for a couple of days at the end of December, to celebrate New Year's Eve. On the afternoon of January 1, 1980, she brought her brother by to say hello and I acted aloof and distant. I called her the next day and was told she didn't want to talk to me. I had succeeded, I thought, I was now suffering the absolute worst kind of horrible pain imaginable. I had pushed this angel, this wonderful person, my forever soul mate away, but never completely from my heart.

Several years later, I was back at MGM having lunch when I ran into a mutual friend of ours. I would learn that she had married and delivered into the world a beautiful God-sent child.

I had used Patti Davis regularly doing voice-over work on *CHiPs* and she would come by and sign her day-player contracts when she would work. On occasion, she would stop in and we'd chat for a few minutes, mostly about show business; who was doing what, who was going to be doing what, and projects she might be right for. At the time I was almost totally uninformed when it came to current politics. I just didn't have time for it, and I especially didn't know much of her father's (Ronald Reagan) politics, either. I knew only that he had run for the Republican presidential nomination in 1976 and incredibly had received only one electoral vote. I remembered also that Patti had been vocal and not too terribly crazy about her dad's position on some of the issues. We continued chatting as I worked; I remember it like it was yesterday. The conversation had come full circle back to politics when I asked what she thought his chances might be that November. She gazed out the window and pondered the question thoughtfully for a beat, and then came back to me and said, "You know, I really think he's going to do it this time, Mike. I really do." The rest is history; Ronald Reagan was elected that November 1980, getting 489 electoral votes to Carter's forty-nine.

He would be inaugurated as president the following January.

I would finish up the season and return to my post at MGM after a short vacation, to begin pre-production of my third season. In early June 1980, I was summoned to Cy Chermak's office and he informed me that he had decided to bring in someone new to do the casting for *CHiPs*. He thanked me for the great job, saying there had been some differences of opinion, but what I had contributed overall was very good work. This would be my reward for helping stabilize the show; nobody was to be tossed from any windows but me. I had busted my hump for MGM and especially this production, and this was to be my glorious, grand prize and reward.

The dichotomy was that I actually was very happy and relieved. I'd felt the tension, the pressure, the clash of personalities, if you will, the presence of the aforementioned monolithic ego I'd only heard about, overshadowing me almost from the beginning; now I would be free of it. Maybe being a paddle tennis bum wasn't so bad after all, as it looked like I might very well have more time for it again. I had a short meeting with Mr. Montanus and explained my feelings. He thanked me for a superb job and said, "I won't forget you, Mike." We shook hands and I left.

I was immediately on the phone to John Conboy, who had called again just days before inquiring about my availability. I met with him that afternoon and was successful in consummating an agreement whereby

LADIES OF PASADENA

April 23,1980

Mr.Edward Montanus
President Metro Goldwyn Mayer
Television
10202 W.Washington Blvd.
Culver City,CA. 90230

Greetings Mr. Montanus;

I am writing to you concerning a mutual friend of ours,Mike Hanks;
who was your casting director on "CHIPS".
This man is probably the most creative,dedicated assessor of
talent around today.

He is not afraid of attacking the temples of cliche . His only
desire is to bring the finest calibre of acting to the public.
Like Galileo,he reaches for the highest and most unique stars,
regardless of the adverse circumstances that always are prevelent
when casting.

Some producers,as you may know, have superior or inferior complexes,
sociological hangups,lack of veracity which it takes to have a
colorful and original cast.

Inspite of all the rejections,obstacles and threats confronting
Mr. Hanks,he helped cast your show with spirit and tenacity. Un-
daunted he continued to suggest and submit actors of versatility.

I was one of those who would have never worked in "CHIPS" but because of Mike's artistic perserverance it happened. It took him
two years. I guest starred in the segment "KIDNAP" which when
aired went up some points in the ratings during the second
half of that segment,which proves this man's
credibility.

My friend Tim Carey's reaction to my termination.

AN ACTORS' CASTING DIRECTOR

Mike Hanks Casts CBS's 'Young and Restless'

BY KENT SKOV

After two successful seasons as head television casting director at MGM where his casting instincts helped *CHiPs* rise to prominence, Mike Hanks moved to CBS. He is paired up again with John Conboy, for whom he worked four years ago, and is casting one of the most popular daytime soaps, *The Young and the Restless.* Hanks is an actors' casting director: sensitive, honest, receptive and, most of all, being a former actor, aware of the heartaches. He spots talent like Sherlock Holmes spots clues. But it didn't happen overnight for Mike Hanks.

When you started as an actor did you have any idea you wanted to get into casting?

No. When I started acting it enabled me to meet some casting people and I found I liked working with my fellow actors. My door has always been open to anybody who said they wanted to be an actor. I spent a lot of time acting and I couldn't get to first base. I got my first taste of being in front of the camera when I was 11 years old and I tried to stimulate my career and couldn't get anywhere or get an agent. I got into casting and was sort of sidetracked and it absorbed some of my creative energies.

Tell us a little about your background

When I was a kid my father, Vernon, became good friends with Clark Gable. Gable wouldn't let anyone touch his car except my dad. I have a special feeling for MGM, having grown up around here. I started as an actor when I was about 20. I didn't feel I had learned my craft in college so I also studied with various coaches around the city. While I was going to college, I worked at 20th Century-Fox for four years part-time as an assistant in the casting department.

How did you get the job?

My ability to work with actors. I knew a lot of actors and it was also the fact that I was here. I was a body and enthusiastic about learning and getting ahead. I was willing to do a lot of the dirty work, the casting stuff nobody else wanted to do. I sort of hustled myself into the job and as time went on, I became more needed. Then I started assisting directly to Joe D'Agosta, Joe Scully, Phil Benjamin and Bill Kenney. They were at 20th at the time and we worked on *Hello, Dolly!, Star, The Sound of Music, Patton, Butch Cassidy and the Sundance Kid,* the TV series *Peyton Place, Batman, The Green Hornet* and all sorts of projects. I did that from around 21 through 26 years old. Then I went to Paramount, thanks to a wonderful guy by the name of Thom Miller of Milkus, Miller and Marshall. He invited me to work over at Paramount with Bill Kenney, who at the time was head of casting. I was Kenney's assistant and very shortly I became a full-fledged casting director. Immediately I started casting *Love American Style* off and on, *The Odd Couple* and *The Brady Bunch.* From there I went to Columbia where I did Robert Urich's first show, *Bob, Carol, Ted and Alice, The Lindberg Kidnapping Case* with Renee Valente; a lot of pilots and daytime shows: *Days of Our Lives, The Young and the Restless* and *That's My Mama.* From there I went independent and cast the *All American Girl Robbery, Kentucky Fried Movie,* and a few other fiascos.

Do you prefer film over television casting?

No, it's all fun from this point of view. There may be more money in film, but I get a great deal of joy just casting the smallest one-liners. There are no small casting directors, only small budgets.

Do you prefer studio or independent casting?

I prefer both at the same time. If you work at a studio you'd like to have the freedom to work on an outside project for the additional income as well as doing something different. Right now, I can work on outside projects as long as it doesn't conflict with my duties at CBS. I was exclusive to MGM when I was there.

Is that the case with most casting directors?

Networks, yes; however, there are a number of independent casting people who come in from time to time to work for us — they come in, do the project, and leave.

Do you miss acting?

Lots of times I wonder. But I've done a few independent jobs: a voice-over in Spielberg's *Close Encounters* and a lead in a couple of independent movies that will never see the light of a screening room. But *I* saw them and it was very gratifying for me to see my work after all these years, and feel proud of it. So I really identify with the actor, his rejection and frustrations.

Do you have any method you use to find new faces, i.e. pictures and resumes, going to see a show, recommendations?

I have all those, and some that are instincts that I can't put into words. If you were on this side of the desk and you were looking for talent, what would really interest you? It's that little spark. I was once in the projection room with Robert Wise. We were discussing what he was really looking for in terms of a star, and he said, "I'm looking for star quality, Mike." And that's all he said. It's really in the eyes of the beholder, some little special spark you see in somebody that makes them exciting, interesting, that you can identify with. If they can take all of that and use it in a creative performance then you've got a great actor.

How easy is it for you to sell an unknown actor to producers?

I would rather trust my own instincts than those of another producer, director, agent or other actor, although sometimes that can get me into trouble as a casting director. I'd prefer seeing an actor act for me and then, based on my own judgment determine if he is good. I don't care if he has one credit or 100, if I see him and I'm casting a specific role and like him, I'll do everything I can to push that person. Sometimes you're up against a wall, a barrier you can't get over: an acceptable, bankable name. And I understand that, but it's not going to stop me from trying to be creative. If I think an actor's right or good enough I will at least pitch him or her to whomever I am working for. Then they have the right to cross the line through the name and say he's not recognizable enough, he's not a big enough name. But at least I've done my job, by saying you should take a look at Nick Nolte or this new Steve McQueen.

How many people do you see for one role?

[Hanks shows me his clipboard with an endless number of name actors.] Does that answer your question? How many would you say? This is just one small list.

Is that for leading roles?

That's just one guest lead of a pilot, and there're probably 70 good ideas there. When I cast something I try to think of everyone I possibly can and then narrow it down. But I think anyone of those 70 people, if you went in their direction, could play that role.

Those people all have a name?

Yes, most of them. You have to be realistic and realize that certain parts are not going to be played by beginners.

Is it true you can do a good job in a small part and be forgotten quickly? Why do you think that happens?

There are a lot of variables involved. Maybe the agent's not enough of a hustler, maybe he didn't see the show and doesn't know what the actor can do and maybe the actors don't persevere. I believe very strongly that the cream will rise to the top. And the cream will one way or another get into my office. I hope it's not sour, but I mean the strong, the ones who persevere, will always get through that door one way or another. I'm happy to see that ABC's trying to initiate a new policy about the acquisition of new talent. I really think there's a place for each and every one of us in this business. It's not an easy craft. It's a hard business and one full of heartbreaks. But if you hang in there, sooner or later, it's going to happen. Believe in yourself! ☆

Photo by Michael Papo

I would return to the staff of the Columbia Pictures Television Casting Department, but be exclusive to *The Young And The Restless* at CBS TV City, to start immediately on Monday of the next week with a very nice contract. I was thrilled; more money and way, way less ego-stress. John Conboy was very bright, a wee bit high strung but we had worked extremely well together in the past; we liked each other. We would always be searching for humor in our creative exchanges, it would be fun again. In some ways I was very sad to leave MGM. I loved Ann Jarboe and would miss her. She was almost ready to retire, and couldn't and wouldn't be persuaded to leave and join me.

CHAPTER EIGHT

Back to The Young and The Restless

The dynamics of *The Young and The Restless* were slightly different from that of the seven-day shoot schedule of a filmed show. A segment of *Y&R* was shot daily, with often a number of supporting freelance principal roles, as well as the roles that were categorized as being under five lines or less. I loved doing *Y&R* and being back there. I was warmly received by all the *Y&R* cast and staff, some of whom I hadn't seen in almost seven years since I had left; it felt like a homecoming. Among others, I was greeted by my personal finds: Jamie Lyn Baur and Carolyn Conwell, and a very different David Hasselhoff, now with more maturity, more confidence, and certainly more experience. All stopped by and welcomed me back. I also felt the change of scenery at CBS was a good distraction from those items of my personal life I was anguished over. My life was a soap opera and I would again be casting a soap opera; it seemed fitting. There would be a number of new characters evolving into the *Y&R* story line, as well as several artists where contract renewal was very near and the probability of obtaining contractual renewal was unlikely. David Hasselhoff was at the top of that list. I was told he was very anxious to move on after his seven-year stint as Snapper Foster. In addition, I had originally found Beau Kayzer for the role of Brock, and was informed that Beau was not interested in returning and would continue to explore other venues. I would be sent in all directions, canvassing and culling through what the world would offer by way of the talented, and always for the soaps, the very good-looking and beautiful artist. I was almost immediately sent to New York to see theater, interview, and meet every available possibility. While there, I met a newcomer named Lee Horsley, a possible replacement for the Snapper Foster role. On my return, I set up meetings for him to meet and read for John Conboy, but he wasn't interested in what we had to offer, and especially in doing daytime. He was a good actor, very handsome, and was being wined and dined by numerous prime-time prospects, soon to land the title role in a pilot entitled *Matt Houston.*

During the next months I would find exciting and wonderful additions for *Y&R.* Among them were John Elerick, Lilibet Stern, Dennis Cole, Loyita Chapel, Michael Damian, Steven Ford, Deborah Adair, Cindy Fisher, William Long Jr., Cindy Eilbacher, Sean Garrison, Melinda Cordell, Brett Hadley, Brett Halsey, Tom Havens, Ty Hardin, Terry Lester, Jerry Douglas, Kathy Kelly Lang, and John Gibson, to name a few. They brought a new sparkle to the show and helped lift the ratings. John Conboy was extremely happy. A few of these had been huge stars of both television and film, and didn't really aspire to do daytime, but finally considered it a place to either just work and make a very good living and/or grow and develop stronger, more disciplined skills. I would always sell the concept of steady work

JOHN GIBSON
would like to thank
John Conboy, CBS and Columbia Pictures TV
for a rewarding 15 months as
'CASH'
on
"The Young and the Restless"

Special Thanks
to all of the Soap Opera
Press and Mike Hanks.

Management
Theatrical: Commercials Public Relations NOW AVAILABLE
Dade Rosen Wilhelmina Artists Dena Brein for
276-7977 461-6744 174-1866 Films & Series

and the fact that it's truly a different audience. That is, the viewer that watches soaps isn't the same viewer, for the most part, that watches prime time and goes to the movies.

John Gibson was a former Chippendale's dancer. He looked great and had an interesting vocal quality and natural delivery, but had very little real formal acting training, certainly the least amount of any actor I brought to the *Y&R* cast. We read him and hired him for a role that would evolve slowly, depending on how well he did. We watched him, much like a screen test. He was immediately sent him to an acting coach, and I myself was instructed to be his dialogue coach for each and every day (episode) he was scheduled to work. For over a year he would stop by prior to going to rehearsal, where I would coach and line feed him; direct his performance so that when he entered rehearsal he had already explored the range of my thinking and his own. He would know how his words might sound and be delivered differently.

As I pointed out previously, I've found everyone's acting experience slightly different, and as long as you don't stray an actor too far away from his real life, if it's not a vast stretch from his true personality, he can more easily understand who his character is and what he must do and say. I'm convinced, whether we realize it or not, the average person who has watched thousand of hours of television or film has in effect observed thousands of hours of acting lessons, and perhaps already knows good actor choices from bad ones. I feel most people have thought that they could act, and the process of watching and making choices is certainly central to becoming a good, competent actor. The artist takes from what he observes and practices it, often very badly as he first trains. He or she must bomb/die, be bad first, to know what it is to be good. As I said, a few lines at first, and the character must be very close to who the person really is in life. John Gibson was a good-looking, macho stud and that was the character he was playing, not much of a stretch. The daytime drama is more inclined to do this; that is, test and try the newcomer, if the talent has something this exciting to invest in and explore. If it doesn't work, they edit and write the character out or someone new shows up in the role in the next daily episode. John's character was written, tailored, and developed to fit him like a glove. He began learning and growing, as did his popularity and fan mail. He started getting a lot of fan mail, and when one gets plenty of fan mail, those in charge aren't given to quickly throwing them away. He and I had become friends, and I was proud that he had taken some of my direction and gone to the next level of performance with it.

John Conboy and I still had a wonderfully creative and successful connection, he was like an older brother to me. He would always listen to my casting ideas mindfully and then add his own precepts. Most times he accepted my views, but often he would add flavor by some dimension based on discussion of those actors that were available. Occasionally that extra quality would be engendered and spawned by the actors themselves that had come in to audition. That individual artist might possess something appealing we were looking for, but not quite enough to prompt the sought-after screen test. Maybe they weren't tall enough or had bad teeth, or maybe they were terrific-looking but simply couldn't act.

Once this nice-looking chap came in and read for a possible replacement for the role of Snapper Foster. It had been suggested to John from some source that he be considered. This guy was about six foot four and had Robert Redford good looks and qualities. He had created a very successful chain of men's clothing stores that encompassed both Miami and Palm Beach, Florida. He confided in me once that he had become successful, not so much by selling clothing in his stores, but at the many social functions and parties he would be invited to. He was a very humble chap, but said that he had discovered he could easily sell what he wore because all the other studs and stud wannabes wanted to look and be like him. He pointed to the slacks he was wearing and said that he had worn a pair like them to a recent party, and the very next day his stores sold out the entire inventory of that item. John and I thought we had discovered a star, and our discovery was very interested in this new endeavor he had stepped into.

We met with him several times and I read with him and coached him, but at that time it was impossible for him to transpose his real-life personality into a character-acting role. He could intellectualize what we wanted in the performance and would get very close. He was this guy naturally but when he tried to act he would get very stiff. And this was a very demanding established character, where we needed someone with his looks and natural appealing qualities, but with more trained in-depth acting ability. He was a really nice guy, and I advised him that if he studied for a while, and really wanted it—that is, a career as an actor—he could have it. He gave me his killer smile and told me in confidence he would take it under consideration, but that he was already making plenty of money, had lots of beautiful and successful ladies in his life, and was happy in business. The last time I saw him he was inviting me to a Palm Beach party, and for a beat I thought it might be nice to be around to meet the ladies he's just too busy for.

Another interview tale revolved around the casting for the replacement for the role of Brock. Again, the requirements for the role had been clearly detailed for talent agent/manager representatives. The character should be a wonderful actor, very handsome, and be able to sing like Sinatra, and of course have stage experience. A simple task, as usual I had already seen tons of possibilities. John and I jointly had seen dozens of people and had found no one that we thought could sing worth a hoot, or that we felt a daytime audience would be attracted to and would want to watch on a regular basis. Choices were dismal, to say the least.

We always held auditions in one of the many very large rehearsal halls late in the afternoon, at the conclusion of rehearsal and the daily shoot. For these auditions, I had asked the talent to bring accompaniment, if they so desired, for the singing portion. After the readings, they would invite their pianist or guitar-playing accompanist in for the song, or they could accompany themselves if they played an instrument. John Conboy always had the same reaction to everyone, unless he liked them. He would wrinkle up his nose and say something about the talent being as ugly as a "pan full of butt wrinkles".

During this session, we had seen a lot of people and we were both getting tired, and I had heard his favorite saying often. I ushered in the next and last possibility from my secretary, who was stationed outside the rehearsal hall. She then returned to our offices. He was a tall, dark, and a very handsome actor, and suddenly John woke up and became very attentive. He looked at me and whispered "great-looking," and then smiled. We read the assigned scenes and this guy was dynamite; a fine actor. He was very good in the dramatic scene and equally good in lighter moments of the second scene. John was looking at his resume again and asking him questions of where he had received his training. I could see John beaming with excitement and interest; maybe we'd found our replacement. When John concluded these additional questions, the actor explained that he didn't have accompaniment but could sing a cappella. He walked away from us toward the piano. John then turned to me and almost exploded with excitement, attempting a high five, whispering, "A cappella! He must know how to sing." John smiled big; the talent had moved and positioned himself next to the piano, asking, "Is this okay?" John nearly jumped out of his chair, saying, "Anywhere you want." We waited another beat that was like an eternity. He seemed to go into character; he suddenly looked around from side to side, stomped on the floor with his right foot several times, and started singing and yodeling a rendition of "Desperado" like neither of us had had ever heard before. John's mouth dropped open slightly and he kept looking out of the corner of his eye at me. I think I knew what he was thinking. Obviously, this guy couldn't sing worth a hoot and knew it, but he had the nerve, the chutzpah to try. John Conboy sat there with a look of total disbelief and when he finished, John quipped "nice try" and told him that he liked his acting a lot, but we weren't casting *The Beverly Hillbillies,* and we all broke into a kind of controlled chuckle. John shook the actor's hand and said that we'd find something for him. "Mike will find you something to pay for more voice lessons." I thanked him for coming in, shook his hand again, and escorted him out of the rehearsal hall. When I had fully closed the heavy soundproof door, John Conboy almost fell on the floor. It was the end of the day's auditions and we both very quietly howled and snickered. When John started sitting up straight in his chair, I tapped my foot on the floor and started a softer, even more ghastly version of the song. John couldn't get up; he fell back in his chair, laughing and clutching his sides, whispering, "Stop! Just stop now! Stop!" We couldn't; we'd lost control. We continued snickering all the way back to our offices, and we laughed for days thereafter. From that time forward, when one of us wanted to make the other smile, all he had to do was just stomp a few times on the floor and start yodeling or humming out "Desperado". I loved working with this guy; we always could find something to break each other up.

Several weeks passed and my regular duties had become just that, regular. There weren't any new characters evolving and the producers had decided to write out the character of Brock indefinitely, or until such time as I felt I had someone that we should consider and test.

One afternoon I got the usual summons to come to John's office. He informed me that he was developing a new daytime drama entitled *Capitol.* He summarized briefly and explained that the crux of the drama revolved around government and those folks very near the elected officials. It was to be produced under his own banner, John Conboy Productions, one of many he was developing in his continued and rising success. He asked me to have a look at the first draft and make suggestion lists for the four or five lead roles. I was delighted for him and myself as well, with the possible additional assignment to come. I never said a word about my exclusive pact to *Y&R* and Columbia Pictures Television. I didn't want to make any waves, and felt if indeed the project sold I would gain the additional assignment and accrue remuneration for my added endeavors. I went to work on *Capitol* and made lists and started meeting people under the guise that these were new characters being added to *Y&R.* When I had culled through all the current possibilities, John and I started reading and meeting people; those I thought the best of what the current talent pools of both New York and Los Angeles had to offer. We made our notes and discussed who I liked and who he liked; there was some slight difference of opinion. I really hadn't paid any attention to our differences, as we weren't a "go" yet. I knew if we were to get the "go" green light from the network, my experience with working with John Conboy told me that he usually would settle down and lean toward my choices when the real casting began. That is, if there was a difference of opinion when the final draft of the script came in, and usually by that point there wasn't.

Recent Nielsen ratings had indicated *Y&R* had moved some four points higher since my return, and I was elated. My contract agreement with *Y&R* and Columbia Television was coming up for renewal, and I drafted a note to John asking simply for an increase in salary, a two-year contract, and that I be given the opportunity to direct two episodes of *Y&R* per calendar year. That's two daily episodes out of a possible two hundred and sixty. After consulting with Hal Gefsky and several casting director colleagues, I thought my request for a salary increase was in line with what others were getting on daytime, especially in light of the fact that we were again being touted as the number one daytime drama. Very reasonable requests, I thought. I had presented the request outlining these items, and John had received them in very good spirits and said he would see what he could do. Several days had passed when John called me to a meeting in his office. Immediately, I could feel my old friend playing the somber corporate businessman; aloof, distant. As I sat down across from him at my usual perch, I sensed it was probably a no, too much of an increase. Maybe he'd let me observe a few directors for a while and then do an episode if somebody was sick;

this raced across my thoughts. He was impassive as he fiddled with the document I had previously given him. He then said to me that he had thought long and hard about my requests, and that after careful consideration he had concluded that he did not want a casting director on his staff that aspired to be a director. He said he was going to bring in a new casting director to cast the show. I went into complete shock. I was astounded; my mouth gaped open. I responded with, "Let's negotiate, John. I don't have to direct, and I certainly didn't mean to price myself out of a job that I love. I just want to grow and do other creative things. You want to do other things, why am I any different?" I asked. In a huff now, he said that he had made his decision; he was going to bring in another casting director. I reminded him that we had been down that path before and it was a mistake then, and that if he did this now it would be a bigger mistake. Again, he stated that he had made his decision.

As I departed, I rattled off stuff about who and what I had again brought to the show, and the show's climb again in the ratings. He said absolutely nothing as I walked out of his office. Shock and disbelief was an understatement. Upset, I checked out for lunch, and on the way back from Studio City I took Mulholland for the drive and to calm my thoughts some. Even after lunch, I was still so upset that I crashed my car at Benedict Canyon and Mulholland as a result of mindlessly running a stop sign. Fortunately, nobody had more than minor scrapes and bruises, but both cars were toast. I caught a cab back to the office to tie up some loose ends for the next week's schedule. I felt betrayed, and now banged and bruised, I felt just awful. I had busted my butt for *Y&R* again and had gotten the shaft, and also had expended a lot of time and energy on *Capitol* and received nothing more than the Fred Allen oath of sincerity. But the real irony was yet to come.

When *Capitol* was finally sold, John Conboy had to step away from *The Young and the Restless*. When it aired, I tuned in and watched for several weeks, and couldn't believe what I saw. He had hired actors for the lead roles that I had voted against. Of the many actors we had interviewed and auditioned, he had selected and hired folks that were at the very bottom of my lists as real possibilities. He had hired the absolute polar opposites of what my recommendations had been. Had he gotten deliriously confused? I thought. I watched in absolute disbelief. Perhaps it was those network jerks again, cooking and stirring the caldron beyond my removal. The story and the production values were mere drivel. The writing was not that of Lee Philip and Bill Bell, or staff; it was dreadful stuff. The direction was slow, the performances were slow, and the story had no sparkle whatsoever. There were no real dazzling, charismatic actors to enthrall and excite, or to carry a show. Dull was what it was, just plain dull. My instincts told me it was in big trouble. It lasted longer than anyone had anticipated, to everyone's surprise, several years, and was finally cancelled. A short life for a daytime drama, and then John Conboy was out of work.

I never got any other explanation concerning his decision in discharging me, but I believe unequivocally that if he had taken me with him to *Capitol,* it most definitely would have had a much more exciting cast and I believe it would have had a much longer life as well. We both might even still be doing it. But he chose the bullet to the foot instead, proving once and for all that what goes around comes around.

The casting business seemed to be going through enormous changes. There were a lot of experienced people around that just couldn't get arrested, as they say. Suddenly, it seemed people nobody had heard of were getting the big jobs. They had cast one or two successful films and were now department heads, and those new department heads brought in more new people nobody had heard of. For the years I was around I knew everyone in town, and then almost overnight I knew no one. And the newcomers didn't know us and were now in charge, and there seemed to be few jobs being offered to the local seasoned veteran.

Funny thing, though, I had been contemplating a life change anyway. I loved casting; I had a very good memory for all of it—the vocal qualities, the heights and weights, who could do what. The art of casting was a natural gift for me, but I was tired of taking scripts home and working until late making suggestion lists, and I was especially tired of the of the constant pressure. I wanted to just take a break and explore some other things. And above all, I wanted to try and get back to focusing some on an acting career for myself. Almost immediately, I told my agents I was back and available to go out on interviews for anything, and for well over a year I did exactly that. I explored other business ventures and went out on commercial and television acting auditions. Several of my former casting colleagues—Joe D'Agosta, Joe Scully, Shelly Ellison, Alice Cassidy—had me in to read for some supporting roles. And I worked; I started getting jobs, both on-camera and voice-over work. I even picked up a couple of good credits, but it's never enough. My resources had once again come near depletion and again, after carefully considering my options, I determined that I should bite the bullet and explore finding a staff casting job again. I began making calls.

CHAPTER NINE

Back To 20th Century Fox and the future

In early 1983, I received a call from Rochelle Farberman. At first, I didn't know who was calling. I had to inquire of her secretary who she was, and was told that it was Shelly Ellison—Rochelle had gone back to her maiden name. We had both worked as staff casting directors under her aunt, Renee Valente, the executive vice president of talent at Columbia Pictures Television. I had called Shelly several weeks before, inquiring about any openings she might know of. I really didn't think anything much would come of our conversation, as she didn't know of anything. Shelly jumped on the line, snickering and saying, "But Mike, you can still call me Shelly." She informed me that Renee had finally stepped away from casting after recently finalizing a very nice contract for herself, and would be co-executive producing at least one show with Glen Larson at 20th Century Fox Studios. An excellent association, I thought, as Glen Larson was one of the all-time most prolific and successful television producers ever.

Mr. Larson was a singer originally with the very popular Four Preps, 1956–1964, with numerous hits, of which "26 Miles (Santa Catalina)" was one of their biggest. He had turned his creative juices in every direction, writing and creating for television. To name just a few of his most successful shows there was *Quincy, Knight Rider, Magnum P.I., Battlestar Galactica, BJ and The Bear, Switch, The Six Million Dollar Man, It Takes a Thief, Alias Smith and Jones,* and many, many more. Some were more critically acclaimed than others, but most were huge financial successes. He had also written the theme music for most of these as well. At the time of my return to my alma mater, the beautiful 20th Century Fox Studios, he still was in production on the long run of *The Fall Guy,* which Shelly had been casting.

Renee had also retained Shelly's services as casting executive on all shows that she produced. And not just because she was related, but because Shelly had always been considered a top-drawer, first-caliber casting person, one of the brightest, most creative, and knowledgeable of her era. I was deliriously happy when I got her call, as I was again very hungry. I loved working for them both. Demanding sometimes, yes. Often a little testy, and extremely opinionated sometimes, yes. But I thought, it goes with the territory and I could take it. It would be a very creative, high-energy-driven environment again and I was elated to be a part of it. Shelly would continue casting *The Fall Guy* and then supervise my assignments, two of which I immediately thought to be basic sci-fi junk, *Manimal* and *Automan*. *Manimal* was again the human who has animal powers, which could be manifested at will and then used to fight the criminal elements of New York City. Simon MacCorkindale, Melody Anderson, and Reni Santoni (the *Seinfeld* chef, Poppy, with poopy hands) starred. *Automan* was the same, a piece about a man who generates a computer superhero to fight crime in his city, starring Desi Arnaz Jr. Both half-hour shows were truly dreadful, but I didn't judge or care. I needed to work. I fought hard to sell and present them as upcoming hit sci-fi shows, and like me, the talent that needed a paycheck would do them. I would often meet any negative agent reaction with the explanation that I was sure someone must have shared the same opinion of *The Six Million Dollar Man* when Mr. Larson presented that original show concept. *Manimal* and *Automan* weren't that fortunate; they were extremely short-lived. I recall we shot approximately a dozen episodes of each and aired about half of what we had in the film container can, or had been finished.

The third show of my assignment was *Masquerade*, produced by Renee Valente. I was really excited about its possibilities. It was totally different; a very sophisticated, smart, chic, contemporary one-hour spy drama. It was very well written, with production values and direction that were second to none. Renee fought hard to select and carefully place each director she felt was best suited to tell a specific episodic story, sometimes adjusting a far-off scheduled story to accommodate a specific director she wanted. It was a lovely show to watch and starred a wonderful cast, with Rod Taylor at the helm as the seasoned spy chief and Kirstie Alley and Greg Evigan as his protégé assistants. Fox allowed us to spare no expense in getting as many big-name actors that were interested in doing the one-hour show. We were shooting second unit in Europe and spending in excess of a million dollars an episode, per week, for location shots. I was having great fun, most times working very late, but exhilarated to the next level. We were having enormous success assembling wonderful casts. The network had bought and we were firm for twenty-four episodes, and that would take us well into the next year.

My intuition and the consensus of opinion said that we'd probably run long enough to go into syndication, which was usually five years. It looked like we might have a huge hit and be around for a long time. We had shot nearly all the network order but one or two and had aired more than half of what had been completed. But the ratings were mixed, there were overages in the shooting schedules, and overall production costs were mounting. I was certain at this point in time that the powers that be, those creative minds at the network, weren't really jerks. This was a great show, and I was confident that they knew Glen Larson's *Masquerade* would find an audience if they gave it enough time. I think it was a complete surprise to everyone involved that next year when those network executives pulled the plug and again revealed their true selves as being spineless shortsighted network jerks. It had been a very nice run, almost a year and a half, and I was again at a "wrap" production party of a show that shouldn't have been wrapped. And, I was probably having one or two too many and again saying good-bye, leaving friends and an association and a lot that I truly loved. But this time I had made a decision.

CHAPTER TEN

I Told You, I Want to Act!

I had always had agents for both commercial and theatrical acting work, so that when it was slow or I was on a hiatus from a staff position they could send me out for auditions. I had turned forty, and some said I was going through a life crisis. I said hogwash; that I was just getting back on track. I think I always knew my casting career would be short-lived and transient. I always felt like I was in training, just studying the craft of acting and filmmaking. I kept telling myself that next year I'd make the change, next year. Now, next year was here. Those other business endeavors would give me the real freedom to audition for acting work, and possibly work once in a while in that capacity and live my life's dream. I'd been studying real estate principles for years; maybe I'd finally get my license and give that kind of selling a try. If a casting job was offered, or an interview evolved for me to meet someone for a casting job, I would be there. But when I left Fox, *Masquerade,* and my good friends Renee Valente and Rochelle (Shelly) Farberman, I told myself I would no longer actively seek out casting jobs.

Sonja Brandon's Commercials Unlimited had been representing me for just a short time, and I'd informed them that I'd now be more available for interviews. When I told them I wasn't going to do casting anymore they didn't believe me; nobody believed that I wanted out. It was just a few days later when Sonja's number one creative workhorse, Randi Rubenstein, called me and said she had submitted me for several TV commercial ads. She and her associate, John Fisher, commenced by sending me out all over town, and I started running into a lot of my actor friends, most of whom liked seeing me out there, rooted for me, and encouraged me. But some resented my being there. I think some thought I had special connections, but I didn't; I just had me. It was about three weeks later when Randi called to inform me that I had a callback for a commercial spot. I honestly couldn't remember the audition or what I had done on it. She said they wanted to see me again for Republic Airlines, a national commercial that Robert Giraldi was set to direct. On the second callback interview, one of the casting assistants asked if I had ever heard of "the great Giraldi." I confessed that frankly I hadn't, and that I was more familiar with television and film directors. He informed me that Robert Giraldi was considered the Fellini of commercial directors. I was up next, and there was only one simple sentence, "It's my birthday," and one word of dialogue that my character kept saying, "perks." Not much to read or memorize. The ad consisted mostly of reactions.

My perception and experience told me that it was a specific look and a quality they were seeking. I was very happy to still be in the hunt, as a callback always gives the agent greater confidence in one's talent and abilities. It usually brings forth more interviews, and it did. Almost immediately, Randi and John had me going out three and four times a week.

Then, a few more weeks passed before Randi called and said Giraldi and Republic Airlines wanted to see me a third time. Again, I had almost forgotten about the ad spot. I guess I was used to more immediate decision making. It's like you don't hear anything, and I thought it must have been cast. Okay, a third callback. I started to get a little nervous; that is, during the time I was waiting to be seen for this third callback I started to hear more about the spot from different people. I learned that they had seen a ton of people in both New York and Los Angeles, well over five hundred actors had been considered; that it was a big commercial production; that they would need my character at least three days, maybe four, instead of the usual one-day shoot.

When I finally met them again I had calmed down and decided to leave the nerves outside where they belonged. I went in with great confidence, presence, and humble charm. I told myself even if they didn't hire me for this one they were going to remember me for something else. This was a huge advertising agency, and they had other clients they created advertisements for. The room was more filled this time, like a small party, and I was the life of it and the one everyone was waiting to meet. Giraldi spun me around the gathering for a moment, meeting folks, and then directed me to center stage and into some related improvisations of slight comedic whimsy. There were some laughter and chuckles when I looked around for a second, but I was more focused on Giraldi than on audience reaction. He then gave me an additional premise and I went with it until he said, "Okay, fine, very nice. Thanks, Mike, for coming in again." I thanked him again, waved to every-one, and made my exit from the festivities. I was in and out in probably less than six minutes. I guess when I left the room I knew they liked me (they had videotaped me three times), but I couldn't really tell how much they liked me. I knew there was at least one more actor they were seeing for the same role, and didn't necessarily feel I had done my best work at anything Giraldi had asked me to do.

On the way home, I started doing what actors do to themselves after they leave an audition. I started to think about what I should have done and could have done. Then, I remembered what Ed Griffith had reminded me of and had advised me to do, and that was to just forget about it. Richard Roat, a mutual actor friend of both Ed's and mine, had advised me that auditions are like little plays. You go in and do your best work, the play closes, and then you forget about it. I didn't have Ed's or Richard's experience yet, and it was hard not to rehash the actor choices I'd made. I had beaten myself up so badly that it was getting easier to forget about it.

I went by to see my parents and told them casually that I didn't think I had gotten the job. My dear moth-er handed me a bowl of fresh homemade corn-clam chowder and a piece of fresh-baked bread, and said, "It's their loss if they don't hire you. There'll be other jobs. Eat." My old dad leaned to me from his wheelchair and whispered, "Well, we love you, Mike. It's a tough business. Have a yam, it'll make you feel better." And with a twinkle in his eye, he added, "They're lucky." By the time I finally got home, I had convinced myself

I hadn't gotten the job, and I had eaten one of my dad's yams, too, and I didn't feel any better.

All my boys were there to greet me with inquiries, as Jon had arrived a few days previously to stay with us for an extended period. Chris knew better what a third callback meant, but Doyle and Jon were just as excited, firing questions at me about how I thought I had done. I handed them Grandma's container of chowder and a loaf of warm fresh bread, and told them I thought I had blown it. But then I smiled at them warmly and told them I had given it my best shot, and if they didn't use me it was their loss. I added that those were Grandma's sentiments. After some high fives, and slurping up the chowder and buttering warm bread slices, they jumped up and started helping with the burgers and salad I had begun making. Then it happened, the phone rang. We all ran to it, and there was more clowning excitement, high fives, and a pretend fight for the phone, which they finally let me win. It was Randi Rubenstein, and I knew when she drew out the M in my name that she was very excited. "Mmmmike, you got the commercial!" I repeated her words for my boys and they started doing the Dad-got-the-job dance. Randi was so excited for me. She said they had a very tentative hold on me for three days, that it might work longer, and she would call me in the morning with more information. She congratulated me again and hung up. Now we were all dancing the Dad-got-the-job dance all over the house. I then called my parents, told them, and thanked them both for their love and support, with a special thanks to my dad for the yam. He replied, "Yams are lucky, I told you."

I suddenly felt hot; Randi, Sonja, and John Fisher were sending me everywhere. They had firmed up the dates for three or maybe four days, but definitely three. I ended up working just the three days; my character was central to the ad. Everything revolved around scenes my character was involved in: parties, family gatherings, birthday festivities, at work, dinner out with the wife, at the airport, on the plane, and more. I had twenty-seven wardrobe changes. It may have been my first national commercial, and I didn't have Ed or Richard's experience yet, but I knew for a commercial production that was a lot of scenes and wardrobe changes. A few days into the shoot, one of Robert Giraldi's longtime assistants informed me that Giraldi really liked what I was doing, but that I shouldn't be surprised if I never worked for him again. He said that he's just a little quirky that way; he never used the same actor twice. A couple of months passed before I heard that they would begin airing the ad for the first time in November, the evening of the 1984 presidential election returns—at that time, the most expensive of all air times. There was a full minute version, a thirty-second version, and a fifteen-second version. We saw them all that evening and my phone started ringing off the hook. My fifteen minutes of fame wasn't over.

Some months after it began running, I got the best phone call from longtime family friend and neighbor, Woody Tolkien (formerly Woody Wilson, a big bandleader and MGM contract player), who was on vacation with his wife, Martha, in Michigan. He said at that very moment, he was sitting with the family and looking out a huge bay window onto Lake Michigan, talking and watching the television, which sat just below window level. He said he was looking back and forth from the television to the serenity and beauty of the lake, talking to relatives, and the commercial I was in came up on the tube at the exact moment when he and Martha were talking about me and my boys. We lived just down the street from them in Culver City. He said he couldn't believe it; just when he mentioned my name, there I was, on the tube in the foreground, with Lake Michigan in the background. We laughed, and I told him that's about as close as I probably would ever get to the beautiful lake—too cold for me. He said he loved seeing me, that I was great in the commercial. Another truly great artist, to this day I cherish the memory of Woody's call.

I was a very happy camper, but then I started to get recognized. Most times, it was the happy, kindhearted person that was startled to see the fellow in the commercial standing next to him or her at the market. It seemed as though I couldn't go anywhere without someone pointing a finger and recognizing me. I heard people say that it was their favorite commercial and had made them laugh, which pleased me greatly. I was on a roll commercially, as I landed another central character for a Schick Hospital ad, which ran for about the same amount of time, roughly six months. I was the chap pitching the benefits of the program to his business partner with the alcohol problem—"It's only ten days and a two-day follow-up." Almost from the beginning of its run I experienced rudeness. It seemed to bring out the worst in people, folks who probably were in need of the program and couldn't separate the ad from reality, and that I was just an actor playing a role. Never before had I realized how much I loved my privacy. I would think, no wonder the really big television and film personalities hide from the public.

Then, I did a commercial for Security Pacific Bank, where I was one of a dozen or so principal characters in the ad. The day of the shoot, the director, Lee Teirs, called me aside and asked if I knew why he had decided on casting me. Kidding around, I responded with, "Well, it must be because I'm a brilliant actor." I'll never forget his reply to my smugness. He said, "Yes of course, that, too, but mostly it's because you remind me of Stan Laurel." Immediately, I went into my very best Stan Laurel impression and Lee Teirs said, "Yes, yes, exactly; that's exactly what I want you to do." In the commercial, my character receives a free VCR from the bank. Later, when finally placed in front of the camera, he directed me to play my moments with those confused, befuddled, and dumbfounded looks and reactions of Stan Laurel while trying to comprehend the electronic components and how to set up the bank's gift. My character seems to understand the instructions, gets the VCR set up, and connects the wiring to the TV. He turns on the TV, smiles that smile, and presses the play button on the VCR. It then blows up and blackens his face, giving his hair that shocked, electrocuted look. For years I had been friends with Lois Laurel, Stan's daughter, and I couldn't wait to get home and call to tell her why director Teirs had selected me for my most recent work. Lois was thrilled for me. My fifteen

Your Life Daily Paks™
"Couple" :30

SHE: And then what did he say?

HE: He said I'm not twenty-five any more.

SHE: C'mon.

HE: He said my cholesterol is high.

ANNCR: High cholesterol is a major factor in heart disease.
SHE: And????

HE: He suggested I get serious.

ANNCR: Introducing the Cholesterol Control Pak, a serious lifestyle and dietary program

including MaxEPA fish oil, plus vitamins, minerals and fiber.

HE: You think I'll ever be twenty-five again?
SHE: (Laughs)

ANNCR: The Cholesterol Control Pak, with MaxEPA. From Your Life, America's leader in vitamin packs.

Poindexter/Osaki/Nissman

Scored another commercial with the talented
Jennifer Rhodes.

minutes had not yet ended, as I got recognized from that commercial as well. It was like someone coming to visit backstage at the conclusion of an evening's performance; the actor's greatest reward, someone telling him how much they had laughed and enjoyed his work. This was the same type of recognition, and a very rewarding feeling indeed. Nothing really compares to warm and friendly praise; to an artist it's very nurturing, and a delight to receive.

By this point in time I had done some work in episodic television and other commercials. I did another amusing spot for Your Life vitamin products opposite the fine actress Jennifer Rhodes. The work and the jobs were coming, but it's just never enough, unless one supplements one's income from another more financially productive source. I had to get rolling in business so that I could further finance my quest to be a successful actor.

That year I founded Fred C. Dobbs (the name of the character Humphrey Bogart played in *The Treasure of the Sierra Madre*) Wholesale Automobiles, and rented an office in downtown Culver City. I would buy cars from dealers and sell them to other dealers or at the various California auctions. It didn't work. I had been optimistic about it, but I'd never be around when my agents were trying to find me; I was always collecting cars or delivering cars. The money was rolling in, but I was becoming even less available, late in getting messages and returning calls. Then one day I had in excess of forty cars parked in my driveway, my backyard, and in the neighborhood and missed a callback request for another national commercial because I was moving those cars around the city. That was my last month in the car business. I closed up my office and told my agents I would not let that happen again; that I'd be available whenever they needed me.

Like any other actor, I started hustling and began getting jobs. I worked more episodic television: an episode of a new show, *Jesse*, for Joe D'Agosta, a *Cagney & Lacey*, a *Mike Hammer* for director Mike Vejar. Supporting roles, nothing terribly large, just a scene or two, a few days, a few lines, day-player work—but I was proud, as I had gotten them like any other actor. I went in and read for the roles, and was hired—oh, happy day.

Then, I got a call from Ann Lockhart, June Lockhart's daughter. We'd been friends for some time and I had always admired Ann's work. She had worked an episode of *CHiPs* for me at MGM, and I was sure she was destined for at least a regular on a series. She informed me that her brother, Lance Lindsay, was preparing a project called *Malibu Beach*, and that he didn't have a casting director and I should contact him. She gave me his numbers and told me to call him. I had taken a couple of meetings for casting positions during my car-dealing period, but I think I was making too much money and probably came off as a little cocky with some new department heads whose casting experience was considerably less than mine. I called Lance the next morning, set up a meeting, we met, he retained me, and I went to work.

Malibu Beach revolved around a very successful family that lived and did business in the Los Angeles seaside community populated by celebrities. It was very much of the *Dallas* genre, but in a beach setting with good-looking guys and bikini-clad babes. Ironically, I had the distinct pleasure of hiring Gregory Walcott, who I'd worked alongside of when I was ten years old in *The Jackie Jensen Story* for Four Star Television, for the *Malibu Beach* pilot, to portray the family patriarch. As we continued the casting process, Lance decided he wanted me to play something in the pilot. One afternoon, he informed me the writers were writing in the character of the family butler, and he wanted me to do it with a British accent. I was delighted. The finished product was very good, much better than I expected for an independent project. It had a very rich, opulent look, a strong ensemble cast, good performances, and was nicely directed by Lance, but without a clear commitment from a major or cable network, it's a roll of the dice. Those boys at the networks don't like it when you bring something to them that has been produced for less money and actually looks as good as, if not better than, their product.

Not two years later, David Hasselhoff won out and broke down this sort of barrier when he produced a similar waterfront drama entitled *Baywatch*.

CHAPTER ELEVEN

The Casting Couch Potato

Yes, both do exist. Temptations exist in any business where there are people who are excitingly alive and there is money and power, from the White House and celebrity status to Joe's car lot in Burbank, and a lot of places in between where there isn't room for a couch. The excitement and especially the glamour of show business can act as an aphrodisiac to some, stimulating and arousing their libidos on their first steps onto a studio lot. For the neophyte it can be intoxicating, especially for those that have only the physical attributes of being sexy, the hustle and bustle of creative activity can be stirring to the senses.

I had a general meeting scheduled with a young woman one very hectic morning. Already fifteen to twenty minutes behind schedule, I retrieved her from Betty Scott in reception and headed back to my office. I know she felt the energy, as everyone was rushing about and the place was abuzz and busy with the many shows we had in production. I guess she felt rushed, or that I was rushed, since she immediately began selling her recent work/credits and telling me about herself. I was listening and reading her resume as we went to my office and sat down. A lot of New York theater, and I remembered her agent saying she had a lot of theater experience. I like her already, I thought.

I apologized for my tardiness and explained that it was due to a problem on a show shooting on the stage, and that our meeting might be interrupted. Immediately, everyone concerned—the agent, the producer—were rushing me. It's always the same. After two or three interruptions while she attempted to tell me something, her presentation seemed to drift and focus more on a steamy, sexy scene she had recently viewed in a popular film. It was if she was frustrated by having to compete with the phone interruptions and wanted to complete a sentence.

This New York actress was going to get my attention by doing what she was there to do—act—for the last row, and in a way that each person in that row would understand everything of the play. I liked this lady instinctively; she was acting already. I was half listening while on hold when her performance intensified with the revelation that she had retained her virginity until the ripe old age of twenty-five. I made a face in response and tried to focus on her, but I'd have to jump back into a phone conversation. I thought, I have this amazing, hot-looking, great-smelling, tanned young woman, a Venus, a centerfold-plus type endowed with more-than-ample sex appeal sitting in front of me, telling me that she was able to fend off the boys, if I'd heard her story right, until recently. I'd tune in and tune out when I had to excuse myself for another phone interruption. I was also thinking that I found it hard to believe. I heard Betty Scott cackling about the person on line three who needed to speak to me. But my eyes hardly escaped her, I didn't want to stare but I looked at her a lot. I was just not engaged and couldn't concentrate on more than my immediate problem needs would allow. For some minutes we intermittently tried to have a meaningful dialogue; that is, more than a couple of rushed sentences at a time.

When she spoke and moved, I would get a horndog's view of her beautiful, perfectly shaped features in her pretty, yellow-flowered, slim-fitting, spaghetti-strap summer dress. She was lean, with great legs and strong-looking arms. I almost always looked at the arms second. Arms always tell the tale. If they're flabby, it's a "least desirable"; that is, for me personally, and for the camera most of the time. It tells me the person is not in good shape physically. He or she is not an athletic-type person, perhaps flabby all over, and nobody likes flabby. I've always liked athletic. Picky, picky, picky, I know. I'm not saying wrestler-arms physical; I'm just saying fit, lean, and athletic. A little definition is always more attractive. Madonna—no, too muscular; Danica Patrick—yes, lean and fit-looking, yet still feminine. This is what personally appealed to me as a person that hired for the camera. Besides assessing acting talent, I looked for what I viewed as photographic perfection also. She was absolutely beautiful to look at, perfect in every way. If she had been plain-looking she still would have turned heads.

It was when she started talking about her boyfriend again that I was finally able to tune in, after the problem on the stage had resolved itself. As I hung up the phone I could feel her delivery again intensify. She continued with her story and said that she had learned to satisfy her boyfriend's needs in other ways. I never expected the details to follow, but she kept going without my asking and I didn't say stop. She was beginning to defeat the phone interruptions; when Betty Scott buzzed me again, echoing resolution to the problem and I cut her off with, "Call you back." She got even bigger as I hung up and said she was of the opinion that sex was as natural as breathing; that her boyfriend was young and hot, and she would arouse him and ultimately please him by her teasing. Unsure of what she had just said, and meant, I responded, "Oh?" In a softer, sexier, more innocent voice, she said, "I would tease him for a long time until he would, I think, explode." Playing my reaction like a very nervous, hard-swallowing Barney Fife, I repeated, "Explode?" She then got up from her chair and walked toward me, as if she had stepped to the edge of the stage to be closer and more intimate with an audience. She gazed at me and said, "I like to tease. I'd like to tease you." Almost at that very instant, Betty Scott buzzed again and cackled that another urgent call was on line two, and I nearly fell out of my leaned-back office chair. Betty was still cackling as we hung up. Too much time at reception, I thought. This beautiful young woman could hear and see that I was frantic, in more ways than one, and she was teasing. As I hung up, I said, "You're teasing, you are teasing, I'm feeling teased. But can you do comedy?" She smiled at me and I then took another final call from an assistant director, confirming that everything was okay on the stage, over an hour late but the talent had finally arrived. She had turned and moved back to her seat on the other side of my desk.

I told her that she had won, had gotten my attention, and that I had enjoyed her story and wonderful performance. I apologized for the rude interruptions and repeated that I had loved hearing her erotic story, but that I should go to the stage to check and double-check. She seemed to change from the attention-getting seductress and became a very real, different, natural, down-home young woman from Ohio. I promised that next time I would give her my undivided attention. She offered that she wanted to hear more about me, perhaps over coffee or a glass of wine, and jotted down her phone number on the back of her picture and resume.

As we left my office she shyly confessed that she liked me immediately, that she honestly didn't have a boyfriend at present, and didn't know why she was being so aggressive. I told her not to worry about that; it hadn't bothered me, in a bad way, in the slightest. I explained that I'd seen it before; that I thought it was the aphrodisiac effect of the big studio lot, and it had that effect on some folks.

As we parted I got an enticing whiff of her scent—not a perfume fragrance, but a clean, natural smell that lingered in my nostrils until it finally compelled me to call her later that afternoon. She invited me to come by for a glass of wine on my way home. While walking in her apartment door, I started explaining that I seldom dated actresses, for the obvious reasons, and if we were to become friends I would give her the same consideration as any other artist, no more and no less. She said she understood (yeah, right). I offered to buy dinner at a great little spot I knew within walking distance on

Sunset Boulevard. On our return, and after still another small glass of wine, she again expressed to me that she really was attracted, and wanted to go jogging, play tennis, and go roller-skating with me. I was truly flattered when she kissed me. I breathed heavily into her ear and said, "If I wasn't a casting director, would you still like me?" She whispered that she would and I kissed her back. Yeah, right, I thought again. Then, she coyly said, "What I didn't finish in my story today was that my boyfriend and I only did it a few times. I was just getting the hang of it when we broke up. It's been almost a year for me." I nodded and said I thought that was a long—a very long—time. But then I suggested that, like riding a bicycle, "It'll come back to you."

In reality, and I think Dr. Phil would agree, this young woman wasn't about acting or her career; she simply liked me and had a good case of the horny-horns. I could have met her at Baskin-Robbins over selection of a bubble gum cone and I think the perception and conversation would have been the same. She felt comfortable. We could have been sitting next to each other on a plane, and one of us would have changed plans and we'd have gone to the same hotel after we landed.

I always expected this kind of performance commitment, as the trained actors/artists/performers are about the pursuit of honesty, or honest portrayal, and when they get to a "power-broker station," they're almost compelled to present and perform even with a broken leg. It's the energy of creative opportunity.

But again, this was something not quite as cerebral as all that. I think this was just simple, lustful, horny, workplace attraction, like falling in "like" with a long-running show cast member or an office coworker. In the weeks that followed we started a sex/jog/workout/breakfast/sex program.

I would come to know her well, and she was really a very intelligent, normal, and moral young woman, but not stapled to any kind of fundamental religious dogma. The whole sexy act in my office was a total façade; an act to get my attention away from the intrusions, she would tell me. She was much broader intellectually and more theatrically complex than that easily played character she had improvised. But apparently she needed to play it out at what she perceived as a power-broker station—my office. She lived freely and judged only those that hurt others; she had no tolerance especially for those that hurt or molested children. We had great fun for a long time. I was never able to get her a job on anything I was doing for scheduling or money reasons and she never seemed to give a damn. "It makes no never mind," she'd say, and laugh like a country yokel.

Another time, I got involved with the mother of a child I had cast in a show. My secretary buzzed me one morning to say that one of the mothers had come over to pick up a script, and wanted to personally thank me for being nice to her daughter and hiring her for the job. I was up to my neck in stuff, as usual. I asked her to tell the woman to come on down for a New York minute. When she entered my office I was instantly taken aback, as she was a stunning Asian woman with all the physical attributes of a model: full mouth and lips, slim, busty, with thick black waist-length hair that she had in a braid down her back. I immediately thought she must be a model. A gorgeous woman. I don't know where she was during the interviews; if I'd seen her I surely would have remembered because, like her daughter, she was a standout.

I've always found intelligence and an inventive wit to be the most attractive features, especially in a beautiful woman, and when those qualities accompany sensuality I'm mesmerized. She was instantly inventive, and I was energized and quickly stirred by her fervor. I would come to learn she was very well educated, with a master's in business. Almost at once, she began thanking me for the job for her daughter and started to tell me, in her broken English, that she liked me and had watched me during the interviews. "I rike yo stire (I like your style)...I think yo soo cooolll." She kept saying it, again and again, "I rike yo stire, I think you ah soo cooolll." At first, I couldn't get what she was saying, and then she slowed and I understood. I was flattered, my ego beaming some, but I was very busy. I thanked her and got up to open the door to prompt her exit, but she approached me and said she thought I was "most handsome" and again said, "Sooo cooolll, except for one thing." I released the door and let it shut and she continued. She said that I ought to roll up the cuffs of my shirt some. She came to me, started unbuttoning and rolling up my sleeves, and touched my hands and arms, saying, "I rike yo stire, I think you sooo cooolll, I like kiss you all over." Again she said, "I like kiss you all over." More than pleasantly surprised, I told her that I thought perhaps I might like that, too, but I didn't think this was the time or especially the place. She then said, "You come by to see me, I live not far away. I make you a little tea, you relax for a while and I like kiss you all over. You come today."

And I did, later that day; I couldn't get her out of my mind. I was surprised by the expensive, upscale neighborhood she lived in; equestrian estates, with a horse for her daughter, no less. The first few times I was apprehensive about just dropping in on her, but she encouraged me to do so. She would welcome me anytime. She always seemed very busy, and I almost immediately would feel like I was intruding and would say something about having to get back to work. She would say, "Oh, no, don't go. I, I like kiss you all over."

Sometimes, I would drop by and take her to lunch or an early dinner. I noticed that whenever I would come to visit and inadvertently rattle my keys, she would say, "Oh, no, don't go. I like kiss you all over." As time went by, she would take longer with making the tea, sometimes lay out a buffet of delicacies fit for a king, tease me some, and then we would eat a wonderful lunch or dinner. How could I refuse? I liked her, too. Then, with a massage she would relax me into a heavenly state that would sometimes last for days. This would be the beginning of a wonderfully loving and beautiful friendship.

I related this "I like kiss you all over" tale to my buddy Joe Dorgan at his Burbank car lot one day, and he laughed and asked if I had heard the hit song by the pop group Exile with almost the same lyrics. I told him that I hadn't. A few days later I heard it on the radio; it was called "Kiss You All Over." I then told her about the song and she, too, listened for it, and then started singing it to me as I would start to leave. I would come to learn that she had inherited a bundle of money from an uncle, as well as his very lucrative import/export furniture business she had worked in since her divorce. She had people that worked for her at various locations, but managed most of her business from her home office, as her child was her main focus.

Without a doubt, these were some of the best and most relaxing and fun times I ever had experienced, and I cared for her a great deal. Another one I let get away. For a very long time after that I was partial to Asian women, and all of their very feminine methods and their relaxing tea and massages. I definitely like their style.

Columbia Pictures

Dec. 20.

Mike,

Thanks for cleaning
up my residual problem.
You are a credit to
the family name.

Tom

Tom Hanks

CHAPTER TWELVE

A Tom Hanks tale

In approximately mid-1987, after I had finally left casting, I received a residual check for my work in *Close Encounters of the Third Kind*, forwarded to me from the Screen Actors Guild. It was for the first run on television and was a considerable amount of money, several thousand dollars. It would come, as always, when my reserves were again almost depleted and I especially needed it. How happy I was. It was like found money or hitting the lottery. Then I noticed mixed in amid the half a dozen other residual checks made out to me, there were numerous checks, for many thousands of dollars, made out to my cousin Tom Hanks for his work on *Bosom Buddies*. I couldn't believe my eyes. I decided that instead of sending them back to the Guild I would make some inquires around town and get his personal address. Finally, I located somebody that still remembered me and obtained Tom's address. I then wrote him a short note explaining what had happened, asked him some questions about the Hanks' family history, and sent off his checks. About a week later my phone rang and it was Tom Hanks, thanking me for getting the mailings straightened out. We chatted for a couple of minutes and shared some family history; that we were both related to Nancy Hanks, who was Abraham Lincoln's mother, but that we didn't exactly know how. Another few days passed and I received a note from him simply saying I was a credit to the family name. In spite of our family connection, I thought, what a nice man this chap is; my "easier to hire the good guy" rule at play here. As I had hung up the phone after our conversation, I had hoped that he would get more work and make it really big.

CHAPTER THIRTEEN

Three Advisory Tales:

A Burning Desire

Guru psychologist Dr. Wayne Dyer said, "A burning desire is like having a burning candle within you. It doesn't flicker, it's constant."

If you've decided that it'll be easy to get to the top, or you've come to the conclusion that you want to be an actor based on your personal assessment of your sterling good looks; that you're just plain handsome or beautiful, and because of that it will be easy, stop reading now. Take what you've gotten from this work so far and find something else to focus your life on. I suggest you suck up your losses to date, minimizing any regrets, as it is the most difficult of roads to travel. It's certainly the hardest road to stay on, and the one most likely to "pothole" even the most determined and the best trained to discouragement. Unless, of course, as Mr. Kirk Douglas pointed out, "You're prepared to die for it." In any event, I applaud your courageous choice.

Forget about the classmate or jealous sibling who said to you at an early age, "You can't do that, you'll never be an actor, you're too ugly, you're not smart enough," or "You can't try out for the school play," or "You can't sing." Tell that to Willie Nelson, Rod Stewart, Jimmy Durante, Louie Armstrong, and Ray Charles.

Maybe they're not the most traditional-sounding artists, but they exemplify the beauty and song that lies within us all. It emanates from and is the essence of real desire. Desire is the best defense for rejection, but it must be a real, burning desire; a desire to compete where the waters are rapid and the current moves much faster. To stay afloat requires real commitment; real dedication beyond the realm of mere physical good looks. It requires an inner strength capable of holding on for survival and growth, as defeat and death is not an option. So don't do anything worth doing unless you are prepared for it, and plan to hold on and live for it, with no "flicker."

If it's to perform, and one is lucky, one knows what one wants to do when one comes from the womb and takes one's first breath while hearing the clapping, slapping sounds of an excellent entrance. For the rest of you who have heard the applause at a later time, you are just as noble in your quest; breathe in deeply, for new life to you is forthcoming. Kirk Douglas is quite right, though. It's a very hard struggle, but what isn't? More fall by the wayside than really last to stardom. Andy Warhol's fifteen minutes of fame may exist for only a very few and the term is relative. Be prepared for that, and be prepared to live happily and not die if you don't gain at least day-player actor status.

Another person's reality does not fill our sails with wind to propel us. The real wind comes from within the individual spirit and is created by this burning, bursting, overwhelming desire. Desire is the path, no matter what opposition is confronted. Desire is truly the mother of the inventive soul and the product is creation. Crush all negativity around you, and most of all the "no, no, no's."

Remember, there are a great many people sitting behind desks in places of power that smile but could really care less about taking time to direct you or your career, and/or molding you to fit a certain role. Most want you to be right when you walk through their door. Some want perfection, and the pressure is on, as their careers are suspect as well if you're not so very good in a reading. Most times, after the actor leaves he or she is dissected, sometimes cannibalized. Always consider that success for the long haul is having friends, the network of people buying your services. The more they savor your very versatile, lasting flavors, the greater the possibility of getting closer to a "yes, yes, oh yes." It's always one less role for the casting professional to have to worry about. It's frankly a relief; it's out of the way when they hire you with that big smile and the words you like to hear most, "You've got the part."

Remember, you want be an actor; be that great salesman. Learn to make the sale to the individual or the crowd. Learn to manage and promote, and be thick-skinned when the sales presentation doesn't work. Learn to play the performance very loud and aggressive and learn to play it gentle and soft. Learn what works for different audiences, because they're all different and have different requirements and needs. Learn to sense who and what you're playing to, as the successful gambler senses his opponents' reactions to the cards dealt. Know what intensity is needed to reach everyone in the audience. And, like the great salesman, know your product;

as an actor, know your character. You may not be exactly the artist they're looking for physically, but leave them jotting your name down on the lists for the next project they're doing. Remember, you're here training as a "practicing" actor, like the "practicing" doctor learns to perform with great confidence.

When Garry Marshall sent me to Hawaii to cast those first ten episodes of *The Little People* for Warner Brothers, as noted previously I interviewed everyone on the islands that wanted to act and then some. When you're casting on location, anyone and everyone is a possibility. Through local legends Don and Josie Over, I had met a young doctor named Doug Ostman. Doug was a nice-looking chap, with a nice speaking voice, and was very personable and charming. He presented himself with great confidence, was obviously well educated, and was a fairly decent racquetball player. Because Doug was a medical doctor and Brian Keith's character was a pediatrician, I thought perhaps I'd use him on something, if he had the time. He told me this story that convinced me to take a risk with him in a small part in one of the episodes. While still completing his residency, he was asked to assist in an operation. The older senior doctor in charge asked Doug if he had previous experience in the procedure they were about to perform. Doug responded with an enthusiastic and emphatic, "Oh, yes, yeah." The older surgeon turned the operation over to Doug, who proceeded to remove the patient's damaged spleen and gallbladder. As they exited the operating room, the senior doctor congratulated him on his excellent, very thorough, meticulous, and efficient work. Doug said he shook the older doctor's hand and thanked him in earnest for letting him complete his very first operation of that kind.

He explained that in the operating room you don't really get a chance to do a procedure unless you convince a senior doctor you're experienced at it. Doug explained further that he had enormous experience practicing the procedure on cadavers; he was ready to do it and very confident. So, with knowledge comes confidence, and practice does make a perfect.

Abraham Lincoln was always practicing and rehearsing. He used his tall hat as a kind of computer, carrying small notes to refer to as he rehearsed speeches. So there you have it: desire is the key to success; the practice, rehearsal, and work of it is the fun. Remember what Emerson said: "Do the thing and you will have the power."

One additional tale here. I once noticed that an actor I thought was not very good or versatile kept showing up in every show in town, getting the jobs that some better actors could have been doing. Why? I pondered. I personally found him to be a bit of a pest, a nudge, always showing up when I had left my office door open—until one day when I needed him. My perception of him changed. I came to recognize him as the actor who kept his nose to the grindstone; he wanted to work. The routine of such an actor is, he gets up and starts out before the competition does, ear to the ground. He works when it's cold and rainy, antennae out, listening at social functions and networking with his associates at studio commissaries to learn who's doing what.

He's like the singer who maybe doesn't have the nicest set of pipes but dwells on the dream of singing the song. He has enormous desire. He's maybe three or four down on a suggestion list, but he makes the lists because he's seemingly always available, and he works for what's in the budget. He endeavors to do in reality what the great actor Liam Neeson's character said to Ben Kingsley's character in *Schindler's List*, "You do what you do, and I'll do what I do, which is the presentation." He constantly presents himself, and when he's hired he grows more knowledgeable with each experience, and then he attempts to repeat the process. He works, he continues to market himself around town by spreading word of his recent successes, he sends thank-you cards, birthday cards, flowers, and he attempts to repeat the process. He's a practitioner of the business of his craft, and real success in any business requires real commitment and real work. Remember that it's just that—a business, show business—and there's no business quite like show business.

The Interview/audition

I have always considered myself a people person, and I always used that skill to interact with actors; to get to know something about their uniqueness quickly so that I could later remember those unique qualities by seeing only their name or their picture. I always felt that the very best way to show talent that I was on their side—to put them at ease, so to speak, so that the very best of their abilities could be seen—was to read and act with them, and show them I could do it as well. I always felt that I had to first step down from whatever exalted and commanding position they thought I held and be of service. I wanted to be the exact opposite of the many self-obsessed, egotistical, aloof, power-hungry casting people I'd known and met. No matter how hurried I was, I always would attempt to take a couple of minutes after introductions for some small talk, in an effort to break the ice. Then, as I scanned his or her resume, I would approach the artist and ask if he or she could do a monologue for me. If he or she didn't have one, his or her passion for the craft was immediately suspect. I have always been of the opinion that when people are passionate about something they work hard at it, and thereby are at their leisure, as Picasso said. I always got excited when I would ask talent that question and see their eyes light up with excitement, because they did have one and yearned to perform it for someone. My instincts would immediately tell me this person is probably a very good actor; he or she craves to act. So, if a really passionate person wants to do something and can't find someone to do it with; if one can't find a scene partner, one works and practices alone on a monologue, perhaps a page from the proverbial telephone book.

For me, this approach was a very effective way of knowing and remembering people. There were two schools of thought here. I was once told by one of those self-important casting directors, "I don't teach acting here. If they can't act in my office, what are they going to be like when they get to the stage? Make it hard for them; it's going to get tougher out there." This casting person also didn't have the skills to give even the slightest creative direction to the artist, to change a performance for what they were really looking for. If it wasn't right, he simply kept interviewing by saying "next" to his secretary.

I loved acting first, so my approach to the interview aligned with the artist and was slightly different. Maybe that's why I sometimes heard that I was referred to as an actor's casting director. I was very proud of that. If I had the time I always culled through the fledgling talent pools by either listening to monologues or giving actors a scene and acting with them. I also continued the practice Renee Valente had taught me, of making and taking the time to regularly see three-minute scenes for a two-hour period once a week, without interruptions. I was always of the opinion that any halfway competent casting person knew the people on the A-list and B-list for both television and feature film consideration. Additionally, any halfway intelligent person who watches television regularly and goes to the movies can look through a current copy of the Academy Players Directory, talk to some agents for a few days, or scan a casting.com website and come up with lists of ideas of who is available and who might be right for a project. It's not quantum mechanics; any beginner casting director can come up with recognizable name ideas from this time-tested method. It's the interesting day players and supporting actors that are at times tedious to find and cast, and the casting director needs to be constantly interviewing and on the search for these, because from them will come the "name" actors, the stars of tomorrow, if you will.

Rejecting Rejection

Whenever I have personally been confronted with common garden-variety rejection, or a just a plain "no!" said to my face, I would remember what I had learned from my experiences as a vacuum cleaner salesperson: I was getting closer to a yes. It was drilled into us all that summer that we were just a couple of doors closer to an acceptance and a sale with each and every negative response. No person on this great earth can make the decision to accept rejection as final but oneself. My dad taught me never to go where I wasn't invited, so I'd attempt to find acceptance and an invitation elsewhere if I wasn't invited to the party. Show business is the party and being an actor is very much like being a salesman. The ultimate success of making a sale and getting hired for a job is a very small percentage of all the interviews or presentations one must make. It's a numbers game; sometimes one sale out of one hundred presentations. If one knows what to do when one earns a chance to perform and/or act, and effectively sell the reality of the script or the benefits of a new kind of dirt-sucker vacuum cleaner machine or some other product, using all of one's very unique powers to entertain and persuade and sell, one wins. Remember what Picasso said (and I paraphrase): "To be at one's leisure when one is at work." Or, we're all artists; do what makes you happy as you create. To smile in our heart is more important while we work and earn. When you get the callback or a job with that affirmative yes, consider it a nomination or recognition by your peers for good work. Maybe it's an unexpected compliment from some stranger that blows a great gust of wind into your sails.

Personally, when I feel right about something, "no" is not an option. Sometimes, a big smile comes to me when I'm told "no" repeatedly about something. It conjures up memories of a pubescent girlfriend I once loved who liked to play out her personal drama of "no, no, no" and then finally give in to me with "yes, yes, yes, oh yes" (thanks, Margaret). This went on for a while. I sometimes would act out different characters and voices for her that I knew she would respond to with the old "no, no, no" on the way to the romantic and seductive "yes, yes, yes." Remember, it's a ratio of about sixty to one hundred presentations or interviews to one for getting a job or making a sale. That's a lot of no's and rejection. Thrive on it; the yes's are getting closer. Never despair; always look for the door of opportunity to open and close, open and close. Opportunity is always there; look for it. "Take action and the feeling will follow"; that is, smile and you'll be happy on the inside. Look for the opportunity while you're happily doing what you enjoy and you'll create greatness and discover more new powers.

Some of my most favorite quotes:

"If you think you can do a thing or think you can't do a thing, you're right" – Henry Ford

"Action this day" – Winston Churchill

"Do or do not, there is no try" – Yoda

"Knowledge that you're going to be hanged in the morning concentrates the mind" – Samuel Johnson

"Fall seven times, stand up eight" – Japanese proverb

"You can't get wet with the word water" – Unknown

"To him that is in fear everything rustles" – Sophocles

"She would rather light candles than curse the darkness" – eulogy for Eleanor Roosevelt by Adlai Stevenson

"You can let it happen, you can make it happen, or you can wonder what happened" – Tommy Lasorda

"Eighty percent of success is showing up" – Woody Allen

"My center gives way, my right recedes. The situation is excellent. I shall attack." – Message sent to the rear from the front by General Foch, WWI

"One can never consent to creep when one feels an impulse to soar" – Helen Keller

"Pleasure is a shadow, wealth is vanity, and power is a pageant; but knowledge is ecstatic in enjoyment, perennial in frame, unlimited in space and indefinite in duration" – Dewitt Clinton

"Meet the sun every morning as if it could cast a ballot" – Henry Cabot Lodge to Dwight D. Eisenhower

"We must either find a way or make one" – Hannibal

"The best way to cheer yourself up is to cheer everybody else up" – Mark Twain

"If you fall overboard, you must be an active participant in your own rescue" – Unknown

"The ancestors of every action is a thought" – Emerson

"Chance favors the prepared mind only" – Unknown

"He becomes what he dwells upon" – Unknown

And maybe my most favorite quote:

"Among those I like or admire, I can find no common denominator, but among those whom I love, I can: all of them make me laugh" – W. H. Auden

Remember, the only thing constant in the universe is change; be prepared for it.

Have a wonderful career.

Made in the USA
San Bernardino, CA
30 September 2013